Torill Strand, Merethe Roos (Eds.)

# Education for Social Justice, Equity and Diversity

# Education for Social Justice, Equity and Diversity

## An Honorary Volume for Professor Anne-Lise Arnesen

edited by

Torill Strand and Merethe Roos

LIT

∞

Gedruckt auf alterungsbeständigem Werkdruckpapier entsprechend
ANSI Z3948 DIN ISO 9706

**Bibliographic information published by the Deutsche Nationalbibliothek**
The Deutsche Nationalbibliothek lists this publication in the Deutsche Nationalbibliografie; detailed bibliographic data are available in the Internet at http://dnb.d-nb.de.

ISBN 978-3-643-90255-9

**A catalogue record for this book is available from the British Library**


Klosbachstr. 107
CH-8032 Zürich
Tel. +41 (0) 44-251 75 05
Fax +41 (0) 44-251 75 06
e-Mail: zuerich@lit-verlag.ch
http://www.lit-verlag.ch

LIT VERLAG Dr. W. Hopf
Berlin 2012
Fresnostr. 2
D-48159 Münster
Tel. +49 (0) 2 51-620 320
Fax +49 (0) 2 51-23 19 72
e-Mail: lit@lit-verlag.de
http://www.lit-verlag.de

**Distribution:**
In Germany: LIT Verlag Fresnostr. 2, D-48159 Münster
Tel. +49 (0) 2 51-620 32 22, Fax +49 (0) 2 51-922 60 99, e-mail: vertrieb@lit-verlag.de

In Austria: Medienlogistik Pichler-ÖBZ, e-mail: mlo@medien-logistik.at

In Switzerland: B + M Buch- und Medienvertrieb, e-mail: order@buch-medien.ch

In the UK: Global Book Marketing, e-mail: mo@centralbooks.com

# Foreword

We are delighted to present this Honorary Volume on *Education for Social Justice, Equity and Diversity,* which is edited to honor the research work of Professor Anne-Lise Arnesen. Throughout her working life, Professor Arnesen has shown an impressive effort in educating teachers for a better school. Most lately, this has resulted in the launching of a Master program on "*Diversity and Social Inclusion*" at Østfold University College in Norway.

We have experienced the process of editing this volume as a stimulating collaborative process, implemented through the wholehearted effort of a large number of persons, who never hesitated in their eager of paying tribute to Professor Anne-Lise Arnesen's long-lasting commitment in education. We deeply appreciate their effort, without which the publication of this Honorary Volume had not been possible. First of all, we thank all authors for their stimulating and topical papers, which make this volume an interesting read for educational researchers and graduate students engaged in European teacher education. We were positively surprised that no one hesitated to accept our invitation to write a chapter for this book. Next, we thank the Department of Education at Østfold University College, and in particular Dean Eystein Arntzen, for encouraging our demanding editorial work. The librarian Ketil Modh Isaksen at Østfold University College's library has helped with putting together the bibliography, and Arlyne Moi translated the Norwegian titles into English. Last, but not least, we deeply appreciate the professional guidance and smooth collaboration with Anna Wojtachno, editorial assistant at LIT Verlag. Moreover, we are delighted to know that the Association for Teacher Education in Europe (ATEE) will pay their tribute to Professor Arnesen by promoting this Honorary Volume at the 2012 ATEE annual conference and on their website.

Professor Arnesen has, through her energetic work during a life-long career, focused on ways of educating teachers for a diverse, tolerant and more inclusive society. In doing so, she has contributed tremendously in putting these themes on the political and educational agenda. We are proud to know her, both as a colleague and fellow researcher.

Oslo, Friday, 29th June 2012

Torill Strand & Merethe Roos
Department of Education
Østfold University College
N - 1757 Halden
NORWAY

# *To Professor Anne-Lise Arnesen*

I would like to use this opportunity to thank *you* for all you have done for our department, Norwegian teacher education, and - as a result of that - what you have meant to me. Life is full of coincidences. As newly appointed dean of the department I had to deal with the situation after our former professor of pedagogy resigned. It is not easy for a department of a small University College to recruit such competence. Originally, the position was for a professor in special pedagogy, but since it took about two years to fulfil the process of recruitment, I had become involved in Inclusion and Diversity, so when you applied for the chair it was not difficult to make some adjustments. At that time our department had just started a development for raising our research activities and you were just the right person. In very short time you organized your colleagues in research teams and we could register the results soon after.

During your time at the department the scientific activities have increased tremendously. Although not all of the activities are yours, you have been a central part of this development. Quite often I have changed my mind after discussing with you, and when I look back, usually to the better. I am happy to have been working with you and for our department and children of Norway I hope you still continue to inspire colleagues for many years to come.

Halden, July 2012

Eystein Arntzen
Dean at the Department of Education,
Østfold University College

# Table of contents

# *Education for social justice, equity and diversity*

EDITORIAL

TORILL STRAND AND MERETHE ROOS
Østfold University College, Norway

We are delighted to present this Honorary Volume on *Education for Social Justice, Equity and Diversity,* which we have guest-edited to honor the research work of Professor Anne-Lise Arnesen. This volume consists of topical papers written by colleagues and fellow researchers of Professor Arnesen, who in this way pay their tribute to Professor Arnesen's dedication on educating an inclusive, just, tolerant and democratic society. This collection of topical research papers thus make this book a stimulating and thought-provoking read for educational researchers and graduate students engaged in European teacher education.

Throughout her working life, Professor Arnesen has shown an impressive effort in educating teachers for a diverse, tolerant and inclusive society. In doing so, she has oriented her competencies in building the school for a better future. Most lately, her visions and philosophy of life has also resulted in a Master program on "*Diversity and Social Inclusion*" at Østfold University College in Norway. One of her very early research interest came to the fore in a Nordic study on feminism (Norlilja). Later, she has participated in, and been the leader of, many collaborative research projects, involving international scholars and research milieus (for an overview, see Appendix I). In seeing and valuing fellow researchers and student teachers in an enthusiastic and loving spirit, Professor Arnesen expresses the most needed qualifications of a committed colleague and teacher. Beyond doubt, Professor Anne-Lise Arnesen has been – and is still – genuinely devoted to those who struggle.

The authors of this Honorary Volume are motivated by the same commitment. All papers presented here discuss the current challenges facing European teachers in regards to social justice, equity and diversity. Young Europeans now grow up in an era characterized by escalating economic, political, social and educational inequalities, an increasing racism and xenophobia, a high level of unemployment and a declining trust in nearly all major social and political institutions. But what are the vital characteristics of the emerging processes of marginalization? How are these processes played out within and beyond educational institutions? And how can we educate teachers for the new situation? In exploring these questions, this Honorary Volume focuses on three topics central to Professor Anne-Lise Arnesen's research interests: *Social Justice*, *Equity*, and *Diversity*.

## *Social justice*

In the Nordic countries, the public school system is viewed as an important tool for equalizing social differences. This mission is vital to the Nordic welfare state regimes, which are based on the principles of equality of opportunities, equitable distribution of wealth, and public responsibility for those unable to avail themselves of the minimal provision for a good life. In short, one of the premises of a welfare state is that the state has particular responsibility for the material and social welfare of its population, whether it is about protecting against poverty, or ensuring the health, education, and social participation of its citizens (Pierson 1991). Moreover, the Nordic model – which is a universal model based on citizenship – is upheld by a common norm, saying that "All benefit; all are dependent; and all will presumably feel obliged to pay" (Esping-Andersen, 2000, p. 163). The crucial features are freedom, equality, and solidarity: *Freedom* encompasses freedom from poverty and oppression, as well as opportunities for personal development and creative self-expressions. *Equality* refers to equal rights and obligations for everyone, independent of social background, sex, religion or ethnicity. *Solidarity* comprises solidarity with those less privileged, international solidarity, as well as solidarity with the next generation. The upbringing of active citizens that are enthused and moved by these values has therefore been one of the core ideas of public schooling in the Nordic countries after the Second World War (Arnesen & Lundahl, 2006).

However, taking the current challenges now facing Europe and European teachers in regards to social justice, equity and diversity, several authors now point to the dangers of blindly adopting an outdated image of an ideal citizenship (Beck & Grande, 2007; Benhabib, 2011; Kymlicka, 2007; Strand & Huggler, 2011). The authors of this volume thus point to the pertinence of renewing, strengthening and reinvigorating the Nordic model of citizenship education in order to promote democratic ideals and social justice within a new world order.

In the very first chapter of this volume, Elisabet Öhrn questions the fact that the teaching of democratic values tends to overlook the importance of solidary thought and action, as it focuses largely of individual rights and individual choice. In her paper, *Making a difference. Targets and resources for student influence*, she focuses on students' influence in upper secondary school in Sweden, while drawing on a study of young people's perspectives on power relations in school as well as their attempts to have a say ("Young people as political actors"). This study included four Swedish schools, and the field work was collected between 2001 and 2003. Reporting from this study, Öhrn shows that young people believe in joint action, and that they are not unaware of practices that risk weakening their cohesion. Her study also points to individual teacher's awareness of the importance of collective actions.

In the next chapter, *Rhetorical citizenship; the Norwegian RPE subject and freedom of Speech*, Merethe Roos discusses the Norwegian subject “Religion, Philosophy of Life and Ethics” (RPE) as an arena for developing “rhetorical citizenship”. In doing so, she sheds light on how the RPE subject carries the possibilities of educating mature, responsible citizens who have the ability to discuss and exchange ideas in the public sphere. Roos claims that RPE's potentiality of being an arena of *Bildung* - a place for acculturating young people - can be realized by requiring the youngsters to practice written and oral skills. However, this requires that the teacher is able to communicate in a neutral and objective way. Such communicating skills, Roos asserts, can be developed through a doxological communication model, which is explained by Mats Rosengren's doxology.

However - as Kjetil Steinsholt aptly argues - a systematic application of educational models, a narrow didactical approach or ruled-governed behaviour may undermine our ambition of promoting social justice. In his article *From Ethics to Justice,* he points to the fact that ethical responsibility cannot be transformed into a technology of teaching and learning. Drawing on the theories of Derrida and Levinas, Steinsholt explores what it means to consider justice as an experience of the "undecidable". In doing so, he exposes a link between deconstruction, justice and teaching, because teaching constantly is directed towards the Other; towards the “undecidable”.

## *Equity*

Equity in education comes forward as an affirmative action that benefits underprivileged groups or individuals in order to promote equal opportunities for all. *Equity* is thus linked to *equality* and *affirmative action*. Equity in education concerns the achievement of fairness, social justice, and the equalizing of social differences through the accommodation and meeting of the special needs of specific groups or individuals. It should be said, however, that such needs-based accommodation will not result in equal treatment of all pupils. On the contrary, it is practiced as affirmative actions to benefit underprivileged groups or individuals. Equity can be promoted through educational policies and practices on a structural, institutional, classroom or personal level, and is often justified as a counteraction towards discrimination (i.e. UN, 2007), through the principle of universal right to education (i.e. UN, 1966) or the individuals' rights to basic literacy and numeracy functioning (i.e. OECD, 2008). These ideas and ideals of equity, equality and affirmative actions are well agreed on worldwide. However, taking a short look at the current situation, we realize the distance between these good intentions and the hostile realities experienced by lots of European children today.

A problem pointed to, by Lisbeth Lundahl, is the widespread tendency of young people to leave school without completing upper secondary education. This is problematic, since young people without an upper secondary education face considerably increased risks of unemployment and social exclusion. In her paper *Leaving School for what?,* which is based on empirical data from European and Nordic research, including her own longitudinal research project, she points out four factors that tend to dominate the Nordic discourse: 1) access to education and the labour market, 2) division and integration, 3) the distribution of resources and 4) the placing of responsibilities. However, she also identifies noteworthy differences. In particular, the fact that young Swedes run larger risks of unemployment than Norwegian youth, since Norway has been more proactive than Sweden to facilitate transitions within upper secondary education and between school and work.

Another issue that troubles the idea of equity is gender equality, which unfortunately is still a hot topic within the Nordic countries. Elina Lahelma and Pirkko Hynninen address this issue in their paper on *Gender equality in Finnish teacher education*, in which they explore the history of gender equality work in teacher education during the latest decades. Comparing the early initiatives (among others the joint work with Anne-Lise Arnesen) and the current situation (among others a current Finnish program on Gender Awareness in Teacher Education), they point out what has been achieved and what remain the same. In conclusion, they say that "when one's eyes have been opened to see and recognize gender injustice – how painful and even shocking it might be – it sensitises one to inequalities based on other categorisations as well". Their ambition is to promote such sensitivity among student teachers, in Finland as well as in other countries.

Moreover, there is a paradox of inclusive education, as the policy and practice of promoting special needs education seem to reinforce a non-inclusive trend. In other words, the ambition of promoting inclusion may come forward as the very opposite, as the policies and practices of inclusive education may strengthen social exclusion (Apple, 2006; Slee, 2009). Kjell-Arne Solli discusses this paradox in his paper *Rethinking special education*. Here, he takes the case of Norway as a starting point for pointing out the fact that more pupils than ever receive special education in primary and lower secondary schools. These children are labelled as someone having "special needs" or as someone being "different". Consequently, the pedagogies and policies of special education in many cases act in favour of non-inclusive trends. On the background of this dilemma, Solli calls for a re-conceptualization of special education. Moreover, he identifies some of the challenges in educating student teachers for more inclusive pedagogies.

## Diversity

As the world is becoming a smaller place – and we now experience new patterns of migration, cultural mix, transnational identities and loyalties, and the materialization of a global virtual network society –long-established beliefs, practices and ideals of citizenship and of education are now being contested. Earlier, "the good citizen" often carried virtues and responsibilities promoting "the common culture" of the nation. But with an extensive and intensified contact within and beyond national borders, people now tend to hold hybrid identities and multiple loyalties. Moreover, vital questions of moral, ethical, political and social concerns are being evoked as an altered image of "the good citizen" is at stake. Three of the papers included here take the case of Norway as an example when addressing these issues.

Åse Røthing reports an empirical study on the conceptualization of *Gender equality in Norwegian textbooks and classrooms* as she elaborates on the implications of a specific notion of "Norwegian gender equality" revealed in this study. She points out how this notion seems to "belong" collectively to majority Norwegians in ways that lead to exclusion. This specific way of conceptualizing gender equality depicts equality as something "we" in Norway already have achieved and thus no longer need to pay political attention to. At the same time equality is perceived as a marker of differentiation that characterizes "us Norwegians" *as opposed to* "the others". In this way, the discourse on gender equality tends to veil discrepancies in the field of gender and sexuality in Norway, both related to politics and cultural norms.

In her paper *Beyond the pale* Trine Anker reports a classroom study on how boundaries between "we" and "others" are constructed in a Norwegian multicultural school. The empirical data shows how students enact and discuss respect according to the categories "Norwegians" and "foreigners." However, Norwegians and foreigners are not totally distinct categories. Rather, boundaries between the two groups are constructed as a mix of ethnicity, Norwegian language skills, colour, religion, interests, and peer relations. Anker argues that the Norwegian National Curriculum's call for a respect of "the others" is not mirrored in the pupils' practices. However, she points out that the observed discourses carry a potential for initiating new and thought-provoking discussions on respect and otherness in the curriculum and the classroom.

In her paper on *Democracy and education for a new era*, Torill Strand addresses the fact that our conventional ways of thinking democracy and education seem to be challenged by the new and ugly processes of marginalization that now emerge. In the first part of her paper, Strand explores the concepts of "democracy" and "education" and their mutual interdependence through an analysis of a current event (a young girl's blog after the terrorist attack in Norway, 22nd July, 2011). Drawing on the work of John Dewey, she reads this event to illustrate democracy and education as a way of life, an ideal and an outlook. But as Dewey's harmonious image contrasts the current situation, Strand – in the next part of the paper – elaborates on ways of re-thinking democracy and education this new era. Here, she draws on Chantal Mouffe's model of agonistic democracy and Alain Badiou's ethics to examine the potential possibilities of strengthening and reinvigorating the link between democracy and education in the present.

## *Teaching for social justice, equity and diversity*

So what are the current challenges facing European teachers in regards to social justice, equity and diversity? In what ways should we teach for social justice? These questions are pertinent, as young Europeans now grow up in an era characterized by escalating economic, political, social and educational inequalities, an increasing racism and xenophobia, a high level of unemployment and a declining trust in nearly all major social and political institutions. But is it possible to prevent the emerging processes of marginalization now playing out within and beyond educational institutions? Is it possible to educate teachers for the new situation?

In her paper *Dwelling, hesitating, but still acting* Ann Sofi Larsen pictures an impossible dilemma: She portrays a situation with apparently no possibilities for the teacher to «do the right thing», while she obviously want to do whatever to avoid that which may not be right to do. In exploring this situation, Larsen reveals how this particular case signifies a difficult and impossible ethical dilemma, as the situation implies an opening up of a multitude of differentiated knowledge. By putting Derrida's terms of justice and ethics into work, Larsen here points out the vulnerability of educational practices. She also destabilizes the taken for granted assumptions regarding "neutral" education.

Tove Steen-Olsen portrays the Development of teachers' competences as a struggle for recognition. In elaborating on a project, in which two researchers and a team of seventeen teachers collaborated over a period of two years to improve the teachers' assessments methods, she indicates that these seventeen teachers highly benefited from participating in this collaborative and systematic project. However, Steen-Olsen also point to the fact that the teachers did not collaborate or direct their agencies towards collective actions. On the contrary, they struggled individually for visibility, recognition and influence.

In the last paper, *Developing competences for diversity*, Julie Allan reports on a Council of Europe Project, "Policies and Practices for Socio-cultural Diversity", undertaken between 2006 and 2009 and led by Professor Anne-Lise

Arnesen. The project had three phases and involved a survey of teacher education policies and practices in relation to socio-cultural diversity across Europe, a conceptual analysis and the development of a framework of teacher competences for socio-cultural diversity. Allan portrays the process of developing the framework and reports on the engagement with the key stakeholders. She discusses the key features of the competence framework, which is informed by Levinas' ethics. Allan holds that "Levinas' ethics offers the possibility of rethinking the relationship between teachers and students *as a dialogue*" that has responsibility at its heart. Allan thus shows how this competence framework is re-presenting competences as ethical, while using the recognizable language and structures of the competences themselves.

In sum, while honouring Anne-Lise Arnesen's dedicated research work, the authors in this volume all shed light on themes in constant need of attention and further research and development.

## References

Apple, M. W. (2006). Producing Inequalities: Neo-liberalism, Neo-Conservatism, and the Politics of Educational Reform. In: Lauder, H., Brown, P., Dillabough, J.-A. & Halsey, A. H. (eds.). *Education, Globalization & Social Change* (Pp. 468 – 489). Oxford: Oxford University press.

Arnesen, A.-L. & Lundahl, L. (2006). Still social and democratic? Inclusive education policies in the Nordic welfare states. *Scandinavian Journal of Educational Research,* 50 (3), 285 – 300.

Beck, U. & Grande, E. (2007). *Cosmopolitan Europe*. Cambridge: Polity Press.

Benhabib, S. (2011). *Dignity in Adversity. Human Rights in Troubled Times.* Cambridge: Polity Press.

Esping-Andersen, G. (1990). *Three Worlds of Welfare Capitalism*. Cambridge: Polity Press.

Kymlicka, W. (2007). *Multicultural Odesseys. Navigating the New Politics of Diversity.* Oxford: Oxford University Press.

OECD (2008). Ten Steps to Equity in Education. *Policy Brief,* January 2008. Retrieved June 2012 from www.oecd.org/dataoecd/21/45/39989494.pdf

Pierson, C. (1991). *Beyond the Welfare State? The New Political Economy and Welfare.* University Park, PA: The Pennsylvania State University Press.

Slee, R. (2009). The Inclusion Paradox. The Cultural Politics of Difference. In: Apple, M. W., Au, W. & Gandin, L. A. (eds.). *The Routledge International Handbook of Critical Education* (Pp. 177 – 189). New York & London: Routledge.

Strand, T. & Huggler, J. (2011). Educating the Global Village. *Nordic Studies in Education*, 31 (2), 69 – 76.

UN (1966). International Covenant on Economic, Social and Cultural Rights. *United Nations,* 16. December 1966. Retrieved June 2012 from http://treaties.un.org/Pages/ViewDetailsIII.aspx?&src=TREATY&mtdsg_no=XX~1&chapter=20&Temp=mtdsg3&lang=en

UN (2007). United Nations Declaration on the Rights of Indigenous Peoples. *United Nations,* 13. September 2007. Retrieved June 2012 from http://www.un.org/esa/socdev/unpfii/en/drip.html

EDITORS: Professor Torill Strand is in charge of the Master program on Diversity and Social Inclusion at Østfold University College, Oslo, Norway. She also teaches Philosophy of education at University of Oslo, Norway.
Correspondence: torill.strand@hiof.no

Associate Professor Merethe Roos is Head of Research and Master studies at Østfold University College, Oslo, Norway.
Correspondence: merethe.roos@hiof.no

# *Making a difference*

## TARGETS AND RESOURCES FOR STUDENT INFLUENCE

ELISABET ÖHRN
University of Gothenburg, Sweden

ABSTRACT: *The paper draws on a Swedish study of young people's perspectives on power relations in school, their attempts to influence and the way they draw upon their experiences of power in the wider community to influence in school. This was researched by means of observations and interviews with 9$^{th}$ grade students in seven classes from four schools in urban and rural settings researched in the early 2000s. The paper provides an overall analysis of the studies of the four schools to discuss general patterns and variations. The analysis focuses in particular on the targets and resources of student influence, and also explores students' views on power and influence in school in relation to leisuretime experiences.*

### *Introduction*

This paper aims to add to the discussion about young people's collective actions by analysing their views on power relations in education and their attempts to exert an influence in school. There is a long tradition of researching these issues in the field of education (e.g. Davies, 1984; Willis, 1977), although recently such analyses have been rare. This does not mean that they are deemed to be uninteresting. Researchers have pointed to the importance of addressing them in relation to the increasingly individualised forms of teaching (e.g. Beach, Gordon & Lahelma, 2003) and, especially, the shift in the teaching of democratic values towards a focus on individual rights and freedom of choice rather than collective justice and equality (Englund, 2003; Öhrn, Lundahl & Beach, 2011). As shown by Arnesen and Lundahl (2006), the upbringing of democratic citizens is still one of the core ideas of the Nordic post Second World War educational reforms and it is emphasised in the curricula and legislation of these countries, but there are divergent local practices due to decentralisation and a risk that the "[e]xtensive use of individual working methods in schools risks weakening collective action and the influence of pupils" (p. 294). It has been suggested that the absence of analyses of this constitutes a major limitation of the academic debate on education (e.g. Davies, 2004), and students' collective actions and resistance to risk being rendered largely invisible (Arnesen, Lahelma, Lundahl & Öhrn, 2010). My hope is that this text might add to the visibility of such actions. As will be shown in the analyses, there was a strong collective dimension in the researched schools; the students' actions relied heavily on their joint participation and aimed at their shared practices and conditions.

The paper builds on the results from the study *Young people as political actors,* which aimed to explore young people's perspectives on power relations in school, their experiences of and strategies for using influence in school and the way that they draw on their experiences of power in the wider community to gain influence in school and vice versa. A main concern was to study processes in school as related to those of the surrounding local community. As emphasised in older research (e.g. Hey, 1997; Öhrn, 1997; Smith, 1993) as well as in more recent studies (e.g. Beach & Sernhede, 2011; Sandell, 2007), relations and processes in the local school need to be related to those of the local neighbourhood. This had consequences for the design as well as the choice of schools in the study. Local communities and schools were chosen to include both a large multicultural city and smaller villages, as well as to represent different sets of social structures and class/ethnic relations. Four schools were included. Two of them were located in different parts of a large urban setting and two were located in smaller communities. In all, seven classes from grade nine (students 15-16 years old) from four schools participated in the study.

Schooling in the urban area was highly segregated with respect to ethnicity and socio-economic background and the schools were chosen from two contrasting areas. One (*Birch school*, in Swedish Björkskolan) was located in a neighbourhood largely inhabited by working class people and people born outside Sweden. The other one (*Rowan school*, in Swedish Rönnskolan) had a highly heterogeneous intake, with some of the students living in a local council estate with a large representation of working-class and immigrant people and others living in a middle-class area with private housing. The other two schools were chosen from smaller villages located in the countryside. One school (*Juniper school,* in Swedish Eneskolan) was located in a small village in a rural district with slightly more than 10,000 inhabitants. It had a large reception area and many of the students travelled by bus to school. The other one (*Conifer school*, in Swedish Granskolan) was located in a large rural district, with slightly more than 30,000 inhabitants, most of them living scattered over a large area. It had a very large reception area and students typically had to travel (far) by bus to get to school.

The fieldwork was conducted between 2001 and 2003. In addition to observations and conversations during fieldwork, formal interviews were conducted with students in pairs or groups of three. Also interviewed were head teachers, people from the local youth clubs and a small number of teachers who knew the researched classes well. Parallel with the observations and interviews in school, the two researchers spent time in the surrounding neighbourhood visiting students' home areas. Students and staff were informed about the study and were asked for consent prior to the fieldwork, in accordance with the ethical guidelines of the Swedish Research Council (2002).

The study made use of Giddens' theory of structuration (1984) for analysing dynamics of power relations and the relations between actors and structure. Structures as defined by the theory of structuration refer to rules and resources employed in social interaction. Giddens' stressed the dialectics of control, meaning that even dependency has resources that might be used by subordinated groups in order to influence. The study focussed in particular on students' use of various rules and resources when attempting to influence their schools and schooling.

## Results

Previous reports from this study have focussed on analyses of themes and processes in the schools in rural areas and smaller communities (Kamperin, e.g. 2003, 2005a, 2005b) and the urban schools, respectively, (Öhrn, e.g. 2005, 2009, 2011, 2012). This paper brings together the results from the sub-studies to present an overall analysis of central targets and resources of influence in school, and also provides some references to students' experiences of influencing in their local neighbourhood.

## *Targets of influence in school*

### *Local themes*

In each of the researched schools, some central themes and processes of influence were identified. Some of them reflected or were closely related to the specific conditions in the local neighbourhood. For instance, in the rural schools, where the students had to travel far and their school days - as well as their leisuretime activities - were largely framed by travelling, the schools' schedules and local bus communications posed as targets of influence (Kamperin 2005a, 2005b). The students in the rural *Juniper school* acted during the fieldwork to change the school's schedule in order to make it fit better with the bus timetable, and they managed at least once to negotiate it successfully with a teacher (Kamperin, 2005a). Such success appeared to be related to students' unity, concrete suggestions for change and, also, that the consequences were acceptable to other students and teachers. On the occasions when teachers did not agree to the students' requests for changes, they still often appeared sympathetic to them and allotted time to the students during lessons to formulate and present their suggestions.

Correspondingly, in the urban schools, some local themes stood out as prominent targets of student influence. These were closely related to the classed, gendered and ethnified relations in the school's neighbourhood. For instance, students in the urban school with a highly heterogeneous intake (*Rowan school*) recurrently referred to the segregation of their neighbourhood and how it was reflected in everyday schooling, and their wish for the school to work towards the integration of the different socio-economic and ethnic student groups (Öhrn, 2005, 2011). The school's segregation of students in different teaching groups due to living area were prominent themes for students' concern. However, the students' wishes for less segregated schooling, although largely shared by teachers, were ignored as they were judged to go against the will of middle-class parents. The school leadership felt that they had to comply with these parents in order not to risk that they would move their children to other schools. In the other urban school (*Birch school*), a small group of girls with immigrant background confronted what they considered to be sexist ideas among the young men in their teaching groups and neighbourhood (Öhrn, 2009). Several of the teachers supported the girls and served as a key resource for their challenges of sexist ideas in class. However, the girls' criticism also included a critique of Swedish society for its culturalist representations of patriarchy, which was largely ignored by the teachers. Instead, the teacher support was given in ways that represented sexism as an 'immigrant' problem, located outside the school and not part of Swedish mainstream society or education (Öhrn, 2009).

The prominence of socio-economic and ethnic issues in students' wishes and attempts to change in school can be regarded as a difference between the urban and rural schools in the study. Targets of influence were only seen to be explicitly concerned with relations of ethnicity, class or gender in the urban schools. The material is too small, of course, to allow for any generalisations, but raises questions about whether the obvious contradictions and conflicts between different categories in the urban, segregated contexts (cf. Hamnett, 2001; Sernhede, 2007) made economic and ethnic backgrounds appear to be more salient issues to be influenced. This is not to say that student background is unimportant to the positioning in rural schools, but some research would suggest that social capital in terms of lineage is relatively more prominent when it comes to positioning in these contexts (Holm, 2008).

### *Common themes*

In addition to the specific targets of influence in the four schools, there were some common themes. One such common theme concerned the disbelief that students could actually influence school practices. Students in all the researched schools expressed strong doubts that they would be able to achieve more than marginal changes in school. But as for the wishes for changes that they did mention, the most prominent ones related to the material conditions of schooling, and to teaching and the conditions for learning. The *material conditions of schooling* typically referred to improvements in toilets, teaching materials, school lunches, the standard and equipment of the school building, etc. These were conditions not only of interest from the point of general wellbeing and comfort, but also related to the premises for developing social relations. This was visible, for instance, in one rural school (*Juniper school*) where the students were highly critical of the social consequences of the school's organisation of physical spaces and teaching groups (Kamperin, 2005a). The school was physically organised to avoid large gatherings of students, with student lockers located in individual classrooms (not together in the corridor which is otherwise usual) and had several small recreation areas instead of one common area for all students. Furthermore, students were separated according to teaching teams with breaks at different times of the day and time off for teachers' further training on different days. Some students explicitly referred to this as a strategy to split them and weaken their cohesion; since they were deprived of spaces where they could gather, it became difficult to form groups and develop joint ideas (Kamperin, 2010).

Some material conditions obviously also related to the students' options for learning, such as whether they had up-to-date textbooks or got enough lunch to cope with the afternoon lessons. Students' wishes for change also explicitly targeted *conditions for learning*, as manifested in joint actions for more qualified teaching in some of the classes. For instance, in one rural school (*Jupiner school)* students were displeased with the lack of qualified teaching in Spanish (Kamperin, 2005a). The class in question had been taught by different unqualified substitute teachers for a long time and thought that this was the reason why they lagged behind other classes in Spanish. The students were highly critical of the organisation of their teaching and a group of girls, supported by both parents and teachers, repeatedly tried to influence the school to organise the teaching in a way that assured them qualified teachers. As the situation did not improve, the students decided to quit lessons and go on strike. Similarly, students from one of the city schools (*Birch school*) tried to interfere with the local political process that threatened to severely reduce their school's economy (Öhrn, 2005, 2012), by calling on the local politicians and mobilising students to join in a public protest march.

Wishes and actual struggles that related to the conditions for learning were typically concerned with fears of less qualified teaching due to fewer lessons or less help during lessons, or no substitute teachers or less qualified teachers. This served as a primary target of students' attempts to influence in all the researched schools. This result accords with contemporary studies showing that upper secondary students act to improve their options for qualified teaching and learning (Öhrn, Lundahl & Beach, 2011), and that this is true also in contexts where students are often represented as showing weak academic interest, for instance, in vocational upper-secondary programmes (e.g. Hjelmér, 2011b; Rosvall, 2011). Another common finding in the researched schools was that students rarely discussed or acted in order to influence the content or forms of teaching. However, there was some indication of differences between students' according to social background in this respect; students from middle-class families in the urban areas occasionally voiced their wishes to change the forms of teaching or to focus on a different content (Öhrn, 2005).

### *Resources of influence in school*

A common finding in all settings was that the youngsters considered the schools' formal organisation for student influence to be of little or no importance. The organisation differed somewhat between the four researched schools, but irrespective of form, the students agreed that the formal routes did not offer any effective means for change or even successful negotiations. School councils, for instance, were with few exceptions considered to be ineffective. Some felt that the *organising* of school councils and their internal activities did not work because of inadequacies in election procedures, forms of work, etc. Others pointed to problems related to the school council's difficulties in actually *achieving change*, as the council's suggestions and demands were deemed to go largely unnoticed or to be ignored by the school leadership. This is in line with other studies showing that formal school organisations do not provide any effective means for student influence (Davies, 2002) and that students feel that school councils deal with issues that they deem to be unimportant or uninteresting (Rönnlund, 2011).

This however, does not mean that formal organisations are entirely without value for students' actions. For instance, analyses of students' action groups have shown that they are organised in accordance with, and seemingly influenced by, the routines of school councils (Rönnlund, 2010). Furthermore, school councils have been found to provide potential space for criticism that students might use without having to fight their way to negotiations (Öhrn, 1998). Still, students in the researched settings did not feel that formal organisation provided them with any important resources for their actual influence in school. Instead, they largely relied on informal contacts with individual teachers to make their voices heard in school.

### *The importance of individual teachers*

Judging from the processes observed during fieldwork as well as students' accounts in the interviews about their past attempts at influencing, individual trusted teachers appeared to be an important resource. It should be noted that teachers were not generally seen as a resource in this respect. The students made it clear that only some teachers could be approached and expected to be sympathetic to their requests; teachers were not generally believed to have a favourable attitude towards student influence or even to heed student suggestions that they themselves had asked for (Kamperin, 2005b; Öhrn, 2005). But when trying to negotiate or to otherwise influence in the school setting, the typical choice seemed to be to approach individual trusted teachers. For instance, the students in the rural school who acted for better teaching in Spanish as mentioned earlier, had discussed various options for how to handle the situation with their teachers (Kamperin, 2005a) and teachers served as a key resource for girls in the urban school who acted to counter sexist practices (Öhrn, 2011). Also, there were instances of teachers organising lessons where students practised political reasoning or discussed contemporary political issues (see Öhrn, 2012). Furthermore, there were occasional tales of students' previous and contemporary attempts to influence politicians and administrators outside school, where teachers had an important role in the process as they supported the youngsters and shared ideas about possible strategies with them (Öhrn, 2005). Some students also turned to the school leaders, but the extent to which students were ready to approach the headmaster with suggestions and demands varied between schools. In this respect, the individual headmaster's approachability and his/her attitude towards students seemed vital.

### *The importance of fellow students*

The second resource stressed by students was access to fellow students (see also Schultz et al., 2010), in particular their political knowledge and joint formation of resistance groups. These results support previous research showing students' social networks to be crucial for their positioning in school (e.g. Gordon, Holland & Lahelma, 2000) and point to the importance of political skills and experience in such networks in order to be able to be heard and make a difference (see also Troman, 2003, on teachers' collective organising). Fellow students with knowledge/experience of political activities and a willingness to act as the group's representative proved most important in the researched schools. In everyday instances of protests and attempts to influence, certain groups of youngsters stood out as important for actions being taken. For instance, in one rural school (Kamperin 2005a) small groups of girls were involved whenever action was taken in the researched classes. The girls composed protest songs, they initiated and administered petitions and urged fellow students to go on strike (Kamperin, 2005a). Similarly, in the urban school where students acted against the local politicians' proposal for a reduced school budget, a small group of students held a key position in the organisation of public protests (Öhrn, 2005, 2012). In this school as in others (e.g. Rönnlund, 2011), there were few students who reported having experience of formally organised political activities, but although scarce, good use was made of the political knowledge and experience that existed among them.

Previous research points to gender as important for students' influence in school, although in seemingly contradictory ways. On the one hand, research points to boys' more prominent position in class and to the teaching content being more tuned to boys' interests and practices than girls' (e.g. Gordon & Holland, 2003; Lynch & Lodge, 2002). On the other hand, at least in the Nordic countries, girls appear to more readily pursue their interests in school (see Öhrn, 2002). The results from this study also show that girls in particular act to exert an influence in school. This does not imply that the same girls were always involved or that they acted without the consent and support of others. Rather, small groups of girls were seen to pursue issues, usually with some support from others. For instance, the girls who acted in the rural schools and whose presence appeared almost a prerequisite for things to happen (Kamperin, 2005a) often had prepared their actions through discussions with others. Through the discussions they arrived at suggestions and ideas that they would present to the teachers and school leaders. Curiously enough, the only example during the fieldwork that involved similar numbers of boys and girls was the action mentioned above to influence the local politician in the neighbourhood. This might seem to support the idea that youth influence in school is more readily coded as feminine than youth's attempts to influence in other settings. However, it should be remembered that this particular action differed from most others in the study, also in terms of being more publicly visible and by being concerned with economy, which has appeared in some studies to be more central to boys' explicit interests (e.g. Swedish National Agency for Education, 2003).

### *Local traditions and the media*

The students stressed access to teachers and fellow students as being important in order to be able to exert an influence in school. In addition to these resources, students especially pointed to traditions in the school and its neighbourhood. They described strategies that were said to have been succesful for earlier generations in their school and therefore considered to be worth trying again. Tales of previous (successful) attempts at influencing could live on for a long time. For instance, when students and teachers in one urban school *(Rowan school)* discussed possible strategies for influencing, they frequently referred to the successful student occupation of a youth centre some twenty to twenty five years earlier (Öhrn, 2005). This took place before the researched students were even born and, also, long before many of the teachers started to work in the neighbourhood.

The fieldwork also pointed to the importance of access to media; students called on television channels and newspapers to get publicity for their cause (e.g. Öhrn, 2005) or reported that their strategies developed from having seen similar ones on the news and in soap operas (Kamperin, 2005a).

### *Individual merits and collective strength*

As shown above, students in urban as well as rural schools acted together to exert an influence in school. One group, however, the middle-class students in Rowan school, stood out by taking a somewhat different stance as they emphasised the importance of individual negotiations and, especially, individual merits for their chances of influencing. Rowan school was the only school in the study with a large group of middle-class and upper middle-class students and, unlike their schoolmates with a working-class background, they stressed the importance of individual merits for making a difference. When discussing explicitly how to go about creating change, these students largely viewed their chances as being dependent on their individual skills, reputations and relations with a teacher. They emphasised conversations and negotiations with teachers and appeared to have a strong belief in, and experience of, the powers of talk and consensus. As Li said about how to influence "You cooperate. Teachers and youngsters cooperate." (Öhrn, 2005, p. 40, my translation).

Some of the students in their line of reasoning referred to how they negotiated in their families, which was a model for interactions with teachers as well. Central to this is the belief in conversation and individual negotiations where one can successfully reason with adults to find acceptable solutions. This contrasts with the views expressed by their working-class schoolmates, who usually emphasised the need for collective formations in order to present a strong resistance that the school could not ignore. As one of the boys (Esad) answered in two words when I asked him and his mates what they would do to achieve change: "Riot. Strike" (Öhrn, 2005, p. 42, my translation). The difference between the various social groups in this study is in line in this respect with the suggestions of some previous research, which indicated middle-class students' trust in their individual relations with teachers whereas working-class students voiced a belief in collective actions (Öhrn, 1997). Much in line with Diane Reay's (2003) adult working-class women, our fieldwork with secondary students shows understandings running counter to individualisation among those from working-class backgrounds as positions, identities and influence were understood as relating to collective processes.

### *Influence in the local neighbourhood*

We made inquiries in the interviews about students' influence in school as well as in the local neighbourhood. Many students had problems recalling any instances when they had actually themselves tried to exert an influence in school and even fewer reported having attempted to exert influence in the local neighbourhood. Some of them also expressed uncertainty about how to proceed if they wanted to influence something in the local community. In the urban schools, some students talked about having joined protest marches and other manifestos (Öhrn, 2005). These were often concerned with international political relations – for instance, protests against wars or political acts involving one's former homeland – or general political issues, like the treatment of refugees. Few recalled having acted with others against conditions in the local neighbourhood. Those students who actually had participated in such actions claimed – like those who had done it in school – to have learnt something about political action that might prove useful for future attempts to bring about change (Öhrn, 2012). In line with Hatcher's (2007, p. 14) argument about campaigns being collective experiences where learning takes place, the students seem to have come to realise "the potential power of the strategy of collective action."

As for attempts to influence organised sparetime activities – typically football or horseriding – the students typically considered themselves to have fairly good chances of succeeding. They reported being asked by their coaches about what sport cups they wanted their teams to compete for or what training camps they wanted to participate in. Also, the students tended to feel that their opinions in these settings made a difference. However, the analyses indicated (Kamperin, 2005a; Öhrn, 2005) that there were usually few alternatives to choose from when negotiating with sport coaches, and students also typically seemed to be of one opinion. Furthermore, the coaches were regarded as experts in their field by the students to the extent that their judgements did not need, and should not, be questioned or negotiated. For instance, a student from one of the rural schools explained when talking about the chances of influencing the coach of his team that he was nationally famous and that "he is so good, he doesn't make any mistakes" (Kamperin, 2005a, p. 31 my translation). Negotiating the activities in such cases then appeared unnecessary; the leaders were deemed to know best. No corresponding trust in teachers' expertise could be seen in any of the schools. Teachers were often regarded as competent in their field and knowing their subjects well, but that did not mean that their teaching practices or ideas about students were unchallenged. In this respect, there was a striking difference in the extent to which teachers and other instructors were acknowledged as experts whose judgements should remain uncontested.

## *Concluding remarks*

This paper took as its starting point research that highlights the individualised forms of teaching and the risk that they bring about of a weakening of collective actions and students' influence in school. There is considerable support for such an interpretation; contemporary research points to the strengthening of individualised practices in school (e.g. Dovemark, 2011; Kennelly & Dillabough, 2008) and, also, to the difficulties for students to act collectively and to get a positive response when doing so (e.g. Öhrn, Lundahl & Beach, 2011). But it should also be noted that young people claim to believe in joint action (Schultz et al., 2010) and, as shown in the study reported here, they are not unaware of practices that risk weakening their cohesion. Furthermore, once they acted to influence in school, access to fellow students, alliances and joint action seem to be important. The results indicate less belief in collective action among the middle-class students who instead emphasised the importance of their individual merits, skills and relations with teachers for their chances to influence. But even these students to some extent relied on their joint actions with schoolmates.

This is not to say that any group appeared hopeful about their chances of influencing. The students were painfully aware of the economic constraints of their schools and expected them, as well as the hierarchical relations of schooling, to place students in a rather weak position for negotiations. Furthermore, some school issues were seen as largely refractory, almost natural. This goes for the content of teaching, especially in academic subjects that were positioned as the more prestigious ones, and was most evident in mathematics (see also Henderson & Hudson, 2010; Hjelmér, 2011a). But the students were anxious to gain access to this content. Access to qualified teaching was a prime target for students' wishes and actual struggles for influence in all the researched schools. Such struggles were usually met with some support by teachers. This also goes for actions targeting external causes, such as students' access to school transport and even students' actions to counter sexism when represented as consequences of relations outside school. Previous research suggests that student criticism involving teachers and their teaching is less likely to be met with teacher support (e.g. Dovemark, 2004; Hjelmér, 2011b; Öhrn, 1998).

The students in this study deemed that access to individual supportive teachers was crucial for their ability to exert an influence in school. Such access appeared to be the most important resource together with access to fellow students. The importance of individual teachers was related to their seemingly powerful position, not only in their own subjects and teaching but also in relations with other teachers and the school leadership. They were important in order for students to gain access to other adults who could not be approached directly. Hence, whereas much research on students' protests and resistance regards teachers and students as conflicting groups (see Arnesen et al., 2010), the study reported here shows individual teachers' importance for students' collective actions.

## References

Arnesen, A-L., & Lundahl, L. (2006). Still social and democratic? Inclusive education policies in the Nordic welfare states. *Scandinavian Journal of Educaitonal Research, 50*(3), 285-300.

Arnesen, A-L., Lahelma, E., Lundahl, L., & Öhrn, E. (2010). Introduction: Agency in a changing educational context: negotiations, collective actions and resistance. *European Educational Research Journal, 9(*2), 159-163.

Beach, D,, Gordon, T., & Lahelma, E. (2003). (Eds.). *Democratic education: ethnographic challenges.* London: Tufnell Press.

Beach, D., & Sernhede, O. (2011). From learning to labour to learning for marginality: school segregation and marginalization in Swedish suburbs. *British Journal of Sociology of Education, 32*(2), 257-274.

Davies, L. (1984). *Pupil power. Deviance and gender in school*. Basingstoke: The Falmer Press.

Davies, L. (2002). Pupil voice in Europe, in Schweisfurth, M., Davies, L., & Harber, C., (Eds.). *Learning democracy and citizenship: international experiences*. Oxford: Symposium Books.

Davies, L. (2004). *Education and conflict*. London: Routledge.

Dovemark, M. (2004). *Ansvar – flexibilitet – valfrihet: En etnografisk studie om en skola i förändring* [Responsibility – flexibility – freedom of choice: An ethnographic study of a school in transition, in Swedish with an English summary]. Thesis (PhD). Gothenburg: Acta Universitatis Gothoburgensis.

Dovemark, M. (2011). Can this be called democracy? in Öhrn, E., Lundahl, L., and Beach, D. (Eds) *Young people's influence and democratic education. Ethnographic studies in upper secondary schools*. London: Tufnell Press.

Englund, T. (2003). Skolan och demokratin – på väg mot en skola för deliberative samtal? [School and democracy – towards a school for deliberative communication, in Swedish], in Jonsson, B., & Roth, K. (Eds.). *Demokrati och lärande: om valfrihet, gemenskap och övervägande i skola och samhälle*. Lund: Studentlitteratur.

Giddens, A. (1984). *The constitution of society*. Berkely: University of California Press.

Gordon, T., & Holland, J. (2003). Nation space: the construction of citizenship and difference in schools, in Beach, D., Gordon, T. & Lahelma, E. (Eds.). *Democratic education: ethnographic challenges*. London: Tufnell Press.

Gordon, T., Holland, J., & Lahelma, E. (2000). Friends or foes? Interpreting relations between girls in school. *Genders and sexualities in educational ethnography, 3*, 7-25.

Hamnett, C. (2001). Social segregation and social polarization, in Paddison, R. (Ed.). *Handbook of urban studies*. London: Sage Publications.

Hatcher, R. (2007). 'Yes, but how do we get there?' Alternative visions and the problem of strategy, *Journal for critical education policy studies, 5*(2), 1-19. http://jceps.com/?pageID=article&articleID=98>, Accessed March 21 2011.

Henderson, S., & Hudson, B. (2010). What is subject content knowledge in mathematics? *The 2010 Teacher Education Policy in Europe Conference, Sept 30th – Oct 2nd*, Tallinn, Estonia.

Hey, V. (1997). *The company she keeps*. Buckingham: Open University Press.

Hjelmér, C. (2011a). Collective actions in the Natural Science Programme, in Öhrn, E., Lundahl, L., & Beach, D. (Eds.). *Young people's influence and democratic education. Ethnographic studies in upper secondary schools*. London: Tufnell Press.

Hjelmér, C. (2011b). Negotiations in the Child and Recreation Programme, in Öhrn, E., Lundahl, L., & Beach, D. (Eds.). *Young people's influence and democratic education. Ethnographic studies in upper secondary schools*. London: the Tufnell Press.

Holm, A-S. (2008). *Relationer i skolan. En studie av femininiteter och maskuliniteter i år 9.* [Relations in school. A study of femininities and masculinitieis in the 9th grade, in Swedish with an English summary]. Thesis (PhD). Gothenburg: Acta Universitatis Gothoburgensis.

Kamperin, R. (2003). *Students' attempts to influence in school*. Paper presented at the NERA congress, Copenhagen, March 5-9.

Kamperin, R. (2005a). *Försök att påverka i skolan: delrapport 1: en emprisik studie av ungdomars vilja och möjlighet att förändra: analys av tre påverkanssituationer i skolmiljön* [Attempts to influence: report 1: an empirical study of young people's intentions and possibilities to make changes: analysis of three influencing situations in school, in Swedish]. Department of Education, University of Gothenburg.

Kamperin, R. (2005b). *Försök att påverka i skolan: delrapport 2: en emprisik studie av ungdomars påverkansmöjligheter i tre grundskoleklasser* [Attempts to influence: report 2: an empirical study of young people's possibilities to influence in three compulsory school classes, in Swedish]. Department of Education, University of Gothenburg.

Kamperin, R. (2010). *Villkorad delaktighet. Ungdomars möjligheter till inflytande i skolan* [Conditional participation. Young people's opportunities to exert an influence in school, in Swedish]. Department of Education and Special Education, University of Gothenburg.

Kennelly, J., & Dillabough, J-A. (2008). Young people mobilizing the language of citizenship: struggles for classification and new meaning in an uncertain world. *British Journl of Sociology of Education, 29*(5), 493-508.

Lynch, K., & Lodge, A. (2002). *Equality and power in schools: Redistribution, recognition and representation.* Abingdon: RoutledgeFalmer.

Öhrn, E. (1997). *Elevers inflytande i klassrummet.* [Students' influence in the classroom, in Swedish]. Reports from Department of Education, no 1997:05, University of Gothenburg.

Öhrn, E. (1998). Gender and power in school: On girls' open resistance. *Social Psychology of Education, 1,* 341-357.

Öhrn, E. (2005). *Att göra skillnad. En studie av ungdomar som politiska aktörer i skolans vardag,* [To make a difference. A study of young people as political actors in schools, in Swedish]. Department of Education, University of Gothenburg.

Öhrn, E. (2009). Challenging sexism? Gender and ethnicity in the secondary school. *Scandinavian Journal of Educational Research.* 53(6), 579–590.

Öhrn, E. (2011). *Class and ethnicity at work. Segregation and conflict in a Swedish secondary school.* Education Inquiry, 2(2). 345-357.

Öhrn, E. (2012). *Urban education and segregation: th*e responses from young people. European Educational Research Journal, 11(1), 45-57.

Öhrn, E., Lundahl, L., & Beach, D. (2011). (Eds.). *Young people's influence and democratic education. Ethnographic studies in upper secondary schools.* London: Tufnell Press.

Reay, D. (2003). A risky business? Mature working-class women students and access to higher education. *Gender and Education, 15*(3), 301-317.

Rosvall, P-Å. (2011*)*. Pedagogic practice and influence in a Vehicle Programme Class, in Öhrn, E., Lundahl, L., & Beach, D. (Eds.). *Young people's influence and democratic education. Ethnographic studies in upper secondary schools.* London: the Tufnell Press.

Rönnlund, M. (2010). Student participation in activities with influential outcomes: issues of gender, individuality and collective thinking in Swedish secondary schools. *European Educational Research Journal,* 9(2), 208–219.

Rönnlund, M. (2011). *Demokrati och deltagande: Elevinflytande i grundskolans årskurs 7-9 ur ett könsperspektiv* [Democracy and participation. Pupils' influence in lower secondary schools from a gender perspective]. Thesis (PhD). Institutionen för tillämpad utbildningsvetenskap, Umeå University.

Sandell, A. (2007). Utbildningssegregation och självsortering: Om gymnasieval, genus och lokala praktiker, [Segregation and self-sorting in education: On choice of upper secondary education, gender and local practices, in Swedish]. Thesis (PhD). Malmö University.

Schultz, W., Ainley, J., Fraillon, J., Kerr, D., & Losito, B. (2010). *ICCS 2009 International Report: Civic knowledge, attitudes, and engagement among lower-secondary school students in 38 countries*. Amsterdam: IEA.

Sernhede, O. (2007). Territorial stigmatisation, hip hop and informal schooling, in Pink, W.T., & Noblit, G.W. (Eds.). *International Handbook of Urban Education*. Dordrecht: Springer.

Smith, L.T. (1993). Getting out from down under: Maori women, education and the struggles for Mana Wahine. In Arnot, M., & Weiler, K. (Eds.). *Feminism and social justice in education*. London: Falmer.

Swedish National Agency for Education. (2003). *Ung i demokratin: Gymnasieelevers kunskaper och attityder i demokrati- och samhällsfrågor,* [Young people in democracy: Knowledge and attitudes among upper secondary students, in Swedish]. Stockholm: Skolverket, http://www.skolverket.se/publikationer?id=1180 [Accessed 16 December 2010].

Swedish Research Council. (2002). *Forskningsetiska principer inom humanistisk-samhällsvetenskaplig forskning*. [Ethical principles for research in the humanities and social sciences, in Swedish]. Stockholm: Vetenskapsrådet.

Troman, G. (2003). Coping collectively: the formation of a teacher self-help groups. *British Journal of Sociology of Education, 24*(2), 145-157.

Willis, P. (1977). *Learning to labour*. Farnborough: Saxon House.

AUTHOR: Elisabet Öhrn is Professor at the Department of Education and Special Education, University of Gothenburg, in Sweden. She also holds a position as Visiting Professor at Borås University and is affiliated with Umeå University, Sweden. Her research focuses on power processes and democratic

participation, and gendered and classed relations at different levels of education. This includes studies of sub/urban schooling, patterns of segregation, and young people's understandings of power and how they would act to create change. Elisabet Öhrn has collaborated with Professor Anne-Lise Arnesen for many years in various contexts, lately especially in the Nordic Research Network *NordCrit*.
Correspondence*:* elisabet.ohrn@ped.gu.se

# *Rhetorical citizenship*

## THE NORWEGIAN RPE[1] SUBJECT AND FREEDOM OF SPEECH[2]

MERETHE ROOS
Østfold University College, Norway

ABSTRACT: *The school subject 'RPE' (Religions, Philosophies of Life and Ethics) is, as of 2008, part of Norway's national curricula for primary and secondary schools. In this article, the RPE curriculum's preamble is the starting point for discussing RPE as a possible arena for developing Bildung, that is, for enabling pupils to become responsible and mature citizens, as conceived in the Norwegian Constitution. The article discusses rhetorical citizenship as a possible strategy for achieving this goal. It argues that in order to practice rhetorical citizenship, the classroom should be seen as a deliberative public space, where the concept of 'bridging rhetoric', as explained by John Dryzek, can be a constitutive phenomenon. Teachers must, however, also make sure that their oral presentation and teaching methods do not undermine any of the religious and ideological discourses represented in the classroom. This can be achieved, the article argues, through developing a doxological teaching model as theorized by Mats Rosengren. Rosengren sees conscious and unconscious bodies of knowledge as valid only within their own respective – hence limited – social spaces.*

### *Introduction*

In this article I examine the premises for the RPE school subject (Religion, Livsyn og Etikk / Religion, Philosophies of Life and Ethics) and how these can aid in developing responsible, mature citizens with the ability to exchange ideas in the public sphere. Such a person will henceforth be referred to as the mature individual. The discussion's starting point is the RPE preamble, which outlines the school subject's purpose. The RPE subject is designed to strengthen the

[1] Religion, Philosophies of Life and Ethics (RPE), Norwegian: RLE: Religion, Livssyn og Etikk

[2] This is a translated and sligthly revised version of the Norwegian text RLE-faget og retorisk medborgerskap, *Prismet* 1/2012

knowledge of Religion, Philosophies of Life and Ethics, and it was introduced in the Norwegian school system in 2008, after a long formation process. Its historical roots are in the school subject 'Christianity', which was strongly linked to the Norwegian State Lutheran Church. The country's increasingly multicultural and pluralistically religious population has, however, made it necessary to reconceptualize the school subject. The concept of the mature individual stems from a published study which formed the basis for the latest amendment to the Norwegian Constitution's §100, on freedom of speech (Norwegian Official Report 1999/27). Here the mature individual is understood as a person who is equipped to express himself or herself in a decent, respectful way in the public sphere. I claim that RPE's potential to be an arena for Bildung – a place for acculturating young citizens, where pupils can learn to become responsible, mature individuals – can be realized by requiring pupils to practice oral and written skills, and that the idea of 'rhetorical citizenship' can be a good basis for developing a suitable communication culture in the classroom. John Dryzek's outline of the function of rhetoric in the deliberative democracy can be a fruitful practical and pedagogical strategy for achieving this goal. Another errand in this article is to shed light on how a culture of communication – one where people behave in a proper and fitting way – requires that pupils be able to relate to diverse discourses on religions and philosophies of life in a relevant, non-biased way, particularly as regards the beliefs and ideas of others in the classroom. This, in turn, requires that teachers be well-versed in the pertinent discourses, able to communicate their contents and knowledge in a neutral and objective way. I will, in concluding, argue that teachers can achieve neutrality and objectivity by developing a doxological teaching model. The basis for this is Mats Rosengren's conception of all knowledge being doxological (Rosengren 2008, p. 12), a term he uses to mean that various bodies of knowledge are only valid within their respective and delimited social spheres. In other words: that which is 'knowledge for me there and then', whether I am aware of it or not, is not necessarily knowledge for another person.

Starting from core values such as respect and tolerance, I attempt to illuminate some of the possibilities that can be linked with RPE as a wide and secular school subject. In a society that is undergoing constant change, to discuss values and attitudes requires that participants in the civic debate possess relevant competence, and I will argue that RPE can be an arena where such competence can be developed.

By shedding light on a school subject that is centred on values, and by seeing how RPE can accommodate the divergent values and philosophies of life that are represented in a class room, this article addresses some of the challenges existing in multicultural societies. It is thus also linked with themes central to Anne-Lise Arnesen's own research.

## *Acculturating mature citizens*

One of the presuppositions underlying RPE's stated purpose is that pupils should be taught to be tolerant of those who do not share their views. The subject's national curriculum emphasizes respect for religious values and human rights, and the ability to enter into dialogue with people of different faiths and philosophies of life (National Curriculum/RPE, p. 1). These emphases can also be traced in the competence goals set for pupils completing tenth grade. They therefore appear to be skills which all pupils are expected to acquire by the time they finish secondary school.[3] Such competence goals give RPE a potentially important position in the Norwegian educational system; its focus on dialogue, respect and tolerance opens a window of opportunity for inculcating norms for democratic *Bildung*, where pupils learn to understand themselves as actors in society, with freedom of expression and responsibility for their expressions.

RPE can therefore be a particularly significant arena for fulfilling some of the primary goals set for compulsory schooling, as outlined in the mission statement of the *Opplæringsloven* (the body of laws for Norway's primary and secondary schools). This mission statement underscores that schools should seek to promote a democratic mentality, and that teaching should be based on the fundamental values that are the legacy of the Christian and humanistic traditions (Opplæringsloven, §1). Other school subjects in addition to RPE also have explicit democratic goals involving tolerance, respect and dialogue. This is especially the case for Norwegian as a school subject. The introduction to its curriculum emphasizes how competence in the Norwegian languages (Bokmål and

[3] In the competence goals for the tenth grade, one reads, among other things, that 'the educational goal is that the pupil should be able to discuss questions about different religions and philosophies of life, and to show respect for them' (National Curriculum/RLE, p. 8) (author's translation).

Nynorsk) enables people to participate in a democratic public sphere (National Curriculum/Norwegian, p. 1) One can also find the democratic goal embedded in social studies (*samfunnsfag*), for its curriculum outlines how it seeks to help pupils understand basic human rights, active citizenship, democratic values and democratic participation (National Curriculum/Social Sciences, p. 1). However, just as religious openness and tolerance are important principles in a well-functioning democracy, knowledge about religions is also important because it can be a springboard for interpersonal understanding. In a society such as we find in Norway, which is increasingly marked by religious pluralism, the knowledge and understanding of different religions will be important for developing democratically minded citizens. In light of the RPE preamble's expressed goal – to teach pupils to be tolerant and respectful of others – this school subject holds a unique position in Norwegian compulsory schooling.

A democratic society is characterized in part by how it gives people the right to express themselves publicly. The ability to express oneself through speech and text must be regarded as an absolute precondition for democratic interaction and a well-functioning society. In Norway, freedom of speech expanded in 2004, through an amendment to the Constitution's §100. Not since the Struensee government have Norwegians had as much freedom to express their opinions publically.[4] The constitutional amendment is based on three processes or principles which, in combination, give a universal defence of the right to self-expression. They build on the idea of 'the mature individual'. Such an individual is acculturated through interacting with others, through hearing others' arguments and through testing alternative perspectives (NOU 1999/27, p. 5). Tolerance of multiplicity and respect for divergent views are also basic preconditions for this understanding of the freedom of speech. At the same time, the constitutional amendment rests on the idea that the 'autonomous self' is moulded and refined through interpersonal encounters. Absolutely central to this process of developing mature individuals is the school, understood as 'as the most important of the institutions which the public sector is responsible for as regards building the public sphere', and as 'the most important means for constituting society' (ibid).

[4] Johann Friedrich Struensee, who governed Denmark-Norway from 1770-72, abolished censure and allowed the public to express themselves at will, without restrictions. See, e.g., Roos 2009, p. 144.

The understanding of compulsory schooling which undergirds the constitutional amendment coincides with two basic skills emphasized in *Kunskapsløftet* – 'Knowledge Promotion', a national school reform implemented in 2006 (Berge 2010, p. 7). This reform stresses pupils' ability to express themselves orally and in writing. With *Kunnskapsløftet*, these skills are defined as fundamental to the national curriculum. Oral and written competencies are thus integrated into the competence goals for all school subjects. As well as promoting development, they should always be part of the subject-competence. While this understanding of oral and written communication is emphasized in the curricula and teaching, the authorities have expressed ambitions of strengthening and developing the mandate for building democracy, which the school, since its inception, has always had.[5]

It is along these lines that one can understand the description of speech and writing in RPE. With respect to oral skills in RPE; the national curriculum states that the subject should stimulate pupils to use oral language to communicate and explain religions, ethics and philosophies of life. The document also claims that oral skills – for instance those used in conversations, discussions, explanations, reports and storytelling – are means for wonderment, reflection and argumentation (National Curriculum: Fundamental Competencies for Compulsory School/RPE). The written skills can serve, among other things, as preconditions for good oral communication: *Kunnskapsløftet* specifies that writing in RPE classes clarifies thoughts and opinions, and that writing should help pupils interpret, argue and communicate. When taking into account the vast range of

---

[5] Certain critics claim, however, that the 'democracy mandate' in *Kunnskapsløftet* has been toned down with the increased emphasis on basic skills. Janicke Heldal Stray points out that the Norwegian discourse on *Kunnskapsløftet* is one-sidedly linked to pupils' achievements, and that the idea of democratic citizenship is not taken into account in the reform's steering documents. Stray points out the need for teaching about democracy and demonstrates that Norwegian teachers lack a common understanding of what it means to be a good citizen (Stray 2009, p. 223). Having said this, the International Civic and Citizenship Education Study (ICCS, 2009) has shown that Norwegian pupils achieve remarkably high scores in this area. There is therefore reason to suppose that the increased focus on basic skills has not impaired the understanding of democracy in Norwegian schools. Stray's message is nevertheless important, and if the basic skills are to be seen as crucial for developing the school into an arena where democracy and *Bildung* can develop, then the quality of learning must be treated as being *as* important as the development of democratic identity and democratic citizenship. Since the start of the twenty-first century, as Stray also stresses, these have not received equal emphasis in the Norwegian school- and education-policy guidelines (Stray 2099, p. 223).

knowledge to which RPE applies, one can see that learning about and being trained in oral and written skills in this subject shows the school to have an important potential as an arena for *Bildung*.

Teachers are therefore challenged to find strategies that can translate the possibilities and potentials of RPE into concrete teaching practices. This challenge concerns, not least, finding tools that help pupils communicate orally. Obvious tools here are rhetoric and rhetorical awareness. Since antiquity, rhetoric has been associated with persuasion techniques and strategies for how to seem convincing. Such speech-related strategies have also always been linked to the speaker's ethical responsibility and decency. This is especially stressed in Aristotle's works (Aristotle 2006, p. 28). He designed his *Art of Rhetoric* as an alternative to the sophists' use of rhetoric. The sophists, such as Plato describes them in the *Phaidros* and *Gorgias* dialogues, were considered beguiling and unethical (Berge 2010, p. 2). According to Aristotle's conception of rhetoric, however, a good rhetor is ethical and has good intentions.

## Possible strategies

An interesting approach to the idea of appropriate dialogue in the public sphere, one which has emerged in our own era, is the idea of *rhetorical citizenship*. This concept has come about through an international Nordic research project under the auspices of the University of Copenhagen. The researchers have studied basic questions concerning well-functioning communication in a modern pluralistic society.[6] According to Kjell Lars Berge, one of the project's participants, rhetorical citizenship can be defined as having relevant communicative resources for participating in important arenas for expression (Berge 2010, p. 9). This means, according to Berge, that the individual is a mature creator of texts, a mature user of texts, or both. Rhetorical citizens are able to wield language in responsible ways, and with this as a foundation, it should be possible to develop a healthy and democratic culture of communication. One way to start realizing RPE's achievement goals may therefore be to see the classroom as a place for exercising rhetorical

[6] http://retoriskmedborgerskab.mef.ku.dk/om/ This research project also includes several Norwegian researchers: Kjell Lars Berge, Sverre Blandhoel, Tom Arne Trippestad and Jens Kjelden.

citizenship. This will invariably concern the pupils' awareness of oral skills and of how they actually speak.

This approach to the oral aspects of RPE requires that the classroom be understood as a social and public space. In addition to being a space for discovery and learning, the classroom can also be seen as a deliberative public arena offering possibilities for dialogue and respectful conversations between the different actors who perform there. It can also be useful to link the idea of rhetorical democracy to the idea of the *deliberative democracy*, as formulated by John Dryzek, among others.[7] The deliberative democracy is actually a political model intended for communication between politicians and citizens, and it is increasingly mentioned in national and international debates on democracy. This type of democracy, according to Dryzek, has three hallmarks: it is *authentic, inclusive* and *consequential*. When a society is authentic, it builds on processes that are able to justify one participant's preferences in ways that do not seem coercive to any other participants. These processes also communicate in ways that allow those who do not share a speaker's views to still be able to accept that which is said. An inclusive society gives all parties the opportunity to participate in decision making, while a consequential society recognizes that the decisions reached are in fact genuine reflections of the views expressed in the processes leading to the final decisions. One could therefore say that a deliberative democracy is constituted by rhetorical citizens: individuals who become mature through their participation in public exchanges of words. This democracy's decisions are based on the dialogues and reasoning of its citizens.

RPE's stated goals, as expressed in the preamble of its national curriculum, allow the classroom to appear as just such a democracy – if the pupils learn to communicate the RPE goals in the right way.[8] The concepts 'dialogue' and

---

[7] See especially 'Rhetoric in Democracy: A systemic Appreciation' (Dryzek 2010b, pp. 319-33). See also *Foundations and Frontiers of Deliberative Governance* (2010) and *Deliberative Democracy and Beyond: Liberals, Critics and* Contestations (2000).

[8] It is important to note that the *Ungdommens maktutredning* ('Youth Power Audit', published in December 2011) calls for greater focus on democratic citizenship in Norwegian schools (NOU 2011/20). This report points out that even though the *Opplæringsloven* (the law pertaining to compulsory schooling) recognizes that the school has a mandate to promote democracy in society, it lacks a plan for how this can be realized. The *Ungdommens maktutredning* therefore suggests that a separate school subject called 'democracy' be established. This subject would engage with ideas presented in the school subject' Citizenship', which was implemented in English schools as early as 2002. The report

'respect' enable bridges to be built between groups who have different interests, just as the idea of the school subject as a meeting place for pupils with different backgrounds encourages inclusion and tolerance of multiplicity. These concepts are well-suited for the formation of mature individuals – for forming people with competence and *Bildung* sufficient for communicating in the way outlined in the Norwegian Constitution's article §100 on the freedom of speech.[9] With this mind-set, RPE becomes important, not only as a theoretical discipline, but as having a potential extending beyond the subject's inherent value; it goes hand-in-hand with the ideals about the school which were the impetus for amending article §100 in the Norwegian Constitution. In this way, RPE also becomes an important arena for responding to the discussions about deliberative democracy that have been heard in teachers' training courses in recent years. These discussions have emphasized deliberative (reasoned) classroom discussions that can help strengthen the teaching of democracy, thus also democracy in general (Englund 2007, p. 154). To achieve this, however, requires that the authorities increase their focus on deliberation (Samuelsson 2011, p. 13).[10]

In light of Samuelsson's findings, RPE can, I believe, serve to develop a culture of speech and writing that reflects a deliberative democracy. This can inspire pupils to distance themselves from segregation and the sharp divisions between 'us' and 'them'.[11] John Dryzek has laid down an important premise for developing this type of culture by launching the idea of *bridging rhetoric*

---

explicates, however, that the proposed new subject must be seen in relation to other subjects, not least RLE. For an English summary, see http://www.regjeringen.no/nb/dep/bld/tema/barn_og_ungdom/the-participation-and-influence-of-child.html?id=678673 (accessed 23 May 2012).

[9] The white paper that is the premise for the 2004 constitutional amendment sees *Bildung*, as envisaged by Ludvig Holberg, as a basic precondition for human freedom. This means that the white paper's authors see a tension between the 'paternalistic tendencies in the ideal of *Bildung* and the anarchistic tendencies in the ideal of freedom' (NOU 1999/27, p. 21).

[10] Martin P. Samuelsson, in his MA thesis from the University of Bergen, shows that even though Norwegian youth know a lot about democracy, their knowledge pertains to the formal and symbolic aspects of the concept. That is, they know what it is but are not able to use it in practice. Classroom discussions, such as Samuelsson has studied them in social studies classes and in the work of student councils, seem more to take the form of socio-emotional discussions rather than deliberative (reasoned) discussions (Samuelsson 2011, p.13).

[11] Divisions between 'us' and 'them' are themed in critical discourse analysis. See, e.g., Ruth Wodak (2008, pp. 54-77). By analysing texts from different political discourses, Wodak finds a range of topoi revealing how certain groups are discriminated against on account of race, language and culture.

(Dryzek 2010, p. 328). Following this rhetorical model, a speaker's goal is to build bridges and unite the parties who have different understandings on one and the same issue. The model stands in contrasts to *bonding rhetoric*, which involves strategies for drawing Manichean distinctions between a speaker's own position and the positions of others. Bonding rhetoric, as Dryzik sees it, means that a person uses rhetoric to stimulate conflict, and it is fertile soil for violence.[12] Those who use bridging rhetoric, by contrast, are seriously interested in recognizing the concerns of those with whom they are communicating, yet without supressing the position or view which they themselves hold. Such actors strive to find a language and a point of reference that can be acceptable to all, for these are tools that create community fellowship and forge bonds. Rather than manipulating discussion partners, those who practice bridging rhetoric want everyone to stand as equal partners in dialogue.[13] In practice, this means the speaker will choose a vocabulary and mode of speaking that cut across divergent interests and make visible a set of commonly held values. The bridge-building rhetor is always watchful of changes in the person, the group, or groups with whom he or she is relating, and is always cognizant that the deliberative democracy must never be assumed to exist in advance. At all times, such a democracy needs proactive work in order to function. With this as the starting point, the speaker's important task is to become versed in the discourses existing amongst the other discussion partners, and to try to find points of commonality between his or her own position and these other discourses.[14]

---

[12] Dryzek finds a clear example of 'bonding rhetoric' in George W. Bush's speech after the 11 September 2001 attacks. Bush delineated a division between 'us' and 'others': 'Either you are with us, or you are with the terrorists.' Dryzek shows that this rhetoric unites those Americans who supported the G.W. Bush administration, but that it simultaneously caused the international sympathy, which sprang up in the wake of 11 September, to fragment (Dryzek 2010, p. 330). Cf., for example, also the language used in the conflict between Protestants and Catholics in Northern Ireland.

[13] History, Dryzek asserts, has shown that it is easier to practice bridging rhetoric if the actor comes from a position that is subordinate to or parallel to the position held by the other interlocutors. Bridging rhetoric is unsuccessful if a political leader tries to supress or neutralize groups who can be considered potential trouble makers. His example of this is the British politician Georg Disraili, who, in the 1800s, tried to forge an alliance between workers and the landed gentry. This proposed alliance would, however, be controlled by the Tory Party (Dryzek 2010, p.331).

[14] Dryzek finds a good example of bridge-building rhetoric in the speeches of Martin Luther King Jr. When King was on the speaking circuit he represented more than one

Translated to RPE and the everyday realities of Norwegian primary and secondary schools, bridging rhetoric entails that the teacher's goal should be to cultivate an oral classroom culture where pupils learn to actively participate in a mutual exchange of views. Through relevant and knowledge-oriented argumentation about themes in the curricula, pupils will learn to countenance others – that is, to tolerate, approve, support or encourage others – and in doing so, will gradually develop a sense of security about their own identity. At the same time, they can discover how the very same values and attitudes can be shared by people with different religions and philosophies of life. The classroom discussions can also be enhanced by including representatives for other religious groups and life-philosophies who live in the neighbourhood but are not represented in the school class. It is fully possible to tie these discussions together with teaching in ethics and philosophical topics. Another important task, when planning the RPE class, is to devise several concrete assignments and research questions that will help the bridge-building and democratic classroom culture to grow – also in relation to other competence goals in this subject. Despite the extensive effort needed to set up this kind of a classroom culture, there is much to suggest that it is worthwhile: pupils' experiences of exchanging their views and discovering that they share similarities can help forge links between different discourses. At the same time, it can help pupils learn to respect the differences in various discourses. This, in turn, can help pupils become mature individuals, as envisioned in §100 of the Norwegian Constitution. This form of courteous, dialogue-oriented argumentation, which is the goal of bridge-building rhetoric, can be said to contrast starkly with the rhetoric dominating today's public media culture. Several researchers and experts on rhetoric emphasize how such rhetoric is

discourse: he participated in the African-American discourse and the civil rights discourse. He was simultaneously careful to emphasize that he could not be considered as representing the more radical discourses for black liberation in the USA. King stood out as a bridge builder between groups who initially were opposed to one another. He appealed to the White population by using the American Constitution and the Declaration of Independence. Amongst Americans of European extraction, two discourses were particularly pressing: racism and universal liberalism. Thus Martin Luther King stood out as someone who built bridges between different groups and different discourses in American society: he was himself coloured, he stressed something which was extremely important for America's 'White' population, and he simultaneously distanced himself from the radical Black liberation movement. In this way, he managed to minimalize the racist discourse in the USA during the 1960s (Dryzek 2010, p. 325).

conflict-oriented and characterized by 'battle' (Berge 2010, p. 5, Koch 2003, p. 161).

## *Doxology as the teacher's starting point*

To participate in debates and linguistic public exchanges requires knowledge. The idea of the RPE subject as a deliberative democracy will require that pupils have secure knowledge about the topics covered in the curriculum, and about the various discourses on the religions and philosophies of life represented in the classroom. To establish a basis for relevant, non-biased and factual argumentation, the curriculum's preamble can actually function as a 'midwife'. Here RPE is portrayed as a generally educative and secular subject: it enunciates RPE as an ordinary subject for *all* pupils. Teaching, the preamble argues, should be objective, critical and pluralistic; it should be factual and non-partisan, and all religions and philosophies of life should be presented with respect (National Curriculum, p. 1). Equal-value pedagogical principles should undergird the teaching, and it should be expressly adapted to the particular classroom's pupils (this is called *tilpasset opplæring,* adapted teaching). Further, the curriculum states that in terms of quantity, Christianity should have the largest place. The role awarded Christianity is, however, limited to its position as a precondition for Norwegian cultural heritage and as a cultural current. Following the primary principle of adapted teaching, the teacher should take into consideration the specific group of pupils in the classroom as well as others in the neighbourhood. Provisions can be made for local variations in the space allotted to each of the main areas covered in the curriculum, in order to reach the competence goals.

Since adapted teaching is emphasized so heavily, a considerable part of a teacher's preparations for the RPE class will be devoted to becoming well-versed in the religious and philosophical discourses represented in the classroom and neighbourhood. This should be the starting point for teaching RPE and be the basis for knowledgeable discussions and communication. It will set the stage for pupils to see a potential for dialogue as well as to see the value of finding common reference points. But the teacher must be careful to teach the material in a critical, objective and pluralistic way, as the curriculum requires. Since the curriculum treats the various religions and philosophies as qualitatively equivalent, they must be awarded the same epistemic status in the way they are taught.

As such, being aware of how one speaks applies to the teacher even more than it applies to pupils: it is up to the teacher to find well-reflected teaching methods and strategies that do not undermine anyone or cause any particular religion or philosophy of life to be treated more favourably than any other. One way to do this could be to see the discourses represented in the classroom as the starting point for a *doxological teaching model*. With this concept, I refer to the Swedish philosopher Mats Rosengren's recently expressed postulate that all knowledge should be seen as doxic or doxological. This understanding, which for Rosengren is a purely philosophical theory, can, I believe, be developed in a didactic context. The distinction between *episteme* and *doxa* stems from Classical rhetoric; episteme refers to objective and permanent knowledge, doxa to beliefs or opinions. When Rosengren claims that all knowledge is doxa, this means he considers knowledge as situated, in the sense that an individual's knowledge as well as beliefs, guesses and commitments as regards religions and philosophies of life should be understood as contingent and related to the knowledge and reality which the individual possesses. Rosengren's understanding of the doxa concept can therefore apply to all discourses and be something that forms each individual's thoughts and deeds.[15] His starting point for launching this view of knowledge is the famous *home mensura* thesis – the idea that 'man is the measure of all things' (Rosengren 2008, p. 15). This he interprets as pointing to humanity in general, in the sense that the world appears as it does to a person because of the way that particular person is (ibid, p. 18). At the same time, he asserts that *logos* appears to be the measure of all things. Logos is, in part, operational, meaning that it is the reason which a person possesses and uses to form the world; it is also constant to some extent, meaning that the person must necessarily always

[15] Based on his understanding of *doxa*, Rosengren's view of knowledge is characterized by a will to relativize each and every form of ontology. 1) Many bodies of knowledge exist, rather than only one; 2) all knowledge is preconditioned by the individual, social, historical or discursive conditions that are determined by the context; 3) to study and analyse knowledge in general requires that one pay attention to the discursive realization and practice of knowledge, that is, the researcher must inquire into the person who practices the knowledge and how it is practiced, etc. With these as starting assumptions, Rosengren can also criticize the traditional view of knowledge as being too narrow since it does not recognize the constantly changing, unclear and often occluded contexts that people are always embedded in. This criticizing he does by allowing that knowledge also includes non-discursive aspects of logos (e.g., that which is right behaviour, that which is normal, that which is considered to be prudent, etc.). Rosengren's conception of doxology thus becomes a view of knowledge and being that covers all aspects of human life: facts, ideologies, clothing style, mode of speaking, etc.

relate to or use the concepts, the mind-sets and the languages that exist at any given time (ibid, p. 23). Logos therefore plays an important and formative role as a mediator between the individual person and those things which apply for humanity in general. Rosengren's understanding of knowledge means, in other words, that all knowledge is individual and personal. At the same time, this knowledge has formed the person's entire understanding of reality and his or her entire existence, such that it is possible to have tacit knowledge or knowledge of which the person is unaware.

Even though Rosengren goes to great lengths in linking the idea of all knowledge to that which each individual person knows, I believe his doxology can help a speaker who needs to relate to a multifarious public – in order to lay pluralistic opinions open to view. Its practical value lies at the intersection between rhetoric and the understanding of truth. For Rosengren, rhetoric is the basic characteristic of language; it is intrinsic to language, and a potential force that can explain and show the relevance of what, at any moment, lies before the speaker.[16] Rosengren sees the speaker's specific audience as the starting point for how a given material should be presented: the act of 'taking inventory' – that is, that part of the speech where the speaker plans, organizes and edits what he or she will say – starts by analysing the doxa existing amongst the given audience. With this as the starting point, Rosengren draws attention to ethos, pathos and logos as creative tools for communicating with the group. What the speaker says is consequently rooted in an analysis of both the discursive and the non-discursive aspects of those to whom he or she is relating.

Rosengren's doxology may be a useful for teaching RPE, but even more important might be his understanding of *topos*. This concept usually pertains to the characteristics or stock features of a specific field. In Aristotle's thinking, there are several topoi characterizing modes of speaking, argumentation, human beings and so forth (Aristotle 2006, pp. 177-88). Rosengren takes recourse in the writings of the Belgian philosopher Chaim Perelman, who, based on Aristotle's distinction between general and specific topoi, claims that specific topoi are the

---

[16] Rosengren's understanding of rhetoric has similarities with that of Friedrich Nietzsche. For Nietzsche, the essence of language is not primarily as a sign system and secondarily as expression; instead, the rhetorical nature of language must be understood as its most aspect (see Nietzsche 2001, p. 2-9). A good explanation of the basic rhetorical character of language is also presented in Kjell Lars Berge's article, 'Er språket egentlig retorisk' (Berge 1998, pp. 32-45).

most interesting (Rosengren 2008, p. 91).[17] Rosengren builds on this in order to shed light on Perelman's claim that the antithetical topoi – those that are *not* lasting, enduring or constant – can nevertheless have a special value. Rosengren is here interested in the link between the non-permanent aspects of a given discourse and also the aspects that typify it. The topos, as he sees it, can enable one to see that a certain group's topoi (or opinions) can have validity within their delimited social frame, and that these topoi can have limited duration. The value of this for the RPE teacher should be clear: the topos shows that the characteristics considered true, right and obvious for one religion or philosophy of life can just as easily appear false or wrong in another context and in another religion.

Rosengren outlines a three-part strategy for how the topos can be used: as a *method*, a *map*, and as a *description* of how one tends to express oneself in a group setting. As a method, the researcher looks for the topoi in a particular doxa, seeing these as a collection of related ideas, assumptions and presuppositions. Along with this, Rosengren wants the researcher to inquire into the opinions on the topic at hand: what is considered already given, valuable, true, and so forth. He conjectures that if the researcher can describe what these relationships look like and which structures they create, it will also be possible to say something about the doxa. The value of the topos clearly requires that the researcher already has good knowledge about the doxa's discursive elements. To check whether the identified topos actually gives a good picture of the respective doxa, the researcher can ask: how representative is the topos I have set up for the doxa I am dealing with? Can I really use the topos to understand the doxa's domains, etcetera? As a map, the researcher can use the topos as a controlling mechanism for judging whether the particular group or audience has been correctly understood. Finally, when used as a description, the researcher inquiries into the doxa's visible exterior and asks how those who believe the doxa express themselves: Which language is used? Which clichés are used? Which linguistic genres are used, etcetra? As Rosengren envisages it, the topos can therefore reveal how the various topoi in a school class stand in relation to each other, which are fundamental and absolute, which are more peripheral, and what the relationships between them look like.

---

[17] Aristotle explains general topoi as those that can apply to all sciences rather than being restricted to any particular science. Specific topoi are those that are typical for specific sciences, or within a delimited genre of speech.

Based on the above, one can see the didactic potential of doxology in a pluralistic, fact-based and nonpartisan classroom setting. Its most important strength is that it opens up some 'safe doxa-spaces' that are not internally relativizing – that is, it does not relativize the truth and value of any doxa from the position of those who identity with it. Further, Rosengren's doxology can increase teachers' awareness that the practices they are trying to mediate information about are only relevant within these delimited social domains. Doxology's more or less limited knowledge spaces give pupils competence and assurance of their RPE knowledge, but it also reveals the limited discursive validity of that competence. Furthermore, doxology focuses attention on the specific audience or group of pupils in a way that enables it to be the basis for the teacher's didactic strategy. This understanding of how knowledge is discursively realized makes it easier to emphasize pluralism and critical teaching.

The usefulness of doxology in teaching RPE can immediately be seen in three areas. First, it can illuminate the fact that what the different religions teach and hold as dogmatic truth are to some extent the result of interpretation-related factors (cf. differences between confessions and different faiths). Secondly, it can elucidate that the form of knowledge within a certain religion, confession or faith can appear meaningless or completely different in a different context.[18] Thirdly, doxology can point out how a person can have knowledge about something without realizing it. An example of this would be where a religious practice or custom has become so engrained that an individual actor is no longer aware of why he or she does it. But again, when preparing for the RPE class, an important task is to devise a teaching method that can translate theory into practice in the classroom. This also means that those who are to teach RPE must be schooled in rhetoric as a part of their training to become teachers.

## Conclusion

By way of conclusion, I will summarize the most important arguments in this essay. I have argued that the RPE school subject has the potential to be an

[18] An interesting example of this is the difference between Islam and Christianity. The Bible and the Koran operate to some extent with the same 'gallery of persons', but they attribute completely different functions to these persons. For a Christian, Jesus will be the saviour of mankind; for a Muslim, he will merely be one of several prophets. Similar examples of the same gallery of persons but with divergent functions can be found in many religions.

important arena for achieving the goals stated in the Norwegian Constitution's article §100 on freedom of speech. This arena is established on the basis of the RPE curriculum's preamble and the RPE goal of training pupils in dialogue, tolerance and respect for one another. The classroom arena is linked with two areas of development. First, to achieve tolerance, dialogue and respect, pupils must practice oral and written communication. The RPE teacher must therefore strive to develop a suitable and respectful communication culture that lays aside rhetorical norms of conflict. Here I have suggested that pupils' training in oral skills can be rooted in the idea of the classroom as a deliberative democracy, and that these skills must be practiced through discussing with each other. This involves a communication culture where the pupils strive for bridge-building and dialogue, and where they are made aware of their status as rhetorical citizens. The understanding of and respect for others also requires reliable fact-based knowledge. The second area of development that is related to the classroom arena will be to devise strategies for teaching RPE in a critical, objective and pluralistic way. In this context, Mats Rosengren's doxology can be an adequate strategy. Given how Rosengren sees every form of knowledge as doxological, he reveals how knowledge can also pertain to non-discursive areas. Each and every good mediation of knowledge must therefore start with a thorough analysis of the doxa that are relevant for the specific group of pupils with whom the teacher works.

In order to develop RPE as an arena for democratic Bildung as outlined here, the authorities–must increase their awareness of deliberative discussion and deliberation. In addition, rhetoric and skills for helping pupils engage in such discussions must become a basic part of the curriculum of teachers' education.

## *References*

Aristoteles [ca. 340 f. kr] (2006). *Retorikk.* Oslo: Vidarforlaget.

Berge, Kjell Lars (1998). "Er språket egentlig retorisk?", in Berge, Kjell Lars (ed.) *Vad är Retorik?* (pp. 32-45) Stockholm: MINS.

Berge, Kjell Lars (2010). "Ytringsfrihet og ytringsanstendighet. Om ytringsfrihetens retoriske vilkår", in Stenstadvold, Halvor (ed.): *Georgs bok. Festskrift til Georg Apenes* (pp. 168-85) Oslo: Pax.

Dryzek, John (2000). *Deliberative democracy and beyond: liberals, critics and contestations.* Oxford: Oxford University Press.

Dryzek, John (2010a). *Foundations and Frontiers of Deliberative Governance.* Oxford: Oxford University Press

Dryzek, John (2010b). "Rhetoric in Democracy: A systemic Appreciation", *Political Theory*, April 2010, pp. 319-33.

Englund, Tomas (2007). "Skola för deliberativ kommunikation", in Tomas Englund (ed.) *Utbildning som kommunikation. Deliberativa Samtal som möjlighet* (pp. 153-68) Göteborg: Daidalos.

ICCS International Civic and Citizenship Education Study (2009). Det utdanningsvitenskapelige fakultet, University of Oslo.

Koch, Christian (2003). 'Magtkamp eller statskunst: Politisk kommunikation på mediernes præmiser,' in Berge, Kjell Lars; Meyer, Siri & Trippestad, Tom Are (eds.) *Maktens tekster* (pp. 158-81) Oslo: Universitetsforlaget.

Læreplan i Norsk [National Curriculum, Norwegian], Accessible: http://webcache.googleusercontent.com/search?q=cache:x6bB2ds33wkJ:www.udir.no/upload/larerplaner/Fastsatte_lareplaner_for_Kunnskapsloeftet/Grunnskole_og_gjennomgaende/lareplan_norsk_fastsatt_180808.RTF+l%C3%A6replan+i+norsk&cd=1&hl=no&ct=clnk&gl=no (Accessed 23 May 2012)

Læreplan i Religion, Livssyn og Etikk [National Curriculum, Religion, Philosophies of Life and Ethics], Accessible: http://webcache.googleusercontent.com/search?q=cache:4VOvRMR3KqEJ:www.udir.no/upload/larerplaner/Fastsatte_lareplaner_for_Kunnskapsloeftet/Grunnskole_og_gjennomgaende/lareplan_religion_livssyn_etikk.rtf+l%C3%A6replan+i+RLE&cd=1&hl=no&ct=clnk&gl=no (Accessed 23 May 2012)

Læreplan i Samfunnsfag [National Curriculum, Social Sciences], Accessible: http://www.udir.no/Lareplaner/Grep/Modul/?gmid=0&gmi=158524 (Accessed 23 May 2012)

Nietzsche, Friedrich [1874] (2001) 'Det retoriske og dets forhold til språket,' *Rhetorica Scandinavica* no. 17, March, pp. 2-8.

Norges Offenlige Utredninger. NOU 27/1999. *Ytringsfrihed bør finde sted!* Accessible: http://www.regjeringen.no/nb/dep/jd/dok/nouer/1999/nou-1999-27.html?id=142119 (Accessed 23 May 2012)

Norges Offentlige Utredninger. NOU 2011/20: *Ungdom, makt og medvirkning,* Acessible: http://www.regjeringen.no/nb/dep/bld/dok/nouer/2011/nou-2011-20.html?id=666389 (Accessed 23 May 2012)

Opplæringsloven, Accessible: http://www.lovdata.no/all/tl-19980717-061-001.html (Accessed 23 May 2012).

Roos, Merethe (2009). *Post Struensee. En undersøkelse av Praxis Pietatis i St. Petri menighet i København, med utgangspunkt i Balthasar Münters forfatterskap*. Doctoral thesis. Det teologiske Menighetsfakultet, University of Oslo, Oslo: Unipub.

Rosengren, Mats (2008). Doxologi. *En essä om kunskap* (2. utg.) Retorikförlaget, Åstorp.

Samuelsson, Martin (2011). *Utbildning till demokrati - Utveckling av deliberativa färdigheter i den norske skolan?* Master thesis, Det psykologiske fakultet, University of Bergen.

Stray, Janicke Heldal (2009). *Demokratisk medborgerskap i norsk skole. En kritisk analyse.* Doctoral thesis. Det utdanningsvitenskapelige fakultet, University of Oslo, Oslo: Unipub.

Wodak, Ruth (2008). 'Us' and 'Them': Inclusion and Exclusion - Discrimination via Discourse, in Gerard Delanty, Ruth Wodak and Paul Jones (eds.), *Identity, belonging and migration* (pp. 54-77), Liverpool: Liverpool University Press.

AUTHOR: Merethe Roos is Associate Professor and head of research and Master studies at Østfold University College. Her research focuses on Eighteenth Century Studies, in particular with relation to textual and theological development in Denmark-Norway in late 18th century. She is currently also doing research on democracy and citizenship in Norwegian school. Since 2011, Roos has collaborated with Anne-Lise Arnesen at Østfold University College's Master study in Diversity and Inclusion.
Correspondence: merethe.roos@hiof.no

# *From ethics to justice*

## TOWARDS A MORE HOSPITABLE AND HUMBLE PEDAGOGY

KJETIL STEINSHOLT
Norwegian University of Science and Technology & Østfold University College, Norway

ABSTRACT: *Linking ethics and justice not only means changing our ideas about the very foundation of social justice. It also throws into question our understanding of the conventional basis of justice as something impartial and universal. This is important in an age when justice is increasingly administered, rationalized and masked through detailed rules and regulations and not least through the growing demand for the use of effective methods as the basis for arriving at "good" decisions. Such "good decisions" now seem to be a part of the teaching profession's ethical obligations. In this article, however, I question the idea that a set of laws, rules and methods can be a substitution for ethical responsibility. Drawing on the theories of Levinas and Derrida, I argue that ethical responsibility and justice cannot be transformed into technology. Consequently, I will look into what it means to consider justice as an experience of the "undecidable" or what we can call "the madness of the decision". The word "undecidable" is not paralysis, hesitation, or neutralization, but a promise of the future.*

### *Introduction*

What does taking ethical responsibility mean according to Levinas' perspectives? It is not a question of following rules and methods. Institutions such as schools, kindergartens and legal systems will, if they systematically apply a rules-governed and method-oriented approach, exercise violence against those who are and will be subject to such systems (Levinas 1969). Justice and ethics (and education) are much more than institutionalized sets of rules, however many (Todd 2008). Rules and methods cannot function as a kind of substitution or excuse for ethical openness and responsibility for the Other. In broad terms, it is possible to regard Levinas' works as a comprehensive critical questioning of our everyday conceptions of the knowledge-seeking subject, of our self-awareness and what a self really is. He seeks to show that whenever we adopt a first-person view of the world and interpret it from that perspective, we inevitably exercise a totalizing form of practice. My attitude to other people, from such a perspective, will give rise to an "I-focused" designation: it is my wife, my mother, my brother, my sister, my uncle, my friends, my pupils/students etc. Relations to other people are identified through reference to me and my life as the nub. Other people become part of my totality, something which is like me and can be interpreted by, and be understood as, me; the Other is reduced and made subject to my economy. This means that for each of us our interaction with other people in the world will be egocentric. Levinas therefore asks us to look beyond the confines of this egocentrism and discover other forms of interpersonal relations, particularly those more fundamental and deeper. In doing so, he turns on its head the traditional concept of the rational autonomous subject we recognize so clearly from education and asserts that no self can be found unless there is an Other to awaken it and give it life. For another human being to be an Other, it cannot be part of my totality: it is not a matter of my wife, mother, brother, sister and pupil only, for these terms confine other people to being merely part of my totalizing context. The Other must therefore be different from me, something other than the faithful categories that constitute my world. The Other does not fall into my categories, concepts and expectations: we are talking of a stranger I welcome hospitably into my home (Joldersma 2001). Levinas invokes pluralism because the face-to-face relation must respect the Other's unique subjectivity. I and the Other cannot concur in our cognition because a meeting between you and me breaks with such totality. Through a meeting of this kind I seek in a direct and worthy manner to bid the Other's face welcome.

This is a particularly important reminder. Bidding the Other welcome stands as a criticism of Sartre and his Hegelian discussion of the master–slave dialectic in which the Other represents a threat. Levinas on the other hand wishes to show that we do not stand as isolated and autonomous individuals separate from each other but that we are aesthetically involved in the Other from the first moment. Further, welcoming the Other is not only a modification of Martin Heidegger's notion of "being with the other". Levinas believes that this veiling of the differences between me and the Other is not only phenomenologically inaccurate but downright dangerous. Criticism of Sartre and Heidegger also concerns their depiction of the relation between me and the Other as a conscious conflict or war.

For Levinas the relation is rather one untainted by any struggle for acceptance, a relation sustained by peace and hospitality. The thinking I loses its prioritized central position and an Other appears as subject. There thus exists no self without an Other to call it to responsibility. The crux of the matter is no longer what I do but what is done to me. Levinas thereby rejects the traditional notions of moral responsibility that are primarily concerned with the actions and decisions of autonomous actors and where the weight is on universality and reciprocity. In his book *Totality and Infinity* he argues that the Western ”ontological” tradition has generally been concerned with the self and the question of being. He focuses instead on a “metaphysics” which is oriented towards the Other and compels us to go beyond being. Where the study of being has led to a way of thinking with totalizing ambitions that seek to bind up everything in knowledge systems, metaphysics gives us scope to “think the impossible” in and through a meeting with the infinite. Levinas further argues that all attempts to grasp the Other in Western epistemology have led to a reduction of the genuinely different to something that seems the same. The attempt to gain knowledge of the Other is imperialistic and (possibly) violent because each description or classification of other people always entails a rejection of their unique qualities. In contrast to Buber's distinction between ”I–it” and ”I–you” relations, which assume an ethical position on which we can base our evaluation of such relations, Levinas wishes to establish a normative ethics without norms. The metaphysical structures relating to the Other, i.e. the presence of a concrete person as alterity, provide the foundation of this ethics. Alterity is a relationship to another being «who is recognized as excessive of my capacity to know or understand» (Peters 1998, s. 188). This means that alterity is that which lies outside our understanding of the knowledge-acquiring subject. In contrast to the golden rule that says we should do unto others as we would that they should do unto us, or the Kantian categorical imperative that says we should act only according to the maxim whereby we can at the same time will that it should become a universal law, Levinas suggests that we should «do unto an Other as he or she would have you do unto him or her» (Murray 2003, p. 39).

Levinas therefore forces us to think along different lines that we routinely do. Ideas that open up our minds show that we have not after all thought everything through, that we should not run away from life but into it, and that by doing so we can get a moral lift; ideas that ask us to take a closer look at our loyalty to prevailing pedagogical systems and methods, including our concepts of subjectivity, morality and virtue. And not only that: we must adjust our loyalty to the conventional practice of ethics. If our ethics lets us down, when we fail to do the right thing, when the decisions we make have different results than expected, it might be claimed that this is precisely proof that our ideas or approaches are not clear enough and that we are not yet sufficiently clear about or have adequate evidence for what we should have done. Or that we quite simply have had a moment's *akrasia* in which our intentions have led us astray and played a trick on us. For Levinas (as for Jacques Derrida and a number of other philosophers) answers like these are far from satisfactory. The ethics we have inherited from previous generations is an ethics which has proved wrong at a much deeper level. All philosophical and pedagogical reflection must have a relationship to the Other as an indisputable point of departure. And a relationship of this kind is characterized by limitlessness: there is always something that eludes our grasp. The Other is just that: something that cannot be held in check by totalizing strategies or the confining scope of knowledge.

## *The encounter with the Other's face*

In approaching Levinas, we are immediately confronted by two challenges. It is difficult and at times confusing to be asked to relate to an ethics which is so clearly based on a radical criticism of traditional Western philosophy. He wishes to summarize his philosophy in the words *Aprés vous, Monsieur*, that is, in friendly and convivial everyday actions. It would be a mistake, however, to reduce his ethics to the mere act of recognizing the Other and showing respect in the actual encounter. This can naturally be a tempting ploy to get some kind of hold on the Other, i.e. to return to traditional views of subjectivity and ethical responsibility. But for Levinas there is something in life which is valuable for its very ability to elude our grasp. There is something that grips you but which you yourself cannot grasp. His use of the word «face» is an example: The Other's face takes hold of us, embraces us, captures us – yet remains transparent and shows us the infinite, peace and the «good» (Aarnes 2001). For Levinas, we meet the Other best when we fail even to notice what colour of eyes he has. The face and our relationship to the Other are therefore more fundamental than one may think. Our relationship to the Other's face is deep down already ethical.

Levinas invokes «the face» to explain a kind of ethical relationship to the Other which is not subject to a well-practised temptation: that of reducing the Other to the Same, to that we can know something about. For Levinas the face is not so much something that presents itself to us but rather a call to meet and accommodate the Other.

Levinas' ethics therefore has its foundation in the «meeting» with the Other. By the Other he means another human being whom we meet in a very special way and who is seen as the very source of ethical responsibility. He tries neither to deduce this responsibility from any existing principle, to show that this is a necessary condition for bringing out accepted truths, nor to draw conclusions from results that empirically-oriented research has arrived at. It cannot either be a question of an editing of the experience I have of the Other as a wholly defined object in my own world (Chinnery 2001). My encounter with the Other is the very thing that constitutes me as subject and in general enables me to experience objects. In this meeting I will experience the Other's face as subjectively valuable, as something that gives meaning. It presents itself to me as something new, a kind of revelation. The face tells me something of others' existence and their qualities as a different, unique subject. For Levinas the meeting has the quality of a moral imperative. The Other is raised above me like a Teacher. But at the same time this differentness entreats me like a Beggar. It is as if a person of superior rank issues stern demands and confronts me with my own egoistic qualities. My little sovereign bodily world and my sustaining meaning system are challenged and the Other requires an answer. What makes this demand ethical is that the Other simultaneously asks for my favours. The Other is vulnerable to my behaviour and attitudes, a Beggar, a stranger who exposes himself to my gaze. The Other will not be compelling because of his moral or physical strength. No, the Other will appear as something alien: something on the other side, something homeless, something out of the way, something which can only be beseeched. The Other wishes to appeal to my freedom and neither can nor wishes to use force. At the same time the Other seeks to attract my attention: the meeting encompasses an absolute must.

Through his use of the face, Levinas seeks to bring out two aspects of the Other. He writes that the face is ethical because it simultaneously demands and begs; or because it begs only to the extent that it also demands and demands only to the extent that it also begs. This is a moral imperative for two reasons: in the first place it depends on ethical resistance, moral conviction and recognition, not physical and mental compulsion; in the second place it is a question of an imperative because he wishes to show that responsibility towards the Other comes before both altruism and egoism. The point is that these two aspects of the face stem from what it means to be a human being. We experience others as unique subjects, and not in the same way as trees, houses and landscapes. For the face is the very fact that others move us deeply. We see that the Other stands outside us, that the Other in no way brings with him an ethnocentric magnetism that seeks to attract all others and everything else into its own force field. The Other compels me to regard myself in his light. My conscience awakens and at the same time I learn something about myself. I see more clearly who I am and acknowledge, if I am open enough, that this is only possible through the Other. My stock of meanings is problematized and thrown into relief through such an encounter. The Other forms me and seeks in this way to extend my freedom and cast light on the possibilities that actually lie before me. I am urged to go beyond that which I have previously accepted as part of myself. I acknowledge that there is an unrealized potential there. At the same time, however, the Other is also dependent on my favours and therefore to a great extent on me. The Other is a self which «lives in me» and appeals to me in my freedom. My own responsibility is aroused in my meeting with the Other.

The face is Levinas' symbol for the Other as I encounter him in a context of ethical responsibility. Even though we normally meet other people as objects (we see them and can touch them) he believes that we always meet them from moral positions. Firstly, such a meeting will differ greatly from everyday visual perception. The face is present in the sense that it has refused to be contained. This means that the Other cannot be an object of everyday experience because our experience of the Other cannot be embodied in experiences of that kind. It cannot therefore either be accessible to my comprehension and right of disposal. But this does not of course mean that I and the Other do not share common ground. If we did not have a «common ground or world» it would be impossible to find any basis for Levinas' descriptions. Such a common ground, a world of the «same», would never exist separate from the Other. A relationship to the Other is wholly critical to my ability to appear as a person, not merely as a moral player but also as a reflective being. The world each individual I inhabits exists as a kind of «interiority», something sufficient to itself which has no relation to the «externality» introduced through the Other. From my interiority I am linked to objects in my world, objects I notice because I like them and derive pleasure from them. But descriptions of the internal are only presented as a contrast to the external, concrete world in which the meeting with the Other takes place. The point Levinas makes is that our experience of moral responsibility is an experience of other, unique human beings that places us in an external world quite different from my own internal, narcissistic world of pure enjoyment.

## *The body's internal enjoyment gives the subject its distinctive character*

The unfettered divide between me and the Other, which reveals itself in close relations, is thus accompanied by an internal corporal intimacy. The physical elements are wholly central to Levinas' understanding of responsibility and not least to the question of rehabilitation of what recognition in the final instance is all about. His analyses of enjoyment and sensuality are closely tied to a natural human condition characterized by a mechanical leaning towards the body's wishes and needs (biological impulses). This corporal existence creates a movement towards self-satisfaction, a drive to swallow different «nutrients». Prior to intimacy, therefore, we are guided by the impulse for enjoyment, for living off what the world has to offer. We enjoy our appetite. First the world gives us nourishment and we take pleasure in the world before we use it. For Levinas, this condition is morally neutral, not violent or aggressive, but organic; through such enjoyment I am unconcerned and satisfied, unaware of alterity and conflict. We bathe in a primitive world reminiscent of Rousseau's discussion, not of «the savage», but of the earliest stages in the history of our civilization. It is a matter of an original sensuality, a self-satisfied enjoyment through unproblematic physicality, an undifferentiated unity with the element from which we grow. Enjoyment means living on the basis of a material world that plays its part in developing our bodily self which in turn is capable of constituting intentional objects. Enjoyment points to physical expression, those events in which the subject assumes a position in the world and gives specific form to itself as a unique subject, and absorbs that which seems alien. The subject concretizes itself in and through enjoyment and seeks thus to affirm its position in the world as something entirely unique. Enjoyment turns subjectivity into a process or happening which gives scope for self-identification. Such a process must be related to a continuous mastery of that which is different in some way from the self, a relationship between the same and the other in which the other melds into the same. The other indicates that which stands external to the subject but is also capable of being woven into the texture of the subject. These elements are far more primitive than feelings because they have no reference to an object that evokes them. They are more in the nature of experiences that meet the subject halfway and complement something lacking; experiences that come and go with no particular purpose or reason. Elements of this kind are pure qualities in which the enjoyment-taking subject disports itself, but they come from nowhere (Levinas 1969, p. 136/144).

Nevertheless, the body is not the most central element linked to the germinating self waiting to unfold as the bearer of dialogical fruit. Nor is it like a Buber's self searching for dialogical relations. By differentiating between the intentionality of enjoyment and the pleasure of producing something, Levinas points to the corporal foundation that must be present in all conscious activities. The capacity to experience enjoyment means being at home in the world, before common sense knocks on the door. In line with the biologically self-evident, Levinas argues that the body takes precedence and is seen as the necessary source of our consciousness. This also means that all ethical relations will have their basis in the corporeal. The body is our material rock, what we base our life on. Living means feeling that we are alive and that life strives to intensify itself by deriving enjoyment from its own vitality. Living means enjoying one's own enjoyment. But enjoyment is also basically physical. That is why Levinas in *Totality and Infinity* describes the Other's face as a bodily expression (Ibid, p. 258). This naturally does not mean only a physical body which can be objectivized and made the object of scientific study, although these too are aspects of the corporeal. In addition to being something physical, the body is a living body that communicates the subject's experiences of the world. It is in this context that Levinas introduces enjoyment, and the fact that enjoyment of being in the world is the very foundation of what it means to be a subject: enjoyment gives the subject a distinctive concrete character.

It is in the meeting with the Other, face to face, that I acknowledge the Other's right over my own egoism, over my own desire to own everything, to gather everything under my own wings. It is therefore not my own thinking but the Other, who «unreceptive to classification» leads to a break with totality. The Other's otherness overwhelms me and confuses my thoughts and what I feel sure about. The impossibility of reducing him to me reveals itself in its true form as a modest question about my spontaneity as something ethical. To make this quite clear, Levinas looks closer at the tension between devotion and the face, between experience of myself and experience of the Other, for the self's affection must be conditional on the Other's absolute differentness (Cinnery 2001, Chinnery/Bai 2008). The Other can only be another in relation to something which at its heart is the same, namely the self's corporeal identity. In relation to the self I live completely separate and take pleasure in all the things I can enjoy and which give me the strength to live. In this differentness I live happily and seek continuously to fulfil my own existence. I try to conquer everything, even the Other, whom I seek to gain mastery over by every means. But the Other's face resists any attempt to do so. It destroys, breaks down and overruns the rigid picture I have created of myself. It is something that comes to me from the outside, it expresses itself and instructs me that I must be filled with more than I actually contain. The message is immediate and allows absolutely no form of classification; it breaks with any systematic determination of type, nature and character (Kemp 1988). It is because of such detachedness (as an important part of enjoyment) that responsibility can be expressed through the Other's face. This means that responsibility can only manifest itself directly in the encounter with the Other. It is not a matter of any general mandate or universal call for responsibility. Everything has to do with me. I have been chosen for responsibility. It has been imposed on me. But how can I know that? I see it in the Other's face. I become aware of it when the Other looks at me. To be honestly myself, to be open to the call from the Other, I must meet him directly in a discrete relationship. Enjoyment is a necessary condition for being honest. Even though the Other makes me uneasy, disturbs the enjoyment I have in living a happy life, it is this very ability to rejoice in life that enables me to meet the Other in his face. It is because of enjoyment that I can be responsible.

## *Objections and counter-objections*

Although Levinas claims to think in terms of face-to-face relations, it can seem as if the subject in these encounters either looks up at the Other as being on a superior level or down at the Other who needs help and who bears the face of the poor, the stranger, the widow and orphan. But if we take a closer look at all the situations in which we are confronted by another who attacks us, abjures all forms of hospitality and who has absolutely no desire to help us the day we really need it, Levinas has perhaps not so much to tell us. If the Other I meet on life's way wishes to harm me, should I then comply with his commands? And if someone disagrees with me, should I then without blinking accept his criticism as a principle which cannot be questioned?

Questions like these show that Levinas perhaps does not construct his ethics on a mutual encounter (Hägglund 2008, p. 84-92). Instead, he assumes that an ethical meeting exposes a basic asymmetry in which the Other is an absolute Other who reveals the transcendence of the good. The Other takes precedence. The Other is in a sense raised up, he is high and mighty. This naturally does not mean that the Other is my superior in questions of intelligence, skills, talent, virtue or piety. We refer rather to a human existence, which in «need and want», surprises me and inescapably puts me under a moral obligation. The relationship revealed in every encounter is one associated with inequality: that is, an asymmetric relation. The appearance of an Other in the world, which also is mine, reveals to me that I am a servant responsible for the Other's life and destiny. Levinas rejects any kind of self-affection and regards it as a break with all forms of ethical relation-building. Any subject must dedicate himself completely to the Other. For Levinas, being ethical means being unselfish, taking responsibility for the Other and without recognition being centred on me. It is sufficient to stand face to face with another to see that the asymmetry Levinas presents to us is in many ways self-contradictory. If we stand there, face to face, who then is really the Other? The answer is quite simply doubly affirmative, since the Other is a changing dimension, shifting referent according to who expresses the words. I am another for the Other and vice versa. Saying that I should subordinate and dedicate myself to the Other is the same as saying that the Other should dedicate himself to me, since I am a you and you a me when we are another to each other. Condemning the I's self-love is in the same breath to condemn the Other's self-love (ibid, p. 89ff). Irrespectively, anyone defending Levinas' ethics will be confronted with a merciless irony immediately one meets anyone else in a face-to-face relation and insists you must subordinate yourself to the Other. This may mean quite simply that you should subordinate yourself to me and observe my laws. According to Hägglund (2008) and Derrida (1978) it is difficult for Levinas to accept this mirror version because in his philosophy alterity cannot be ethical as such. Alterity suggests that nothing can exist in itself. In the final instance his philosophy requires that alterity must relate to the good. Even when Levinas openly describes the ethical in violent terms, in which the Other «accuses», «torments» and «traumatizes» the subject, he interprets this as being close to the good which will help to break down the subject's negative egoism. If one subjects oneself to the demands of the Other, this malignity will be broken down. It is therefore important for Levinas to show that the act of submitting to a brutal tyrant who demands that we obey his orders can be separated from that of subjecting oneself to an ethical other. It is however this very possibility of distinguishing between a good and a bad other for which he has been criticized (Herbert 2010, Hägglund 2008, Wall 2010). Suggesting that the Other is basically good helps to weaken the indeterminate aspect of alterity. We cannot anticipate anything about the Other, nor can we know in advance how we will behave in the encounter with him. There will therefore be nothing basically ethical in subjecting oneself to the Other, for the Other can naturally always be a tyrant. No encounters will precede this risk as it is presumably a factor that will mark all relationships from their inception. We can therefore raise the objection that it is quite simply impossible to know if the meeting with the Other will be a gamble or a threat, acceptance or rejection, a life revelation or a violent death. Levinas writes that transcending an internal existence does not consist of gaining recognition from the Other but rather of offering my existence. Being present in oneself means expressing oneself, meaning that we already serve the Other. The very basis for any expression is goodness. Existence is being good (Levinas 1961, p. 158).

We have seen that for Levinas the I arises in enjoyment itself, where I have my centre in myself. That means I am egoistic. But through the Other's face desire awakens in me. This distinction is made possible not from a totalizing I but because it has a presence in me based on a conception of something infinite. The fact of existing has meaning derived from another dimension that that of expanding such a totality; I can transcend myself in moving towards the good. I am responsible. But the good, in Levinas' defence, is nevertheless not something that exists as a matter of course. The good is by no means the highest we can aspire to. The good is not governed through principles inscribed in our nature and something we are capable of expressing (Kunz 1998). The good is not something rooted in some form or other of common philosophy, for that would only create a new totality. The good is also revealed in face-to-face relations; it is quite simply an event over and above any being. Goodness means going beyond oneself without knowing where. It is almost the opposite of a single good thing. For Levinas it is not a matter of the good serving some ideal form. Rather, the good asks daring and lethal questions about all ideals. Not least, the good asks questions about the idealization of the ethical relation. Goodness is not a goal I can hope to realize. It remains an event which simply happens.

The idea of the Other being absolutely an Other can be deduced from the fact that he cannot be compared with anyone or anything else. The Other is precisely his face because he cannot be reduced to "an example", "a case", "an essence" or a "sort" or "series". Such a reduction would be involved in every case in which a person's individuality is directly tied to a formal structure. For Levinas, any human being first becomes an Other when he shows deep respect for all others. The Other belongs to no series; the Other as another is not embedded in any logic and is in no way reversible or "something in common". The Other is the unique, unrivalled and exceptional one *par excellence*. It will never be possible to grasp the Other once and for all. Of course he has his own distinctive physiognomy, so it will actually be possible to photograph him. But the Other's face reveals itself when it breaks through its form and external image, and by transcending this any expression of the Other's differentness will appear a mystery. It would therefore perhaps be better to «forbid» photographs of the Other, quite simply because, through the photograph, we reduce the Other to that which makes him visible; we freeze him to a single moment and thus regard him as an object like other objects. The Other is strictly speaking outside any typology, characterology, diagnosis and classification, beyond any attempt to obtain knowledge of him and by so doing attempt to build a tangible frame around him. We cannot know if the Other is a tyrant or not: it is beyond my reach, beyond anything I can know about. He is something ungraspable, something "greatly unrecognizable" – and that is absolute. I can be hospitable to the Other for there is no other possible relation without ignoring the Other's presence.

It is also important to emphasize that those who criticize Levinas for treating the Other as an absolute Other, as pure alterity, a pure difference without having anything in common with the ego he meets face to face, may have got things wrong. This has caused a number of people to claim that Levinas offers «a pure thought of pure difference» (Derrida 1978, p. 151). It is therefore not so remarkable that he is credited with the idea that the fact of recognizing the Other means quite simply recognizing the Other as another me, another alter ego: «The other is absolutely other only if he is an ego, that is, in certain way, if he is the same as I» (ibid. p. 127, cf. Hägglund 2008). From this angle it would be very difficult to respect the Other if the Other in his alterity is not seen as an ego; as an alter ego. But is it true that Levinas has no wish at all to regard the Other as an alter ego? In both *Totality and Infinity* and other texts (Sheffler Manning 2001) Levinas shows that he incorporates an intentional transformation of the ego through the notion of the face: «The way in which the other presents himself, exceeding the idea of the other in me, we here name face» (Levinas 1969, p. 50). It is quite clear here that I already bring with me into my relation with the Other an idea of the Other as both an Other and an alter ego, an idea that shows that a meeting with the Other face to face will break through and override the Other's character of being infinite and absolute. The Other is for Levinas like an Other, not only an alter ego. The Other is what I am not.

## *The Third and justice as a limitless responsibility for each of us*

For Levinas the most basic dimension of responsibility is justice, a term he ranks higher than the general concept of love. His reason for this is that in everyday communication we too frequently attach love to simple emotions which can activate an ambiguous and "seductive" character and in turn lead to misuse. Attaching responsibility itself to love can give the false impression that responsibility stems from a kind of feeling for the Other and not from an unconditional call from the Other. Many people will say of course that one should love one's nearest and that this clearly has the character of an order. Levinas turns to the biblical tradition that takes for granted that loving one's nearest is a command, in the same way as Kant writes that we must not treat another person as a means but only as an end in themselves. The call for responsibility that comes to us from another face is not based on personal preferences for a particular human being we experience as pleasant, interesting and perhaps a little roguish. This is not really love. The Face demands that we respect the Other as an Other and not in reference to a set preference but quite simply because the face gives me a categorical order. The Other's rights come before mine, regardless of any dispositions and goodwill from my side. Justice as the Other's right is an absolute and inescapable decree. This has no basis in any form of empathy. Justice stems from the inescapable ethical call for responsibility for the Other emanating from the meeting with his face. Levinas' concept of justice means being just towards the Other, respecting him as an Other and in the light of this evoking his concerns before dealing with our own.

Justice for Levinas cannot be tied to process or development. It is not true that justice can be deduced from an interaction related to Hegel's right to recognition or Habermas' rules for the reciprocity hidden in every communicative action. Levinas' concept of justice has its nerve in a form of non-reciprocal intersubjectivity. The task in one way is to direct attention to the breakdown of the ethical meeting in the midst of the communal diversity. Justice stands here in an area of tension and, it is just this tension or conflict that makes justice possible. This notion of justice is closely linked to the criteria applicable to the ethical relation; it is derived from the original distinction between the subject and the call from my neighbour. At the same time, however, it invites the impossible: that these criteria should be transgressed. This transgression occurs when a third person appears in the area for the ethical meeting. Towards the end of *Otherwise Than Being* the Third person turns up, and it has been customary to interpret this as a kind of addendum or retroactive supplement to the discourse on alterity which is a central topic in the book. It has often been interpreted to mean that Levinas, by introducing the Third, will be able to throw new light on common everyday problematics such as judicial justice, government institutions and not least how reciprocal relations between people are developed socially. In *Totality and Infinity* the Other reveals himself to an already established «I». As long as the Other is regarded as a specific exteriority to the self, the meeting with the Other through face-to-face relations operates on an ego-oriented level. In *Otherwise Than Being,* on the other hand, Levinas goes behind the back of the I's consciousness so that there is no longer any danger of him being read to mean that the ethical appears as a concrete event in life to an already constituted ego. The transition to the Third shows that the discourse is no longer limited to the meeting between a single self and a unique Other. Now the alterity perspective is raised and put into a societal context. But Levinas does not break with his previous lines of argument. He presents, and takes an important step into, a remarkably consistent and continually developing ethics. In *De Dieu qui vient à l'idée* he writes that the Third is also my nearest, but that the relationship to the Other is never exclusively a relationship to the Other; from the very outset the Third is represented in the Other – in the Other's appearance the Third is already looking at me (Levinas 1986, p. 132f). This means that the Other without a third party would exclusively be a «you».

The third party interrupts my limitless obligation to the one and questions me about the need for justice for the many. This calls for the use of means and reference to objectivity. Proximity to the Third may necessitate the use of generalizations and comparisons abhorrent in the intimate encounter between two parties. But it is important to note that the order to strive immediately for justice stems from the ancient dawn of ethical relations. The imperative qualities of justice cannot therefore be deduced from any contemporary universal or teleological objectives. Justice is born out of the diachrony of ethical relations that tears up all forms of universality and instrumentality. Justice is neither a pedagogical afterthought nor a practical impossibility. It is incumbent on me from the very outset. My relationship to justice is neither causal nor optional; it is my uncompromising duty to strive actively towards it in all pedagogical situations. Just like the ethical relation from which justice stems, the call for justice is mandatory on us all. All is laid bare before justice's altar.

In the transition from ethics to justice, Levinas seeks to preserve the integrity of the ethical relation. Without this, justice could not be just. For him, it is important that the intimate ethical relation should not be altered or eliminated by the Third party's appearance. If the ethical relation is transmuted into justice, this will break with every ethical relation and undermine any possibility of justice. Nor is it possible for reciprocal intersubjectivity to form the foundation for justice. Proximity is naturally essential but not the critical goal of justice. The asymmetric ethical relation is simultaneously the factor that both divides and drives commonality onwards. Even though the appearance of the Third party will clearly stimulate the work of justice, the command itself will be carried by an ancient ethical relation. History is therefore what gives and maintains the integrity of the ethical relation. But what effect can this have on justice? It is proximity itself that calls out for justice, and that must surely require goals and knowledge? How can the common landscape of justice be constructed on the absolute distinctiveness of the ethical relation? The answer derives from the arrival of the Third party that disrupts the ethical twosomeness. The question of justice is therefore not posed before the entry of the Third party on the scene. As with the ethical meeting one to one, the Third challenges us to responsibility. But, as we have seen, responsibility within a wide diversity obliges us to turn our gaze towards that which is forbidden: generalizations, universality and rational decisions. It is these tools, which have no application whatsoever in ethical relations, that therefore become the invisible and impossible basis for Levinas' notion of justice.

Levinas does not believe either that justice is derivable from reciprocity and recognition, but he claims nevertheless that it is necessary. The historical factor (diachrony) is ethical because it is witness to the Other's particularity and separateness. Our relationship to the Third opens up the possibility of fellowship and allows us to set aside our subjective positions. The Third awakens the need for justice as commanded, but not necessarily on the basis of the historically-delivered ethical relation. When the third party breaks up the ethical idyll, the exclusive proximity is also disrupted. Now we are no longer merely face to face with our neighbour but also with someone who is perhaps neighbour to the Other and myself. The possibility of showing responsibility towards many others makes the close one-way responsibility towards the other complicated. The third party invites me to justice, to set up different cases against each other and to think aloud. If I am to do the right thing in relation to the Other, I must answer with responsibility and not establish a knowledge-oriented relation to him in the form of recognition. But in my encounter with the Third much of this will change. It will involve more a correction of the ethical relation's non-reversibility. Since the ethics disturbs recognition, justice requires, as we have seen, a form of intersubjective recognition. This is despite the fact that justice is constructed on an asymmetric and non-calculable proximity. When the Third turns up, and there will always be a third, I shall also be ethically bound to give him answers. In our meeting with the Third, how shall we decide how to make peace both with those close to us and those distant? How can we create a just fellowship which is both inclusive and which obliges us to preserve the differences in the Other? A meeting with the Third therefore requires systematic and conscious thought; in other words, totalitarian tools.

I can immediately meet the Other in an ethical relation without knowing the colour of his eyes. My relationship with him is material, concrete and ethical.

But I do not know him; nor is a reciprocally close recognition between two subjects necessary or possible here. But when the Third shows up I must have means at my disposal to make a decision. If not, it will be difficult to be just to everyone. I must engage in reciprocal relations with others whom I accept as my equals. To a certain extent I must be able to regard them as objects in the sense that I must identify their needs and the opportunities available for satisfying them. Levinas' justice therefore does not have recognition as its point of departure but as a loose «final point»

Regardless of the colour of their eyes: there are tears which a public official cannot see—the tears of the Other. This thought alone, where a rational and proper hierarchy fails to see the individual, is one of the liberating features of Levinas' work. Someone must be there to see the tears. «The I alone can perceive the 'secret tears' of the Other, which are caused by the functioning – albeit reasonable – of the hierarchy» (Levinas 1996, p. 11f). In many ways this is Levinas' non-liberal defence of a form of liberal individualism in which the individual has the highest value, but only because he can see the Other's tears (Alford 2004). Much of Levinas' political theory can appear relatively commonplace on the surface. The institutions and laws (and the bureaucrats that often accompany them) we have developed in our contemporary Western democracies are something he views as important. This is because political theory does not concern two people, but many – symbolized by the Third, the others to the Other. The introduction of the Third changes everything and nothing. I may owe the Other everything but when there are many others I must share my obligations among them. When there are many others I also become another towards whom others in turn will be obligated. I must be willing to sacrifice myself but others need not ask me to. The question of justice takes on a wholly different character when the Third appears on the scene. The question of distributive justice (Johnston 2012) did not arise earlier because there was never any question about how much I sacrificed to the Other in relation to myself: namely everything. Now I have to re-assess how to distribute or spread my responsibility. Even though my responsibility remains limitless, resources such as time and attention are not. Considerations of this kind are not much different from traditional procedures for distributive justice. "Comparison is superimposed onto my relationship with the unique and the incomparable, and, in view of equity and equality, a weighing, a thinking, a calculation» (Levinas 1996, p. 168). Regarding distributive justice as a superimposition can be taken to mean that justice is not conditional on the original meeting with the Other. Levinas' point is surely that others are present all the time, they are encompassed by my original encounter with the Other's face. This means that the imperative that says we must show care for all others is itself part of the original meeting with the Other. How we do this is therefore what justice is all about. But it is not a justice in which I become like the Other but rather that we are actually different from and for each other. If it treats everyone the same way, justice will contribute to what Levinas calls a totalizing, making subjectivity and particularity subject to universal and comprehensive categories. Justice is the cardinal virtue of mass democracy but it is also ambivalent. Treating everyone the same way is naturally better than unfortunate discrimination, but it offends against the individual's wholly unique humanity. For Levinas it is not the case that I do not deserve to be treated like everyone else: I deserve to be treated as me! Instead of creating a symmetric relation between equals, Levinas asserts something impossible: that I am responsible for all others in the same way as I am towards the Other. It is not only this one person who conquers me but all others as well. In my meeting with the face I am commanded by all others at the same time. The face is both my neighbour's and that of all others. Levinas here refers back to the enjoyment attached to my body's internal life. I have, and must have, narcissistic life qualities in me before I meet the Other. And these are qualities I never lose. If I become too dependent on others, if I meld with them, I cannot devote myself to their service. If I do not exist as an independent individual in my own right I will be unable to see their tears (ibid).

The term justice therefore means an arena in which there are many Others, and in which we are bound not only to answer the call from a given individual but must also consider the possibility of negotiating between different competing calls. The transition from ethics to justice is problematic and unclear in Levinas (Taureck 1991). This is because he gives no clear answer to the question of how we should relate to a multiplicity of ethical commitments and how specifically we should assess and if necessary rank them. How can I share my limitless obligations to the Other in a world of many others? Levinas' answer is «as equably as possible», even though in his later works he stresses my duties to my neighbours, no longer the abstract other but real people who stand close to me. He warns us against applying different judicial systems and methods where they are inappropriate, because this can lead to subjugation. He is far more concerned with the call from outside that perturbs the self than attempting to define methods for confirming the validity of our own decisions. But this does not mean that we can simply act without systems or methods when making decisions in situations of urgency. We cannot remain silent in the face of the troubled call from the Other, but we never know if the decision we make is the right one. Nevertheless we must act. Levinas does not give us a system that tells us what justice is or shows us how his ethics can form a basis for being able to arrive at «good» decisions. «Justice is not a legality regulating human masses» (Levinas 1981, p. 159). Justice is something more than a system of rules and methods. His ethics is not comparable to a judicial system because the Other's individuality and alterity can never be adapted to fit universal rules and totalizing forms of practice. The danger of homogenizing individuals into a clear «other», is that individuals who do not share other people's experiences and needs may be marginalized and brought to silence (Murray 2003). Levinas' philosophy therefore does not seek to provide normative rules for ethical (and pedagogical) decisions. Instead, he gives a phenomenological description of how ethics is experienced in the light of the Other's call. The ethical obligation that comes from a specific other is the true basis for making a decision. Theoretically, my obligations towards each individual are limitless. In practice, this would be impossible. How can we relate to this differential dilemma? Levinas has no answer to offer. He is humble—and that's fine! If he had given us an answer it would have required some form or other of universal approach to ethics. All Levinas wishes to show is there is no solution, only a specific commitment to a multiplicity of others. No solution can be found because his project is aimed at challenging principles, methods, contracts and rules which he regards as totalizing and which tend to reduce the individual to a case or a link in a bigger chain (Alford 2004). It then becomes a matter of involving other people in projects not their own: a totalizing strategy in which I relate to others in a way that contributes to overwhelming them and «functionalizing» them. It is a form of cannibalism with different forms of brutality. We can talk about «murder» in the sense that it is a form of intentionality that obliterates and wipes the Other away. As an alternative to universal principles, justice presents itself as the open-ended answer for each individual. This will also have pedagogical consequences. If Levinas has a pedagogical theory it can perhaps be outlined thus: the concept of justice tells us that making pedagogical decisions (irrespective of how evidence-based they are) is downright impossible. There are namely no theoretical recipes for meeting the indefinable. It would be impossible to relate to each individual and all other individuals as if they were part of my world. In other words, justice is the answer or response to the impossibility of ethics. For Levinas, however, justice will never take precedence over ethics: it is always with origin in the face and responsibility for the Other that justice manifests itself. Ethics is the fundament on which justice rests. Ethics is both that which demands justice and makes justice possible. And we have to live with this impossible task.

## *Educational hospitality: being humble in the face of the indefinable*

For Derrida, justice is not an abstract concept hovering over all our undertakings. On the basis of Levinas' theories of justice, which he believes to be quite minimal but nevertheless loves (Derrida 1997), justice is for Derrida like a relation to the Other, «and that's that» (ibid, p. 17). If justice is care for the Other as being an "other" , for the Other's differentness, for a differentness that cannot be foreseen or totalized, justice will always be directed towards, and be open and attentive to, the Other's particular character. In the name of justice we are committed to «keep the unforeseen possibility of the in-coming of the other, the surprise of the invention of the other, open (Biesta 2009, p. 103f). Levinas' interest in the Other, what Derrida calls his «ethical ethics» is in turn the basis for a possible justice. The question then is how it is possible to go from ethics' ethics to a more «concrete» policy/educational theory. How can a hospitable ethics as described by Levinas be applied to government institutions? This question is what informs Derrida's theory(-ies) of ethics, justice and the law: what he calls in various parts of his writings (see Derrida 1997, p. 33) the gruesome and inescapable double bind introduced by the Third party. If I have limitless responsibility for the Other I can never measure the call to be just to the face that meets me. But to top it all there is another Other always present on the scene already: the Third. What shall I do if I have limitless obligations to the first Other and can never measure this call for justice, when a completely different Other shows up? As Levinas also discusses, the Third will open my eyes to the impossible: how can we judge between competing but limitless obligations? With the Third arises also the question of politics and society, what Levinas calls justice. Derrida argues more cogently than Levinas for a clear divide between the ethical and the societal subject—a distinction between a purely ethical responsibility and a form of political responsibility. He believes that the disturbance from the Third in itself protects us from ethical violence in that we are not then consumed by our commitments to the first Other (Smith 2005).

Critchley (2008) also thinks there are close ties between Derrida and Levinas, and that this is shown in the question of justice. In many ways, Derrida goes beyond the point where Levinas ended, by further elaborating the distinction between law (what Levinas calls the straight line of justice) and justice. The law is a set of rules that can guarantee justice understood vaguely (as in Levinas) as fair treatment for all. But as both Levinas and Derrida suggest, the application of a set of rules will entail our doing some people an injustice. This is because a rule that is justified in some cases may be unfair to some people in others. For Levinas it is important in this context to emphasize that no systems of justice, however good and effective, will be just because there will always be some people who do not share this kind of system. It is therefore possible to deconstruct any legal system by showing how it may not be consistent in terms of its own justice-related objectives. But if it is possible to deconstruct the law, justice – in the light of the laws to be deconstructed – cannot be deconstructed. Derrida therefore also writes that deconstruction is justice. Justice is the experience of something mystical and impossible; justice is an experience of the indefinable. We hear here the echo from Levinas: an indeterminate experience of justice does not arise through intellectual intuitions or theoretical reflections but in relation to the Other's uniqueness. Our experience of the Other (and of justice) is indefinable because the Other's individual qualities are beyond the grasp of my cognitive abilities to the extent that no clear reasons can be given for just decisions. The madness of decision (to quote Søren Kierkegaard), the experience of justice, resembles in many ways Levinas' interpretation of what is means to experience the Other (Gutting 2011).

We may often wish we could find effective solutions to problems we are faced with. But what we wish for is utterly impossible: things will never work out the way we think. For Derrida the possible is related to what we can expect, what «fits» within a horizon of planned, calculable assumptions/ideas and known possibilities. His «ethical» perspectives on the other hand are directed more towards «the impossibility of the possible: an openness towards, and a desire to affirm, that which cannot be expected or planned in advance. He recognizes that exaggerated attention to the ethical aspect of responsibility, which necessarily involves general norms, can easily mask the genuine responsibility we have for the concrete decisions we must inescapably make and which entail our having a unique responsibility for the Other. On the other hand he warns us that an automatic observance of individual and absolute obligations outside the ethical can be equally catastrophic, exemplified by the tragic wars between «those holding the book», as he calls the heirs of Abraham. There is no responsibility without ethical norms and rules, but these must remain open if we are to bear responsibility. For Derrida the concept of responsibility is one of those curious notions that give food for thought without turning to thematization. It presents itself neither as theme nor thesis. And more importantly: it must always put itself in jeopardy in conversation and natural social intercourse. There is no responsibility without aberration and inventive breaches of tradition, authority, orthodoxy, rules or doctrines (Derrida 1995). For him, justice is the name of openness in the face of such inventive breaches. Justice is seen as something impossible, something that does not show itself as such.

Derrida supplements and continues Levinas' distinction between two types of justice: law (droit) and justice (juste). He also further develops his analyses through a closer scrutiny of Benjamin's text *Zur Kritik Der Gewalt* (1965) which problematizes the demand imposed on the subject by the unauthorized and unique authority of the call. The law is universal and understandable; it can be written down and used to direct future decisions. But it is not a question of any idealization of how the law or ethical rules work. Rather, it is an expression of our attempts to be just, attempts which may or may not naturally follow an ethical pattern. The way in which we explain things to ourselves – be it a body of laws, when we try to give someone concrete advice or when someone is asked to give an account of something they have learned – takes place within the law's domain. The history of political decisions, debates and so on also take place in this area. Everyone strives to be generally understood. Justice, on the other hand, can be translated to mean justice in the sense of an inclination towards a bold empirical openness in the face of the Other and something which to a high degree is concerned with responsibility and the Other (Edgoose 2001). For Levinas, it is a question of an infinite and unknown area that reveals itself in the meeting with the Other: «In reality, justice does not include me in the equilibrium of its universality – justice summons me to go beyond the straight line of justice, and consequently nothing marks the limits of this march» (Levinas 1969, p. 245). Openness towards the Other is therefore a critical condition for a decision to be just. The authority on which a decision is based cannot be assured or determined by reference to a thematized law. Rather, the authority for justice has an integral quality related to a call. The proper quality of such a call expresses both a humble uncertainty and an ability to escape from the hard-frozen and "sure" character of the law and from questions, repetitiveness and the daily routine. One way of approaching Derrida's concept of justice is to look more closely at the thought that «nothing repeats itself in exactly the same way.» All situations in which we must make decisions are inevitably new and special, and any attempt to show that we have been just will be impossible if we simply refer to, or apply, previous decisions or laws –however similar the circumstances. For if we refer to an earlier decision and only apply it in another situation, i.e. if a decision is reached through simply repeating an existing method, theory, experience or practice (no matter how effective it might be), we cannot talk about a decision at all. It is merely the action of a clerk. We fail to do the new situation justice. We stifle its uniqueness. We do not see the Other's tears. All decisions lack a secure basis and in the final instance are random and indeterminate.

A decision cannot only entail our weighing up advantages and disadvantages, what works and doesn't work, and in doing so marking out a problem as if it were a mathematical equation (ibid). We can naturally base ourselves on sure scientific knowledge— knowledge that has shown itself to be watertight—, effective methods and diagnostic tools or common sense. Nevertheless, the decision itself will not follow automatically from all that. It must still be made, and that requires us to look beyond what we have acquired as a «sensible» basis for the decision. What Derrida insists on is that if a decision is to be genuine it must invoke the Other who lies outside our control, and that it must therefore be mad. In emphasizing the undecidability involved in any decision, he naturally does not wish to create a kind of equanimity of doubt. In a number of places in his writings he has pointed out that the madness of decision also requires necessity and haste. Irrespectively: what happens is described as the «trial of undecidability», and it seems that this may entail a relatively painful process. In an interview, Derrida writes that no matter how careful we may be in preparing ourselves theoretically and methodologically for making a decision, the very moment in which the decision is made (if there is any question of a decision at all) will be disorderly and confusing when it comes to putting knowledge into practice (Derrida 1995). If this is not so, no responsibility can be attached to the decision. A person making a decision accordingly need not know everything. The decision is made and cast towards a future we know nothing about and which cannot be grasped. The future is not something that springs directly out of the present. For Levinas the future is a result of a meeting between a self and an Other I am incapable of understanding and who cannot be reduced to my totality. It will therefore always be able to surprise me. The future is both mine and not mine. My possibility but also a possibility for the Other. But it can never be a matter of logical possibilities. My future will lie far beyond what I believe can be realized, for this belief will always be mine. Since the future depends on me and an Other who is completely different, the future can surprise me. An assumption that decisions cannot anticipate the future may seem a little strange, if not trivial. Is it not the case that the ability to decide something is at least dependent on the ability to anticipate something on the basis of the situation in which we are and the experience we have acquired? And that even though, correctly, the anticipated results naturally do not have to be realized? Derrida's rejection of anticipation is not only a rejection of the traditional notion of what it means to make a decision on the basis of measuring, weighing and describing concrete possibilities. In suggesting that it is not possible to anticipate anything, he is trying to make a more general point: no matter how much we try to anticipate events, every decision must always break with expected confines, even though these are constructed from the habits that mark our physical behaviour towards the world. Derrida's main intention is therefore once more to emphasize that a decision must be fundamentally different from the preparatory work we have done, in other words that there is a marked difference between preparing ourselves to make a decision and actually deciding something (Reynolds/Roffe 2007).

Derrida takes a step further towards something enigmatic. Any decision must invoke change. And not only that: every change must surprise our subjectivity. This does not mean of course that he is reverting to some idea or other of free will, for he always makes a decision with the Other in mind, meaning that it is basically passive. He therefore concludes that decisions are unconscious in the sense that they can appear mad but that they are always pursued by an absolute responsibility. The reason a decision cannot be anticipated is that it is always in part unconscious, which assumes that our conscious reflections in connection with the decision must always give way to the mad. It is in this very leap away from calculating reason that responsibility lies. It is what Derrida calls aporia, a flash of undecidability we must all experience when making genuine decisions. He argues that the making of a decision requires us to behave justly both towards the actual decision-making process itself (which must always be undecidable so that every decision will be a form of experimentation or trial) and to those the decision affects (which must never be decided in advance, even though such prior decisions are grounded in most «laws»). There is thus no contradiction between the undecidable and making a decision. On the contrary: it is because the future cannot be determined in advance that we must make a decision. If the future were predictable, well then there would be nothing to decide. When the decision is made, in the actual aporia moment, we must never look back, never clutch at what has been. For if we blend the new and different with the old and same, the possibilities of the new will be obstructed – we say no to the new. And like Levinas, Derrida always tries to say «Yes, come on! Here I am». For to say no to the new is to hasten a closure – which is unjust. Naturally, no one has ever made a completely just decision. But that is after all what aporia means (Edgoose 2001). We want to make a genuine decision, but we can't: we are always already in the text; always already situated and bound by our past and what we have consciously or unconsciously inherited from it. Nevertheless, even though it is quite impossible, we should attempt to free ourselves as much as we dare from our heritage and what the circumstances allow scope for, so that through our decision we visit the least possible violence on the Other who is its recipient. And it is the Other, the unique other who is affected by our decision, who will be our judge, and it is he who will be able to tell if the decision has been just or not with reference to the situation he is in. If not, it will simply be a matter of ruthlessly incorporating the Other in our own value systems: a reduction of the Other to me, a reduction of the concerns of justice to my concerns. The concept of this undecidable justice is the very condition for the possibility of envisaging justice which rightly concerns us all. And it is precisely aporia which can guarantee that any decision will almost always be a necessarily impossible action. Derrida likes to show that there is still something lurking in the shadows, that in all our hearts there lies a secret, a vestige, a ghost that causes us to always make mistakes – something that should not be avoided but instead appreciated. The structures associated with aporia will always ensure radical doubt and therefore guarantee that it is impossible to arrive at a reliable and complete answer, and therefore – he hopes – a form of totalitarian security (ibid). Undecidability is a necessary condition for all decisions. There is nothing obscure about this. For a decision to be both possible and necessary there must be undecidability, a humility between determined choices. If there is not, there will be nothing to decide. And even when we make a decision, the undecidability will never quite disappear, a truth many sleepless nights can confirm (Hill 2008).

Undecidability continues to trouble every decision. It is never absolutely final and concluded, and although it may be behind us in time, it hovers there as if still out there somewhere in the future. In one way, the decision was never correctly made that time, and we shall be confronted with it over and over again. This has often been misunderstood by Derrida's critics. He has occasionally considered abandoning the entire concept of undecidability. As he says in an interview on French radio in December 1998: «I hesitate to use the word undecidable now because it has too often been interpreted, in ridiculous fashion, as paralysis, hesitation, or neutralization, in the negative sense. For me, the undecidable is the very condition of any decision, of any event, and since you're referring to pleasure and desire, it is obvious that I knew and could decide in advance that the other is indeed the identifiable other who is accessible to the movement of my desire, if there weren't always the risk that the other might be somewhere else, that I might have made a mistake, that my desire might not reach its destination, that the movement of love that I intend for the other might get lost en route or meet with no response, if there weren't this risk, marked with undecidability, then there would be no desire… So I think that, just like death, undecidability, or what I also call desinerrance, i.e., the possibility for an action not to reach its destination, is the condition of the movement of desire, which otherwise would expire before it happened. I conclude from this that the undecidable, and all the other values that may be associated with it, are anything but negative, paralyzing or immobilizing. For me it is exactly the reverse» (Derrida i Hill 2008:111).

The relationship between deconstruction, justice and teaching is not one that appears out of the blue. To the extent that teaching is something other and more than a technical and instrumental occupation, this something must necessarily lie in its orientation towards the Other. Levinas and Derrida show that Western thinking has not been capable of recognizing the significance of the Other because it has primarily understood the relationship between people and the world to be epistemological: one in which an isolated ego seeks to obtain accurate and reliable knowledge of something in the external world. The Other can therefore only stand as an object of knowledge. But for something to be an object of knowledge, it must be conceptualized, meaning in turn that it must be identified as part of a more general concept. If the Other can only be regarded as a result of an ego's conceptualizing actions, it can however only be seen as part of something more general. The other can therefore never then appear as special and unique and as an absolute Other. I do not meet the Other as an object for my or others' use but rather as something inaccessible. When I bring my power to bear on him, trying to lead him towards goals that suit me, it means attacking the Other's existence. Or, as Levinas often writes: «Any attempt to instrumentalize the Other means that I am trying to «kill» him, which in turn means that I am trying to act as if the Other did not exist at all».

## *References*

Alford, F. C. (2004). Levinas and Political Theory. *Political Theory*. Vol. 32, No 2, p. 146-171.

Benjamin, W. (1965). *Zur Kritik Der Gewalt und Andere Aufsatze*. Frakfurt am Main: Suhrkamp.

Bernstein, R. (1991). *The New Constellation.* Oxford: Polity Press.

Biesta, G. (2009). Education after Deconstruction: Between Event and Invention. In Peters, M. A./Biesta, G., *Derrida, Deconstruction, and the Politics of Pedagogy.* New York: Peter Lang.

Boler, M. (1999). *Feeling power. Emotions and education*. London: Routledge.

Chinnery, A. H. (2003). *Response and Responsibility.* Wellington: UMI.

Cinnery, Ann./Bai, Heesoon. (2008). Justice in the Name of the Other. In Egéa-Kuehne, D (ed.), *Levinas and Education. At the Intersection of Faith and Reason.* New York: Routledge.

Cohen, R. A. (1986). *Face to Face with Levinas.* Albany: State University of New York Press.

Cornell, D. (1992). *The Philosophy of the Limit.* New York: Routledge.

Critchley, S. (2008). *Infinitely Demarking: Ethics of Commitment, Politics of Resistance.* London: Verso.

Derrida, J. (1997). *Adieu a Emmanuel Levinas.* Paris: Galilee.

Derrida, J. (1995). *Points.....: Interviews, 1974-1994*. Stanford University Press, Palo Alto

Derrida, J. (1992). The Force of Law: The "Mystical Foundation of Authority». In Cornell, D./Rosenfeld, M./Carlsson, D. G. (eds.), *Deconstruction and the Possibility of Justice.* Cambridge: Harvard University Press.

Derrida, J. (1978). *Writing and Difference*. Chicago: University of Chicago Press.

Diamantides, M. (ed.). (2007). *Levinas, Law, Politics.* London: Routledge Cavendish.

Edgoose, J. (2001). Just decide! Derrida and the ethical aporias of education. In Biesta, G./Egéa-Kuehne. (ed.). *Derrida & Education.* London: Routledge.

Egéa-Kuehne, D. (2008). *Levinas and Education. At the Intersection of Faith and Reason.* New York: Routledge.

Gutting, G. (2011). *Thinking the Impossible. French Philosophy Since 1960.* New York: Oxford University Press.

Düwell, M./Hofmeyr, B. (ed.). (2009). *Radical Passivity: Rethinking Ethical Agency in Levinas.* Dordrecht:Springer.

Hägglund, M. (2008). *Radical Atheism. Derrida and the Time of Life.* Stanford: Stanford University Press.

Herbert, A. (2010). *The Pedagogy of Creativity.* London: Routledge.

Hill, L. (2007). *The Cambridge Introduction to Jacques Derrida*. Cambridge: Cambridge University Press.

Johnston, D. (2012). *A Brief History of Justice.* Malden: Wiley-Blackwell.

Joldersma, C. (2008). The Importance of Enjoyment and Inspiration for Learning from a Teacher. In D. Egéa-Kuehne, *Levinas and Education. At the Intersection of Faith and Reason.* New York: Routledge.

Kemp, P. (1988). Nærhedsetikkens begrænsning. In Schuster, B. G, *Moral & Etik.* København: Forlaget Anis.

Kunz, G. (1998). *The Paradox of Power and Weakness*. Albany: The University of New York Press.

Levinas, E. (1969). *Totality and Infinity.* Pittsburg: Duquesne University Press.

Levinas, E. (1981). *Otherwise than being or beyond essence.* The Hague: Martinus Nijhoff.

Levinas, E. (1985). *Ethics and infinity.* Pittsburg: Duquesne University Press.

Levinas, E. (1986). *De Dieu qui vient à l'idée.* Paris: Vrin.

Levinas, E. (1996). God and Philosophy. In Peperzak,A. T/Critchley, S/Bernasconi, R (eds.). *Emmanuel Levinas: Basic philosophical writing.* Bloomington: Indiana University Press.

Murray, J. (2003). *Face to Face in Dialogue.* New York: University Press of America.

Peters, M., (ed.). (1998). *Naming the Multiple. Poststructuralism and Education.* Westport: Bergin & Garvey.

Rynolds, J./Roffe, J. (eds.). (2007). *Understanding Derrida.* New York: Continuum.

Sheffler M. R. (2001). *Beyond Ethics To Justice. Through Levinas and Derrida.* Illinois Franciscan Press.

Smith, J. A. (2005). *Jacques Derrida. Live Theory.* New York: Continuum.

Taureck, B. (1991). *Levinas zur Einführung.* Hamburg: Junius Verlag.

Thomas, E. (2004). *Emmanuel Levinas. Ethics, Justice, and the Human beyond Being. New* York: Routledge.

Todd, S. (2008). *Att lära av den Andre.* Stockholm: Studentlitteratur.

Todd, S. (2002). On Not Knowing the Other, or Learning from Levinas. In Rice, S. (ed.). *Philosophy of Education 2001*. Illinois: Philosophy of Education Society.

Wall, J. (2010). *Ethics in Light of Childhood.* Washington: Georgetown University Press.

Aarnes, A. (2001). *Ut av fatning. I samtale med Hall Bjørnstad.* Oslo: Aschehoug.

AUTHOR: Kjetil Steinsholt is Professor at the Department of Education, Norwegian University of Science and Technology (NTNU). He also holds a position as Adjunct Professor at Østfold University College. His research focuses on philosophy of play, democratic participation and childhood studies.
Correspondence: Kjetil.steinsholt@svt.ntnu.no

# *Leaving school for what?*

## NOTES ON SCHOOL-TO-WORK TRANSITIONS AND SCHOOL DROPOUT IN NORWAY AND SWEDEN

LISBETH LUNDAHL
Umeå University, Sweden

ABSTRACT: *Young people without an upper secondary education face considerably increased risks of unemployment and social exclusion. In this article, Norwegian and Swedish policies aiming to support young people's school-to-work transitions and minimize school dropout are analysed and compared, applying a categorisation of social inclusion from Arnesen & Lundahl (2006). It is concluded that the similarities between Norway and Sweden with regard to four factors - access to education and the labour market, division and integration, the distribution of resources and the placing of responsibilities - tend to dominate the picture. There are, however, also a number of noteworthy differences. In particular, young Swedes run larger risks of unemployment than Norwegian youth. Norway has been more proactive and has taken more comprehensive approaches than Sweden to facilitate transitions within upper secondary education and between school and work.*

### *Introduction*

Is it a problem that young people leave school without completing upper secondary education? If someone had posed that question in the 1960s, no one would have understood it. At that time, just a small percentage of young people entered upper secondary school and there were plenty of jobs for boys and girls who had left compulsory education. Today the situation is quite different. Not only do most young Europeans at least complete upper secondary education – and, in reality, this has become a minimum requirement to become employed - but the path to adulthood and economic independence has also been lengthened considerably because of the difficulties in finding a job. In Sweden, the average

age of establishment in the labour market (that is, when 75 percent of a cohort have some kind of employment) thus rose from 21 in the early 1990s to 28 in 2006 (SOU 2006:102), which is a remarkable change over a very short period. All over Europe, the patterns of school-to-work transitions now look different from the rather linear ones that dominated into the 1980s. Reversible and fragmented, so called yo-yo transitions have thus become more and more common. They are characterized by repeated switching between education, training and (often temporary) work, along with spells of unemployment and participation in various youth schemes (Lidström 2009, Walther et al. 2002). It is known from research that unemployment, especially in combination with other risk factors such as difficult home conditions, dropping out of school and receiving social allowance, leaves scars that last several decades when considering unemployment, wages, health and job satisfaction (Hammer 2007; Bell & Blanchflower 2009). Leaving school has thus become a risky endeavour for many young people, in particular those who leave upper secondary education with incomplete grades: this group is markedly over-represented amongst unemployed youth.

In an article from 2006, *Still Social and Democratic? Inclusive Education Policies in the Contemporary Nordic Welfare States*, Anne-Lise Arnesen and I compared the significance attributed to the social-inclusive aspects of education in education policies in the Nordic countries and the extent to which education is regarded as an element in welfare policies. The overriding aim was to analyse if it is still reasonable to speak of a common Nordic model in these respects, in line with Gösta Esping-Andersen´s (1996) welfare state typology. We concluded that the education policies of these countries continued to deviate from other European or OECD countries in a number of important respects, but that profound neo-liberal influences had prevailed, reducing the differences between this and other welfare state regimes. In this article, I will focus on the policies concerning young people´s school-to-work transitions and efforts to minimize school dropout – another part of inclusive welfare politics, even if it is not always named as such. Several European youth researchers have analysed transition policies in terms of different transition regimes, also using the categorisation of Esping-Andersen (see below). Elsewhere I have suggested that it may be time to critically question government thinking in connection to youth transitions, as the explanatory value of this kind of categorisation seems to be limited. For example, the variations both of preconditions, such as the organisation of vocational education and training and of outcomes in, amongst others, youth unemployment and early school leaving are greater *within* national transition regimes than *between* them in many cases (Lundahl 2011). In the following, I will explore this question somewhat further by comparing efforts to prevent and manage school dropout in Sweden and Norway. In the final section, I will tentatively discuss if it is justified to speak of a common youth transition regime within the Nordic countries, a question that is similar to that posed in the article from 2006.

This article is structured as follows: three short introductory sections will serve as the framework for the analysis and discussion of the Norwegian and Swedish examples. First, the problematic 'dropout' in Europe and the Nordic countries, as well as common strategies to combat this is briefly outlined. Second, the concept of youth transition regimes, as developed by Walther and colleagues (2006) is presented. Third, I set out the categorisation of social inclusion, which was introduced by Lundahl (2001), further developed by Arnesen & Lundahl (2006) and is here applied to young people´s transitions from school to work. The rest of the article mainly builds on empirical data and analyses from European and Nordic research and statistical databases, including my own ongoing longitudinal research project *Troublesome Transitions. School-to-work transitions of young people at risk in a longitudinal perspective* (2010-2013)[1]

## *Leaving school early – what´s the problem?*

Early school leavers, a term that today commonly describes young people who leave upper secondary education without having completed their grades or a degree, constitute a growing problem as they run a considerably higher risk of being unemployed, becoming socially marginalised and falling ill than those of the same age who have, at the least, completed upper secondary education (Dale 2010, Hernes 2010, Bäckman et al. 2011, Olofsson & Östh 2011, Wilson et al. 2011). The societal costs associated with school dropout – costs resulting from lower productivity and tax incomes as well as from higher social and health care expenses - are vast (Dale 2010, Hernes 2010). For example, these costs were recently estimated to be 5 billion NOK for each youth cohort in Norway (Hernes 2010, p. 7)[2]. A

---

[1] The project is funded by the Swedish Research Council (VR Dnr 2009-5964).

[2] In the U.S, it has been similarly estimated that approximately 12 million students will dropout over the next decade, costing the U.S. about $3 trillion (American Psychologist

number of factors increase the dropout risk: (a) Family and social factors such as low income and educational level, unemployment, high mobility of the parents and teenage parenthood. Dropout is indeed a matter of social class; (b) School-related factors e.g. social composition, teacher support, school and class size; (c) Factors related to the educational system such as length of compulsory education, teacher/pupil ratio, public expenditure on education and the quality and efficiency of education (Dale 2010). These factors are complexly interlinked and it is reasonable to treat the dropout problem as a *process* rather than a single event; the young person runs the apparent risk of falling into a downward spiral where his/her lack of various resources is gradually amplified over time, as illustrated in figure 1.

Prevention of failure at school and facilitation of school-to-work transitions have become more and more important as topics on political agendas all over Europe. The measures taken at national and local levels can be pre-emptive (e.g. having an extensive system of high quality preschool education), preventive (e.g. higher expenditures on schooling and special needs education) and support to those who have failed (e.g. second chance education, mentoring and counselling services). Preventive measures could be more general or more directed. The most common general measure by far is to strengthen the vocational education and training, situated in schools and/or at places of work (Dale 2010, Bäckman et al. 2011).

---

Association 2010). Also see Rasmussen et al. (2010) on how the long-term social costs of different levels of marginalisation of Norwegian youth can be calculated.

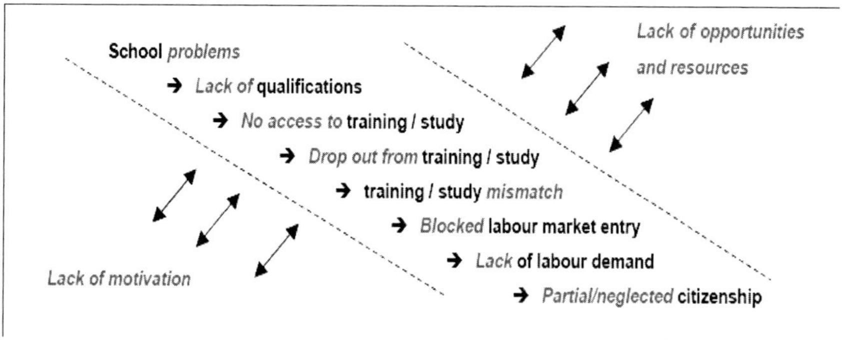


Figure 1. Thwarted Trajectories[3]

## *Youth transition regimes*

A number of studies show that the national policies of school-to-work transitions differ considerably from each other (Bäckman et al. 2011, Olofsson & Panican 2008a, Walther 2006, Walther et al. 2002). Youth researchers, for example, within the European research network EGRIS and the German GLOBALIFE project (Lopéz Blasco et al. 2003, Blossfeld & Hofmeister 2005), use the categorization of welfare state regimes (Esping-Andersen 1996) as a point of departure when they compare school-to-work transitions and the varying strategies and measures adopted to facilitate such transitions. Andreas Walther (2006) distinguished between four youth transition regimes: universalistic, typically represented by the Nordic countries, conservative employment-centred, liberal and conservative sub-protective. They supposedly differ in regard to concepts such as the comprehensiveness and standardization of the educational systems, the degree of openness and regulation of the labour market for young people, the character of social protection and the scope of female employment[4]. Even the ways of conceptualizing youth, youth unemployment, 'at risk' or disadvantaged youth as well as the political strategies to manage school-to-work transitions tend

[3] From Walther and Pohl, 2005, p. 35.

[4] We have also found varying *local transition policy patterns* in Swedish municipalities based on similar distinctions (Lundahl & Rönnberg 2008, Lundahl & Nilsson 2010).

to differ between the regimes (Table 1). One may note that in all four clusters, education and training are central parts of transition policies, but the emphasis differs with regard to the kind of education and training emphasized - more universal or selective educational measures and varying degrees of flexible or standardized education and training.

| *Regime* | *Countries (examples)* | *Dominant conceptualizations and focus* | | | |
|---|---|---|---|---|---|
| | | *of youth* | *of youth unemployment* | *of disadvantage* | *of transition policies* |
| Universalistic | Denmark Sweden | Personal development, citizenship | 'Not foreseen' | Mixed (individualized/ structure-related) | Education, Activation |
| Conservative/ employment-centred | Germany France Netherlands | Adaptation to social positions | Disadvantage (deficit model) | Individualized | (Pre-) vocational training |
| Liberal | UK Ireland | Early economic inde-pendence | Culture of Dependency | Individualized | Employability |
| Conservative/ sub-protective | Italy Spain Portugal | Without distinct Status | Segmented labour market, lack of training | Structure-related | 'Some' status: work, education or training |

Table 1. Youth, unemployment and disadvantage: conceptualizations and policies[5]

[5] Source: Walther 2006, p. 126.

The picture of the universalistic transition regime in Nordic countries is painted in quite bright colours by Walther (2006): it is said to be based on a comprehensive school system and generous social and educational allowances. The employment regime is characterized by an extended public sector, broad access options and high rates of female employment, facilitated by the system of public childcare. Counselling is institutionalized throughout education and the stage of transition from school to work. 'Personal development' is central to the definition of youth, which is also reflected in the transitions policies and measures oriented towards early school leavers. Experimenting with yo-yo transitions within certain frames is encouraged and supported and there is also a strengthened focus on the individualized labour market (ibid. pp. 126-127). All in all, one gets the impression that the Nordic countries have a clear inclusive approach to young people who are preparing to establish themselves as adults in the labour market. However, the analysis of school-to-work transitions in Norway and Sweden somewhat modifies this rather idyllic viewpoint.

## *School-to-work transitions in socially inclusive terms: A categorisation*

Based on a categorisation that was originally developed in a research project on educational governance, social integration and exclusion in Europe (Lundahl 2001) and slightly altered in the article by Arnesen & Lundahl (2006), four comprehensive elements of social inclusion will be used here when discussing and comparing Swedish and Norwegian school-to-work transitions: (a) access to arenas or resources, (b) integration/separation of categories and/or contents, (c) distribution of resources and (d) community versus individual agency orientation.

*(a) Access/non-access*: This element mainly concerns the availability of education at different levels, including the provision of adult education and 'second chance education' in various forms. Additionally, it is about access to qualified special education, counselling and also about young people´s opportunities or difficulties in entering the labour market. Finally, it may also include access to resources and arenas outside education and work such as culture and leisure time activities, but such aspects will not be dealt with in this article.

*(b) Integration/division*: the integration or separation of academic and vocational paths, the latter including apprenticeship training, is one important aspect here. Another is the integration or separation of young people with regard to characteristics such as gender, special needs and immigrant or minority background, both in education and in the labour market.

*(c) Distribution of resources:* When studying transition policies, one distinguishing feature is to what extent a re-distribution of resources, in the form of the tax-funding of measures to support young people at risk of social marginalization – unemployed youth, young people who have not completed their upper secondary education (or equivalent), disabled young people etc. - takes place. Another important aspect concerns the incomes and living standards of young people. Are, for example, special (lower) youth wages introduced with the intention to facilitate employment of young people?

(d) Community versus individual agency: Somewhat simplified, this element deals with the major localisation of responsibility for educational success (or failure) and for success (failure) of the young person´s transition to higher education or establishment within the labour market.

## Paths from education to work in Sweden and Norway

### Education and training

Both the Swedish and Norwegian education systems are characterized by the extensive provision of early childhood education and childcare that reaches more than 80 percent of the youngest children. Norwegian municipalities are obliged to provide such education and care for the one to five-year olds; in Sweden, this provision covers the one to six-year olds. Early childhood education is mainly tax-funded in both countries, but parents pay certain fees. The compulsory comprehensive school – attended for 9 years in Sweden and 10 years in Norway – was introduced through reforms in the 1960s in both countries. Similarly, upper secondary education underwent reforms in the 1970s and 1990s in Norway as well as in Sweden. As a result, all vocational and academic programs are part of the same organisation and last at least 3 years. After the reforms of the 1990s, there are only a rather limited number of programs – originally 13 in Norway (of which 9 are vocational) and 16 in Sweden (14 vocational). In both countries, one of the aims of the reforms at that time was to promote flexibility and to avoid vocational programs becoming dead ends. By this time, young people were entitled by law to receive upper secondary education, in Sweden as well as in Norway. In Sweden, all 3-year programmes thus ensured that all students were eligible for studies at university level. In Norway, the reform called *Kunnskapsløftet* in 2006 added certain revisions to the policy, while a reform in Sweden in 2009 (implemented in 2011) constituted more of a break with earlier trends as it introduced sharper divisions between academic and vocational programs with the latter not automatically giving eligibility to higher education anymore (c.f. Lundahl et al. 2010, Olsen et al. 2008). At the end of the 1970s, two thirds of all Norwegian 17-19 year olds attended academic or vocational education and training at upper secondary level, while the corresponding figure was higher in Sweden – almost 80 percent. Today almost all (98 percent) of Swedish and Norwegian pupils enrol in upper secondary education. In 2009, 53 percent of Swedish girls were enrolled in one of the vocational programmes at upper secondary level, with 46 percent in Norway. The corresponding figures for boys were 60 and 62 percent (Eurostat 2012). In both cases vocational education and training (VET) reflects the highly gender divided labour market. The patterns of transition to *higher education* are rather similar in the two countries. In 2007, 42 percent of Norwegians and 40 percent of Swedes aged 25-34 years received an education at tertiary level[6], with a gender difference of 12 to 14 percent in favour of the females – largest in Norway (Eurostat 2009).

So far, the similarities between the educational systems at preschool, primary and secondary levels and between the contents and timing of the reform processes in the two countries are rather striking. However, there are profound differences as well, mainly in regard to the organisation of VET. From the 1950s, the Swedish VET system has been typically school-based, and apprenticeship training has been rare at upper secondary level. For the last 30 years, there have been repeated, rather fruitless, reform efforts to introduce so-called modern apprenticeship education, the latest but probably not the last being in 2009. Swedish VET followed the model of the 1990s and has been both criticized and blamed for being too 'academic' and causing a high dropout rate – a criticism that was one of the motives behind the 2009 reform (Lundahl et al. 2010). However, this negative picture has been contradicted by the results of research: for example, Bäckman et al. (2011), in their analysis of dropout and labour market

[6] ISCED 5-6

attachment in four Nordic counties, concluded that Swedish young people who follow the vocational path come out best, if the percentage of diplomas awarded seven years after the start is taken as a measure (*ibid.*, p. 36. Also c.f. Svensson, 2007).

Norway has traditionally had a rather unique combination of school-based vocational education and apprenticeship training which were regulated by two different sets of legislation and developed in different directions. Another peculiarity was the potential to attain the status of skilled worker without formal education or training, a status held by almost half of the applicants studied (Olsen et al. 2008). In the 1980s, the old VET system was perceived as increasingly problematic: a lack of flexibility and problems in planning resulted in more and more young people having to wait for education and jobs. The solution, the 1994 reform, meant that vocational education at upper secondary level was organized in a sequential way: during the first two years, students mainly attend theoretical classes on a full-time basis and some then move on to a two-year apprenticeship, while the others move to a third year in school. The reform also meant that there was a bridge between vocational and academic studies. Students on vocational training, provided that they attended certain courses, were considered to be of sufficient standard to study at higher education level (Ure 2007, Olsen et al. 2008). Even after the 1994 reform, adults (older than 20 years) in Norway are allowed to start studying in upper secondary school, but in Sweden there is a limit to entering such studies of 20 years of age. After that, a person is referred to adult education (Olofsson & Panican 2008b).

Another difference relates to how young people with special needs and incomplete grades from compulsory schooling are treated when they reach the upper secondary level. In Sweden, the 1991/92 upper secondary school reform included the establishment of the so-called Individual Programme (IP), initially meant to provide individually tailored studies, normally for one year, for those who were not yet ready to decide which 3-year national programme to choose. Very soon the IP became one of the largest programmes, containing many (but not only) students who lacked complete grades from compulsory schooling and hence were not eligible for a national programme. The IP was often criticised since it largely failed to provide the intended bridge to successful studies on a national program. In 2005, less than half of the students on the Individual Programme went on to undertake a national programme and only one in five completed upper secondary education within four years (Swedish National Agency for Education, 2007). The 2009 reform meant that the IP was replaced by five different introductory programmes, the success of which is still unknown.

As was mentioned previously, the Norwegian 1994 Reform introduced a general right to 3 years of upper secondary education. Before this, young people with special education needs in many cases had not been accepted to study at upper secondary level and Markussen et al. (2009) consequently wrote of a qualitative jump concerning the rights of education (rettighetssprang*)* for this group of students. The white paper *A culture for learning* (Govt bill 2003-2004, no 30) was one of the reports preceding the reform *Kunskapsløftet* of the 13-year long primary and secondary education and proposed increased funding of research, method development and dissemination of results from work aiming to promote adapted education. The reform also intended to strengthen competences in special education and counselling and to evaluate how individualised instruction was dealt with in teacher education. Educational choice ('utdanningsvalg') was introduced as a subject in secondary education (Ure 2007; Markussen et al. 2009). In contrast, the Swedish upper secondary school reforms of the 1990s and 2000s did not include any measures of this kind.

In 2006 and 2007, the proportion of young people who completed upper secondary education after five years ranged from 65 to 70 percent in Norway, Sweden and Denmark and was almost 80 percent in Finland (Wilson et al. 2011.)[7]. In other words, 20 to 35 percent of the young adults may be labelled as early school leavers in the Nordic context. However, such figures are not alarming as long as the labour market is open to people who just have compulsory education. As Hernes (2010) put it: "*Dropout is not a new problem, but it has become more visible when everybody is entitled to upper secondary education – and after upper secondary education became the very portal to a productive adult life*" (ibid., p. 7).

### *Transitions to work*

As in the rest of the Western world, the establishment of young people in the labour market takes place considerably later in Sweden and Norway than two decades ago. While Swedish youth unemployment rates are among the highest in

[7] In Denmark and Finland, this refers to youth entering upper secondary education in 2001, whilst in Norway and Sweden it refers to youth entering upper secondary education in 2002.

Europe, young Norwegians face a relatively low risk of unemployment according to a comparison of Nordic and European nations[8] (Figure 2).

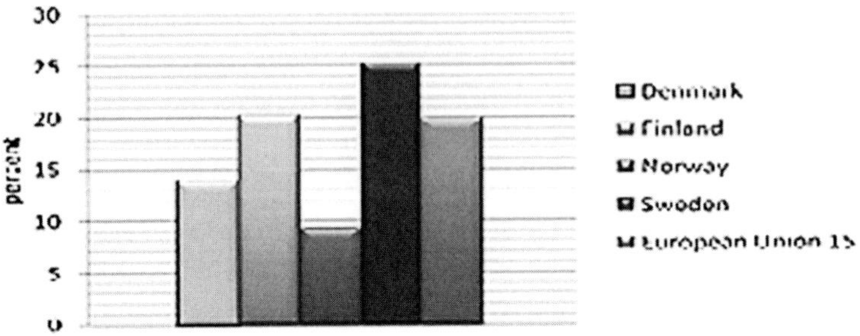


Figure 2. Unemployment for 15-24 year olds in 2010 (%)[9]

However, the differences between the Nordic countries diminish considerably if we look at the rates of young people who are not in employment, education or training (NEET) - to a large extent a group of early school leavers, at 20-24 years of age[10]. These rates have remained between 5 and 7 percent with few exceptions between 1995 and 2007 (Bäckman et al. 2011, p. 24). There is consequently reason to believe that Norway and Sweden have more of a common problem of young people at risk of becoming permanently marginalised than one would believe just looking at youth unemployment figures alone. In their analysis, Rasmussen et al. (2010) estimated that 2-4 percent of young Norwegians under 20 years old are at risk and, considering the labour market and youth unemployment situation, this rate could increase up to 8 percent for 25-30 year olds. It is no overstatement that these percentages are even worse in Sweden. It may be added that the number of young adults (20-34 years) receiving disability pension increased alarmingly from 1995 to 2007 in both Norway and Sweden – in Norway some 45 percent and in Sweden 80 percent. In their analysis of the Swedish situation, Olofsson & Östh (2011) concluded that this increase has more to do with the labour market situation than the deteriorating health of the people concerned.

---

[8] The corresponding average unemployment figure for EU15 was 20 percent.

[9] Source: OECD Stat 2012.

[10] The figures concern native-born and the measurements were conducted over three consecutive years.

Young unemployed people are targeted by a range of schemes, often tailor-made for young people, with benefits that commonly prevent the young person from becoming economically independent. In Sweden, a "job-guarantee" for youth aged 16-25 was introduced in 2007, whereas in Norway a "follow-up guarantee" for youth aged 20-24 as part of a big employment reform in 2006/07 was brought in (Arbetsdepartementet 2006/07). In both countries, as in the rest of Europe, the 'activation line' i.e. the demands on unemployed and recipients of social benefits to actively seek jobs, has become dominant over the last twenty years (Handler, 2003). The activation line implies an emphasis on mutual obligations, laid down in individual action plans, as a precondition to receive income support. But also, as Newman (2007) pointed out, it can be understood as "*opening up more of the person to governmental power, requiring them to collaborate in the development of new subjective orientations to the worlds of work and welfare*" (Newman, 2007, p. 3).

### *'Second chance' education*

In international comparisons, the Nordic countries generally stand out as providing extensive options for so-called life-long learning i.e. opportunities for basic and further education at adult age (Figure 3).

However, the opportunities for second chance education are far less favourable than indicated above, at least in Sweden. The majority of adult Swedes had attended some form of informal learning activities at their places of work, rather than formal education, on average for just four days[11]. The locally administered adult education *(Komvux)* has played a crucial role for adults who wish to complete and supplement their basic education and in the 1990s, a large investment (Kunskapslyftet) was made to strengthen the competence level of adults with little education. However, the number of student places in *Komvux* has undergone a reduction of a fourth from 2004 to 2009. In addition, the number of participants in labour market training (mainly vocational training for the unemployed) has gone down dramatically since the 1990s and today less than 5 percent of unemployed people in some kind of labour market schemes participate in education; such measures have largely been replaced by coaching and practice within the so-called job and development guarantee (Olofsson forthcoming).

[11] Actually, if one measures participation in terms of hours, Sweden not only falls below the average of the Nordic countries, but also that of the nineteen EU countries.

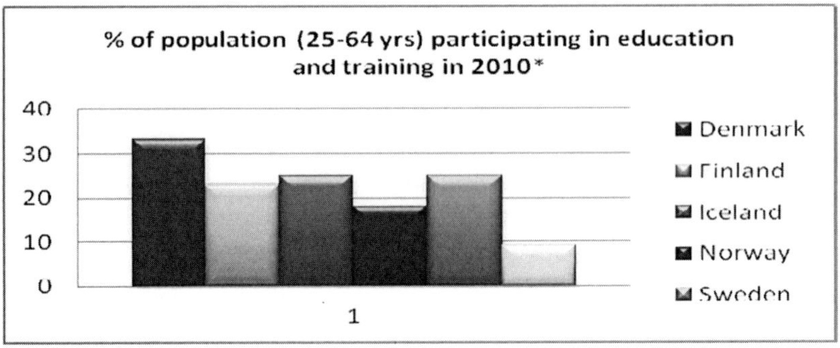


Figure 3. Percent of population (25-64 yrs) participating in education and training in 2010[12]

In Norway, a major reform, the *Competence Reform,* was launched in 1999 with the aim of enhancing Life Long Learning (LLL). It had a variety of components such as changes in legislation giving a legal right to free education at primary and secondary levels and a right to a leave of absence for attending further and continuing training, funding of projects experimenting with work-based training and validation of non-formal and informal competencies. Ure (2007) concluded that the Competence Reform offered improved access to formal education for those in need of a second chance, but it remains a paradox that participation in training has not increased in spite of these lofty ambitions – rather the reverse.

## *Experiences of those who left education without complete grades*

When school failure and dropout is discussed in the media and by decision-makers, some explanations and recommendations stand out over others. One set of explanations attribute the problems to the individuals; young people are allegedly tired of school, lack an entrepreneurial attitude and have unrealistic job and life expectations. Another set of explanations blame education for being too academic and schools for having too little contact with the surrounding society and places of work. In Sweden, the gymnasium (Upper Secondary School) stemming

[12] Eurostat (2012). Criterion: receiving education or training in the four weeks preceding the labour force survey.

from the reform in the 1990s has been attacked on such grounds and apprenticeship training has been advocated as a major solution to the problems (Lundahl et al. 2010). Also, it is common to define the problem in terms of labour legislation that is too strict and to recommend lowered initial salaries for young people in order to make them more employable. The results of our interviews, as part of the ongoing research project *Troublesome Transitions* (2010-2013), with more than 80 young people in Sweden aged 21-22 who left upper secondary school without complete grades[13] complicate the picture considerably and the previous arguments and suggestions that point to just one cause are not shown to be correct. Here, I will give some examples from the first round of interviews that may highlight the problems and requirements of additional resources and competencies within the rough framework described earlier.

Many of the young people describe their social and family situation as unstable with repeated moves within Sweden and from other countries, divorces and changing groups of grown-ups. Alcohol abuse is common and some of the youth in addition describe domestic violence within the families. Also, a number of the young people interviewed started using alcohol at an early stage. Primary education is often perceived as a harmonious time, but at secondary level, the students have increasing problems keeping up with the others in education. The situation is often worsened by truancy and harassment. Young people, later diagnosed as having ADHD, dyslexia or similar, conclude that they have been treated as 'different' not just by the other students but also by the teachers, but seldom received any adequate support for their learning and cognitive difficulties; the school has done little to tackle the harassment. The situation in upper secondary school is unstable: this period is to a high degree characterized by changes of programs, leaving school then returning, attendance and absence.

Some people are described as positive key persons in the lives of young people: the families, in particular the mothers, despite their problems and shortcomings, relatives and committed teachers who have seen the young individual, listened to them and also demanded something from them. In particular, the young

[13] The young men and women come from 20 municipalities representing a wide range of housing conditions and varying success in preventing school dropout and youth unemployment. The study builds on three sub-sets of interviewees: young adults (a) with some kind of disability – in practice cognitive disabilities such as dyslexia and ADHD, (b) of non-European origin, (c) with non-defined background (other than not having completed upper secondary education)

people of non-European origin emphasise the importance of their families *('my family means everything to me')*, but also conclude that their parents have few opportunities to help them with things such as homework or choice of programme. These young people seem to have made a lonely journey through their studies.

At present, a majority of young people attend education of some kind, mostly local adult education *(Komvux)* in order to complete their grades. Practically all of them have experiences of unemployment and difficulties entering the labour market. Generally, their economic situation is precarious and, to a large extent, they have to live with their parents or are dependent on a partner giving economic support as the study and social allowances they receive are too meagre to live on.

The stories from our respondents are not unique within Sweden. They illustrate a complexity of factors at work found in many other countries. In line with this, it was concluded a recent Norwegian report on school dropout at upper secondary level that a broad range of measures are needed from preschool level to vocational education and training in places of work (Hernes 2010).

## *Concluding discussion: Similar or different mechanisms of inclusion and exclusion?*

I will now return to the four elements of social inclusion that I presented earlier in the article and use them to compare Swedish and Norwegian school-to-work transitions. These elements are: (a) *access* to arenas or resources, (b) *integration/separation* of categories and/or contents, (c) *distribution* of resources and (d) *community* versus *individual agency* orientation. Needless to say, this will be a very brief and superficial comparison of the countries, but hopefully it can serve the purpose of starting a discussion about the Nordic transition regime(s) – similarities, variations and marked differences.

### *Access/non-access*

In both Norway and Sweden, young people have extensive access to preschool education, compulsory and post-compulsory education. With the exception of preschool education, where parents have to pay certain fees, all education and training (including higher education) is free of charge, which is a highly significant point. Upper secondary education is designed to receive 100 percent of all young people, including those with special needs.

At present however, Norway seems to invest more actively in life-long learning provision than Sweden. In fact, Sweden has reduced the number of study places in local adult education substantially in the first decade of the twenty first century and has an employment policy which offers very little in the way of educational support. Also, in contrast to Norway, adults older than 20 years are not allowed to enter an upper secondary school programme. In other words, the number of opportunities for a second chance at education is shrinking in Sweden. It is, however, noteworthy that participation in adult education shows a small drop in Norway despite its large Life Long Learning Reform in 1999. Norway has a stronger position than Sweden with regard to commitment and investments in research and development in individually adapted and special needs education and counselling. Considering previous evaluations and the interviews from our ongoing research project, this is probably *one* crucial factor that might prevent study failure and thwarted school-to-work transitions. Finally, Norway has a considerably lower youth unemployment rate than Sweden. In other words, the labour market is more accessible to young people in Norway than in Sweden. However it should be kept in mind that, in both countries, 5 to 7 percent of young people are neither in employment, nor in education or training for a lengthy period and they constitute a group under apparent risk of becoming socially excluded.

### *Integration/division*

The Swedish educational reforms from the 1960s to the early 2000s were oriented towards reducing the barriers and differences between academic and vocational paths at upper secondary level; the Norwegian reform of 1994 had a similar aim. In Sweden, this tendency towards integration stopped with the reform in 2009. For example, students attending the vocational programmes now have to take active steps to choose and supplement courses in order to obtain general eligibility for higher education, which was not the case before. The reduction in the number of applicants to many vocational programmes was almost 10 percent in 2011, a decrease often attributed to this change. The differences between and within academic and vocational programmes have increased in other respects, which will not help facilitate a change of program or flexibility more generally.

Other divisions remain more or less unchanged in both countries, in particular the highly gender-biased educational and job trajectories and the increased risks for young people with an immigrant background of dropping out from upper secondary education. Young Roma people are in an extremely precarious situation: in, for example, Malmö in the south of Sweden, 80 percent of the Roma population is unemployed, almost half of the children do not attend grades 7-9 of compulsory (sic) school and virtually none progress to upper secondary education, although this is a necessity for employment (Söderman & Ström 2008). In both countries, young disabled people run considerably higher risks of being excluded from the labour market than others and the rising number of disability pensions among young people in both countries – especially in Sweden – is alarming.

### *Distribution of resources*

Both Sweden and Norway spend quite high proportions of their GNP on education[14] i.e. at a general level, a substantial redistribution of resources via taxation takes place in order to provide educational services. How much of these expenses that were invested in measures to support young people´s transitions from school to work, in particular youth at risk of social marginalization, would however require a major investigation of its own.

Youth poverty is far more widespread in Europe than is usually acknowledged. Fahmy (2007) concluded:

> ...the experience of poverty is not confined to a small minority of "socially excluded" young people, but is very common for Europe´s young people at various points in their transitions to adulthood. At the same time… young people are also more vulnerable to recurrent poverty than older adults (*ibid.*, p. 54).

Tackling youth poverty is therefore not only an important policy task in its own right but also a way of preventing social marginalisation. In the Nordic countries, as opposed to other European nations, young people leaving school tend to be clearly more poverty-stricken than other age groups, the latter of which display

[14] In 2008 Sweden spent 6.74% of its GNP on education, Norway 6.51% as compared to 5.07 in the 27 EU-countries. In both cases the figures were somewhat higher in 2003 – 7.30% and 7.54% (Eurostat 2012).

lower poverty levels than the rest of Europe. Iacovou & Aassve (2007) related this difference to the early age when Nordic youth leaves the parental home.

### *Community versus individual agency*

Over the last two decades, a marked change has taken place in the localisation of responsibility for young persons' educational success and failure and more or less successful transition from school to work. The tendency to address the autonomous, entrepreneurial and knowledgeable child and youth is seen in education policy documents, in youth policies and in the activation line of employment policies, not least when concerning unemployed youth. In educational practice, teacher instructtion is increasingly replaced by autonomous student work (Österlind 1998). Individual development or action plans become somewhat of a universal instrument, from kindergarten to the employment agency (c.f. Lundahl 2002; Arnesen & Lundahl 2010). If the trajectories after school one generation ago used to be rather linear and visibly driven by tradition, gender and social class, today´s youth is expected to navigate through an endless number of alternatives without such ties - even if the resulting choices indeed are still related to class, gender, ethnicity and geography (Lundahl 2010). Young people are responsible for the design of their 'choice biographies' (Bois-Reymond et al. 1994). The same individual agency thinking is reflected in the narratives of the young people concerned; unemployed youth tend to see themselves as the architects of their own lives (Lidström 2009). Similarly, in our interviews with young adults in the project *Unsafe Transitions,* school dropout is mainly explained by the individual´s shortcomings such as drinking too much alcohol or not taking the situation in school seriously enough.

## *Some final reflections*

One of the initial questions touched upon in this article asked if it is reasonable to speak of a common Nordic transition regime with similar approaches to youth unemployment, dropout, and transition policies, if we take two of the Nordic countries as test cases. For obvious reasons, it is not possible to answer that question other than perfunctorily. All in all, the similarities between Norway and Sweden with regard to the specific factors brought up here - access to education and the labour market, division or integration in some important respects, the distribution of resources and the placing of responsibilities - tend to dominate the picture. There are, however, also a number of noteworthy differences, both with regard to the conditions and policies of school-to-work transitions and dropout from school. In particular, young Swedes run considerably larger risks of unemployment than Norwegian youth. The two countries have initiated reforms of upper secondary education in the 1990s and 2000s, the increased employability of young people being high on the agenda in both cases. But it seems that Norway has been more proactive and has taken more comprehensive approaches than Sweden to facilitate transitions within upper secondary education and between school and work, including efforts to develop special education, counselling and guidance and to promote life-long learning.

## *References*

Arbetsdepartementet (2006/07) Stortingsmelding. nr. 9 (2006-2007) *Arbeid, velferd og inkludering.* Oslo: Arbetsdepartementet.

Arnesen, A.-L. & Lundahl, L. (2006). Still Social and Democratic? Inclusive Education Policies in the Nordic Welfare States. *Scandinavian Journal of Educational Research,* 50(3), 285-300 http://dx.doi.org/10.1080/00313830600743316

Bäckman, O., Jakobsen, V., Lorentzen, T., Österbacka, E. & Dahl, E. (2011). *Dropping out in Scandinavia. Social exclusion and labour market attachment among upper secondary school dropouts in Denmark, Finland, Norway and Sweden.* Arbetsrapport/Institutet för framtidsstudier 2011:8.

Bell, D. N.F & Blanchflower, D. G. (2009) What Should Be Done about Rising Unemployment in the OECD? Forschungsinstitut zur Zukunft der Arbeit/Institute for the Study of Labour, *Discussion Paper* no. 4455.

Blossfeld, H.-P. & Hofmeister, H. (2005). *Life Courses in the Globalization Process. Final Report from the GLOBALIFE project.* Bamberg: University of Bamberg. http://oldsite.soziologie-blossfeld.de/globalife/pdf/final_report.pdf

Bois-Reymond, M., Guit H, Peters E, Ravesloot J, Van Rooijen E (1994). Life-course transition and future orientation of Dutch youth. *Young* 2, 3–20. http://dx.doi.org/10.1177/110330889400200101

Dale, R. (2010). Early School Leaving. Lessons from research for policy makers. *NESSE: An independent expert report submitted to the European Commission.* European Commission.

Esping-Andersen, G. (1996). *The Three Worlds of Welfare Capitalism.* Cambridge: Polity Press.

Eurostat (2009). *The Bologna Process in Higher Education in Europe. Key indicators on the social dimension and mobility.* European Commission and Hochschul-Informations-System G mbH. http://epp.eurostat.ec.europa.eu/cache/ITY_OFFPUB/KS-78-09-653/EN/KS-78-09-653-EN.PDF

Eurostat (2012). *Pupils in upper secondary education enrolled in vocational stream.* http://epp.eurostat.ec.europa.eu/tgm/table.do?tab=table&init=1&plugin=1&language=en&pcode=tps00055

Fahmy, E. (2007). Poverty and youth transitions in Europe: an analysis of the European Communities Household Panel, in Colley, H (Ed.), *Social Inclusion for Young People: Breaking Down the Barriers,* 43-56, Strasbourg: Council of Europe, 2007.

Hammer, T. (2007). Labour market integration of unemployed youth from a life course perspective: the case of Norway. *International Journal of Social Welfare* 16 (3), 249–257. http://dx.doi.org/10.1111/j.1468-2397.2006.00467.x

Hernes, G. (2010). *Gull av gråstein. Tiltak for å redusere frafall i videregående opplæring.* Fafo-rapport 2010:03.

Iacovou, M & .Aassve, A. (2007). *Youth poverty in Europe.* York: Joseph Rowntree Foundation. http://www.jrf.org.uk/publications/youth-poverty-europe

Lidström, L. (2009). *En resa med osäkra mål. Unga vuxnas övergångar från skola till arbete i ett biografiskt perspektiv [A journey with uncertain destinations. Young adults' school-to-work transitions in a biographical perspective].* Umeå: BUSV, Umeå Universitet.

Lopéz Blasco, A.; McNeish, W. & Walther, A., eds. (2003). *Young People and Contradictions of Inclusion.* Bristol: The Policy Press.

Lundahl, L. (2001). Governance of education and its Social Consequences. Interviews with Swedish politicians and administrators. In Lindblad and Popkewitz (Eds), *Listening to Education Actors on Governance and Social Integration and Exclusion. A report from the EGSIE-project. Part II.* Uppsala: Department of Education, 321-343.

Lundahl, L. (2002). Local Youth projects: Political Rhetoric and Strategies. The Swedish Case. *Social Policy & Society*, 1(3), 247-255. http://dx.doi.org/10.1017/S1474746402003093

Lundahl, L., Ed. (2010). *Att bana vägen mot framtiden. Karriärval och vägledning i individuellt och politiskt perspektiv [Paving the way to the future. Career choice and guidance in individual and political perspectives.].* Lund: Studentlitteratur.

Lundahl, L. (2011). Paving the way to the future? Education and young European´s paths to work and independence. *European Educational Research Journal* 10(2), 168-179. http://dx.doi.org/10.2304/eerj.2011.10.2.168

Lundahl, L.; Erixon Arreman, I.; Lundström, U. & Rönnberg, L. (2010). Setting things right? Swedish upper secondary school reform in a 40-year perspective, *European Journal of Education*. 45(1), 49-62. http://dx.doi.org/10.1111/j.1465-3435.2009.01414.x

Lundahl, L. & Rönnberg, L. (2008). Safe Bridges School-to-work transition policies in twelve Swedish municipalities. *Paper presented at the NERA congress in Copenhagen*, 6-8 March 2008.

Lundahl, L. & Nilsson, G. (2010). Vägledning i en tid av decentralisering och avreglering [Career guidance in times of decentralisation and deregulation]. In Lundahl, L. (ed.) *Att bana vägen mot framtiden. Karriärval och vägledning i individuellt och politiskt perspektiv.* Lund: Studentlitteratur (in Swedish).

Markussen, E.; Wigum Frøseth, M. & Grøgaard, J. B. (2009). *Inkludert eller segregert? Om spesialundervisning i videregående opplæring like etter innføringen av Kunnskapsløftet.* Rapport 2009:7. Oslo: NIFU STEP.

Newman, J. (2007). The "double dynamics" of activation. Institutions, citizens and the remaking of welfare governance. *International Journal of Sociology and Social Policy*, 27 (9/10), 364--375. http://dx.doi.org/10.1108/01443330710822066

Olofsson, J. (forthcoming). *On Lifelong Learning – Swedish experiences in international comparison* (unpublished manuscript).

Olofsson, J. & Panican, A., (eds.) (2008a). *Ungdomars väg från skola till arbetsliv. Nordiska erfarenheter [Young people´s paths from school to working-life. Nordic Experiences].* TemaNord 2008:584. Köpenhamn: Nordiska ministerrådet. http://www.senrp.se/content/1/c4/52/86/ungdomars_vag_arbliv.pdf

Olofsson, J. & Panican, A. (2008b). *Ungdomars etableringsförhållanden i de nordiska länderna – en bakgrund.* In J. Olofsson & A. Panican (eds.), 21-52

Olofsson, J. & Östh, J. (2011). Förtidspensionering av unga. En fråga om utsortering efter utbildningsnivå och socioekonomisk bakgrund? *Underlagsrapport till den parlamentariska socialförsäkringsutredningen* (S 2010:04).

Olsen, O. J., Høst, H. & Michelsen, S. (2008). *Veier fra yrkesopplæring til arbeidsliv. En studie av det norske overgangsregimets effektivitet.* In J. Olofsson & A. Panican (eds.), 249- 332.

Österlind, E. (1998). *Disciplinering via frihet. Elevers planering av sitt eget arbete*. Uppsala Studies in Education 75. Uppsala University.

Rasmussen, I.; Dyb, V. A.; Heldal, N. & Strøm, S. (2010). *Samfunnsøkonomiske konsekvenser av marginalisering blant ungdom.* Oslo: Vista Analyse As.

SOU (2006:102) *Samverkan för ungas etablering på arbetsmarknaden [Collaboration for improving young people's establishment at the labour market],* p. 102. Stockholm: Utbildnings- och kulturdepartementet, 334-401.

Swedish National Agency for Education (2007). *Redovisning av uppdrag om Individuella program. Redovisning av regeringsuppdrag 2007-05-13. [Report om Governmental assignment 2007-05-13].* Dnr 2006-03 130.

Svensson, A. (2007). Dagens gymnasieskola – bättre än sitt rykte? *Pedagogisk Forskning i Sverige,* 12 (4), 301-323.

Söderman, E. & Ström, B. (2008) *Romers situation i Malmö. En rapport om Malmös minoritetspolitik utifrån romernas perspektiv*. Malmö: Malmö Stadskontor, Avdelning för Integration och arbetsmarknad.

Ure, O. B. (2007). *Lifelong learning in Norway. A deflating policy balloon or an act of Piecemeal Implementation?* Fafo-rapport 2007:30.

Walther, A. (2006). Regimes of youth transitions: Choice, flexibility and security in young people´s experiences across different European contexts. *Young*, 14:2, 119–139. http://dx.doi.org/10.1177/1103308806062737

Walther, A. and Pohl, A. (2005), Thematic Study on Policy Measures Concerning Disadvantaged Youth, *Study Commissioned by the European Commission, DG Employment and Social Affairs in the Framework of the Community Action Programme to Combat Social Exclusion 2002-2006,* Tübingen: Institute for Regional Innovation and Social Research (IRIS).

Walther, A.; Stauber, B.; Biggart, A.; du Bois-Reymond, M.; Furlong, A.; López B., Andreu; Mørch, S. & Pais, J. M. (2002) (eds.) *Misleading Trajectories – Integration Policies for Young Adults in Europe?* Opladen: Leske + Budrich.

Wilson, S. J.; Tanner-Smith, E. E.; Lipsey, M. W. Steinka-Fry, K. & Morrison, J. (2011). *Dropout prevention and intervention programs: Effects on school completion and dropout among school-aged children and youth.* Campbell Systematic Reviews 2011:8

AUTHOR: Lisbeth Lundahl is Professor in educational work at Umeå University. Her main research interests concern new forms of education governance in Sweden and Europe, youth policies and new patterns of young people´s school-to-work transitions and life-careers. At present she runs the cross-disciplinary research project 'Troublesome transitions. School-to-work transitions of young people at risk in a longitudinal perspective', and she recently finalised another project 'Upper secondary school as a market'. Her collaboration with Anne-Lise Arnesen, which started in the late 1970s, includes joint articles and work within the research network Critical Perspectives on Young People, Welfare and Education (Nord-Crit).

Correspondence: lisbeth.lundahl@edusci.umu.se.

# *Gender equality in Finnish teacher education*

WITH REFLECTIONS ON NORDIC AND EUROPEAN COLLABORATION

ELINA LAHELMA AND PIRKKO HYNNINEN
University of Helsinki, Finland

ABSTRACT: *In this article we examine the history of gender equality work in teacher education during the latest decades. We start with a short review on central concepts and the international background. We then move to the history of our joint work with Anne-Lise Arnesen that started in the 1980s within the working group on gender equality in the Association of Teacher Education in Europe, and continued in the Nordic project on gender equality in teacher education, Nord-Lilia. We reflect on these early initiatives vis-à-vis current situation and on the experience in a Finnish project funded the Ministry of Education called Gender Awareness in Teacher Education (2008-2011). We explore what has changed in the aims, working methods and contexts of this work, as well as what has been achieved and what remained the same.*

## *Introduction*

European collaboration in promoting gender equality in teacher education started in the 1980s in the context of the Association of Teacher Education in Europe (ATEE). The United Nations General Assembly had adopted a global women's rights treaty in 1979, and the elimination of all forms of discrimination against women included education. The treaty is often referred to as the international bill of rights for women. At that time most European countries had instituted gender equality policies. In the Nordic countries, the Nordic Council of Ministers provided resources during the 1980s and 1990s for several conferences and projects with a view to promoting gender equality in education. One of the projects, known as Nord-Lilia (1992-1994), focussed on teacher education. The activities, ideas and innovations that were shared in the early projects have been repeated with some variation nationally and internationally in new projects, including in Finland, especially since it joined the European Union in 1995. Since that time, there has been 'project after project after project' (Brunila & Lahelma 2011). We have to ask whether gender equality in teacher education is 'an impossible mission' (Lahelma 2011).

In this article we examine this history, focussing on the work of gender equality in teacher education conducted in the context of the ATEE and in the project Nord-Lilia. Anne-Lise Arnesen was the initiator and chair and the authors of this article were active in both ATEE and Nord-Lilia. Here we reflect on these early initiatives vis-à-vis current situation and on the experience in a Finnish project funded the Ministry of Education called Gender Awareness in Teacher Education (2008-2011). We explore what has changed in the aims, working methods and contexts of this work, as well as what has been achieved and what remained the same. We will concentrate on developments in Finland. The case is interesting because, along with other Nordic countries, Finland has a reputation for gender equality, and comparative statistics indeed suggest that the position of women in the country is relatively good (e.g. Gender Differences in Educational Outcomes 2010).

The paper draws on documents from the above-mentioned projects and our earlier studies (e.g. Lahelma 1992; Brunila, Heikkinen & Hynninen 2005; Brunila & Lahelma 2011), as well as on our own experiences gathered as activists for gender equality in the field of education. We present our memories in their social, historical and cultural contexts, thereby incorporating some aspects of auto-ethnographical methodologies (e.g. Allen and Piercy 2005).

## Conceptualising gender equality in education

Education in Europe has a history of strict gender and class segregation. At the beginning of organised schooling, education everywhere was the privilege of upper class boys. The question of gender equality in education was a question of girls′ right to participate, as articulated by the pioneers in the women's movement (Wollstonecraft 1792/1983). Globally speaking, this aim has still not been fully achieved, but it is the goal of national and international recommendations, action plans and developmental programmes (see e.g. European Commission

2010; IIEP 2011). In most European countries the right of girls to attend school is realised, and European girls and women generally outnumber boys in higher education. Therefore, it is not unexpected to find that people in education do not always regard their field as the most pressing area demanding gender equality.

The philosophical discussion around the meanings of equality, including gender equality, is endless, and we will not address it deeply in this article. As a reflection on the early discussion of educational equality in more general terms (e.g. Husén 1977), gender equality in education can be understood as equal access to education and equal treatment in educational institutions, irrespective of a person's gender. More profoundly, it can be understood as equal educational outcomes. This means that education is considered a factor in promoting equality in society, for example in opportunities for young people in the labour market. In Finland this perspective was articulated in the Act on Equality between Women and Men in 1987. Gender equality in education can still be discussed in terms of human rights as well, and this issue is acute in several countries. The perspective of social justice offers yet another dimension to the conceptualising: as Nancy Fraser (e.g. Fraser & Honneth 2003) suggests, equality is not only a question of redistribution, but also of recognition. In terms of education, recognition should mean that the experiences of women, as well as those of people of colour, non-heterosexual people, working-class people and people with handicaps are recognised and respected.

In the official documents, for example, of the European Union, the aim of gender equality is often problematic whenever discussions such as those above are considered. The Council of Europe outlines gender equality as follows: 'Gender equality means an equal visibility, empowerment and participation of both sexes in all spheres of public and private life. It requires the acceptance and appreciation of the complementarity of women and men and their diverse roles in society' (Council of Europe). The complementarity of the two genders troubles the definition of equality: if the diverse roles of women and men are accepted as a starting point, then it is difficult to argue for the need to diminish gender segregation in education. A parallel understanding of essential differences in girls and boys can be found in the current Finnish Act on basic education: 'In teaching, special attention should be given to the different needs and the differences in growth and development of girls and boys.' (Act 1435/2001, §4; translation EL).

Understanding girls/women and boys/men as essentially different groups of people is counter to the general reflection on gender neutrality as gender equality, which is problematic as well (Lahelma 2011). The Western concept of equality is rooted in social contract theories.[1] Equality is a relation between impartial, neutral and abstract individuals. Accordingly, all human beings are seen as basically alike. With this definition the discourse of opening up the possibilities to schooling for all makes sense. Equality and difference are theoretically understood as alternative concepts, in which equality has a positive value and difference, a negative value. If one fails to make the most of the possibilities offered, it will easily be read as class- or gender -bound deficiency or even a personal deficiency. Genders are understood as commensurable. The idea of sameness leads to the idea of neutral treatment.

In Finland, formal class and gender equality exist, i.e. there are no legislative hindrances to access to education, but there are gender and class inequalities in institutional practices and in the contents of education. Although different discourses exist, gender equality has, since the 1990s, been largely justified from the perspective of the labour market and the efficiency and productivity of the economy (e.g. Julkunen 2010). The labour market as well as education is gender segregated, and the relative division of the sexes in trades and professions has been used as the main indicator of gender (in)equality. Student counselling has been given the responsibility of lessening the division, and resources have been directed to numerous projects for changing girls' educational and occupational choices (Brunila, Heikkinen & Hynninen 2005). The rhetoric is about encouraging girls to choose branches of learning and work that are traditionally associated with men. This is understandable because the trades men do are more highly paid and highly valued than those performed by women. Yet the efforts have not been very successful (Ministry of Social Affairs and Health 2010).

In Finland the presumption and ideal of gender neutrality in education seem to persist (Lahelma 1992; Lahelma 2011). While gender is a self-evident division, talking about it is avoided and, accordingly, the impact of it is muted. Discussion of gender equality often lacks an analysis of power. This inflates the concept of equality to mean a fifty-fifty division. In schooling this means aiming, on average, for equal performance by girls and boys in the core subjects. When

[1] For example, by men such as Hugo Grotius, Thomas Hobbes, John Locke, Jean-Jacques Rousseau and, in the twentieth century, John Rawls.

boys' performance is on an average poorer than that of girls, it is then addressed as a question of gender equality, and demands for changing the school, pedagogical strategies and teacher education are made. This is often stated in the official documents at the European level (e.g. Gender Difference in Educational Outcomes 2010). In the Finnish Government's new Development Plan for Education and Research, an action programme for promoting equal opportunity in education is planned, with the following task: 'The Government will undertake comprehensive action to even out gender differences in learning outcomes, participation in education and completion of studies and to minimize the effect of the socio-economic background on participation in education' (Ministry of Education and Culture 2010, 10). Whilst Finnish girls, on average, have better learning outcomes than boys and women participate more actively in education than men, this aim can, in principle, be achieved either by lowering the outcomes, participation and completion of education by girls and women or by improving those of boys and men.

## *Decades of equality work*

During the last thirty years, work towards gender equality in education has been repeatedly conducted in various networks and projects. This has been a worldwide mission: again and again the important role of educators in promoting gender equality has been underlined in statements of the United Nations. It has been explicated, for example, in the declarations of the Fourth World Conference on Women (The Beijing Platform for Action 1995), and in The Millennium Development Goals of the United Nations (2001). Recently, Education International celebrated the fifth World Teachers' Day on 10 October 2011 focusing on the theme 'Teachers for gender equality' (Education International 2011). The Council of Europe has made recommendations for gender equality in education, including teacher training (see e.g. Parliamentary Assembly 1995). Gender research and feminist studies in education have achieved a respectable status in universities in several countries around the world.

When Elina Lahelma was in 2008 asked to lead a national development project on gender equality in teacher education, she had a moment of déjà vu (Brunila & Lahelma 2011). Twenty years earlier she had been acting as a secretary to the Commission of Gender Equality in Education in Finland, whose task was to explore changes needed in education as required by the new legislation on gender equality. One of the most important themes in the Commission's recommendations concerned teacher education. The Commission even worked out a provisional framework for a basic course in gender studies for teacher education (Ministry of Education 1988). On returning to the report from 1988, Elina realised that changes in teacher education had been minimal, and the recommendations given in 1988 were still valid. These recommendations, moreover, were very similar to those currently given internationally, e.g. by OECD (CIDA 2010).

Between the 1980s and 2008, more than one hundred gender equality projects in education were undertaken in Finland (Brunila, Heikkinen & Hynninen 2005, Brunila & Lahelma 2011). In retrospect, it seems significant that most of these projects and equality work in education were both initiated and led from outside schools and institutions of teacher education. The Act on Equality between Women and Men (1986/2005) has delineated concrete responsibilities for educational authorities to promote gender equality. One would therefore expect this task to be included in the internal developmental work of educational institutions. Yet support offered from outside has not necessarily been met with enthusiasm by the institutions. Even free-of-charge training in equality (offered by gender equality projects) has been hardly utilised. When asked, teachers and student teachers often do not recognise the need for such training. However, those who have attended classes on gender issues report their usefulness at work. (Vidén & Naskali 2010). The need for knowledge of how to promote gender equality in schools' every day practices, pedagogies or learning contents seems to be understood only when one has faced inequality at the personal level or, as often happens, being informed by change about issues of inequality.

It is interesting to compare education on gender equality with 'multicultural education' and its advances. New posts and courses in multicultural education have been included in several teacher education institutions in Finland, with in-service courses being popular. The aim of the courses is to give teachers and student teachers the facilities for meeting and teaching pupils from diverse cultural backgrounds. Multicultural studies have often been organised inside institutions as internal developmental work and as an answer to socially constructed problems and requests from the field. This is caused especially by the relatively new increase in immigration; in 2009, more than 200,000 Finnish inhabitants (4 per cent) were born outside Finland, whilst in 1990 the number was around 13,000 (Statistics Finland 2010).

There is no such spontaneous request or demand from the field for equality training; gender patterns have not changed equally quickly. Moreover, deconstruction of unquestioned expectations that are embedded in cultural understandings of gender is difficult. It has been argued that gender awareness goes beneath a person's skin. Whenever student teachers start to see how gender difference and gendered inequalities are built into the practices and processes of teaching and learning, they start to see the same patterns in society – and in their own lives and partnerships. Students who take part in voluntary courses in gender studies, especially men, often feel obliged to explain their participation to their mates. Adopting a gender perspective or feminist stance will sometimes cause embarrassment about one's surroundings and even lead to problems in one's personal relationships. Questioning the gender order can be experienced as dangerous. (See e.g. Lahelma 2011; Vidén & Naskali 2010.)

Planning for gender equality seems to remain a separate sector in administration worldwide, and requirements and ideas that are provided in reports concerning equality are best found at the level of statements in documents given by educational authorities. Even if gender equality has been a policy area since the establishment of the European Community in 1957, the integration of a gender dimension in all policy areas has failed. Instead, a special institute for gender equality was established in 2007. One of its tasks is to develop methodological tools for integration (see EIGE). In Finland, the first Governmental Report on Gender Equality given by the Ministry of Health and Social Affairs (2010) includes concrete outlines for education, prepared after thorough research-based analysis. However, the above mentioned Development Plan for Education and Research (2012), given by the Ministry of Education and Culture one year later, does not make any reference to this work. The only gender issue to be addressed, found in the section 'Action programme for equal opportunity in education' (Ministry of Education and Culture 2012, 10), reflects the general concern about boys' problems in schools, a concern that is challenged and analysed in more reflective ways in the documents given by gender equality authorities (e.g. Ministry of Health and Social Affairs 2010).

For equality workers, it is frustrating to see how toothless is school administration in bringing together internationally devised good practices and high-level scientific knowledge in planning and regulating education. Governments, for example, have failed to include gender equality as a mandatory component in the inspection of schools and teacher appraisal. Since the Beijing Conference there has been considerable talk about mainstreaming (see e.g. Council of Europe 2007) and, at the European level, strategies and action plans have been drawn up to include issues impinging on gender equality in all kinds of activities (e.g. EU 2003; EU 2010). The strategy is meant in particular to make better use of women's potential, thereby contributing to the EU's overall economic and social goals, rather than simply promoting the position of women. It can be argued that when grounds for equality lie not in justice, but in worries about a sufficient labour supply (see e.g. EU 2010), governments may take more serious action. For example, in recent decades, gender equality projects with the aim of persuading women to enter professions in technology have been allocated resources, but not projects with the goal of persuading men to enter caring professions.

Above, we have examined the general international trends and problems in promoting gender equality in education. We now turn to discussion of the work of gender equality in teacher education that has been conducted in Europe and the Nordic countries and, finally, in Finland.

## *Networking in the Association for Teacher Education in Europe (ATEE)*

In the 1980s, Anne-Lise Arnesen, the chair of the Standing Working Group 10 of the Association for Teacher Education in Europe invited Elina Lahelma to join the group, whose task was to find methods of supporting equal opportunities of girls and boys in teacher education. The first conference of ATEE attended by Elina to took place in Toulouse in 1985. Pirkko Hynninen joined the group later, whilst working at the Nord-Lilia project. In the Working Group, Elina met an active group of feminist teacher educators and was soon actively involved in drawing up the first European Curriculum Framework for Teacher Education in Gender Equality (Arnesen & Ní Chárhaight 1987). The group also edited a series of booklets for teacher education, published by ATEE and Sheffield Hallam University with the financial support of the Equal Opportunities Unit of the EU. The introductory booklet (Arnesen & Ní Chárhaight 1992) was meant as a guide to curriculum change in the area of equal opportunities in teacher education. The rationale for the work was included, and attempts were made to clarify basic concepts. The booklets that followed dealt with the contexts, approaches and methodology of this work (Boulton, Cohen, Coldron & Povey 1992), practical ideas for classroom interaction (Dolle-Willemsen & Rodenburg-Smit 1993) and transforming the contents of the teacher education curricula in various subjects to be more gender equal (Ruotonen, Lahelma, Boysen, & Krogh-Jespersen 1995).

The network, with joint efforts made toward establishing a Framework Curriculum and the series of booklets, was a very early attempt to share the experience gained in several European countries and in networking across borders, with the idea of providing ideas about gender equality for teacher education. When looking back now on the contents of these booklets, written by dozens of teacher educators and researchers from across Europe, one finds that the variety of themes and ideas is impressive and several of the articles are still relevant. It is difficult to specify what was the impact of this work on teacher education in different countries and how the booklets have been used. In Finland, the work did not really reach teacher education at the university level. Perhaps one reason was that, even if the number of Finnish participants grew year after year, none of us were in positions of power in teacher education. Elina, however, succeeded in having a curriculum framework for an introductory course on gender equality in teacher education included in the Report of the Commission of Equal Opportunities, but only as an appendix (Ministry of Education 1988, 159-162). The framework was based on the work conducted at ATEE. As far as we know, this framework has not been implemented; one reason might be that material in appendices tends not to be read. During the 1990s, the activities of the network gradually diminished and eventually it was merged with a network having multicultural aims.

## *A Nordic project on gender equality in teacher education, Nord-Lilia*

Nord-Lilia (1992-1994) is the acronym that designates the project for Gender Equality in Teacher Education Curricula under the auspices of the Nordic Council of Ministers. The project had a Nordic leader, Anne-Lise Arnesen, and a secretariat composed of national project co-ordinators. The work was carried out in 61 projects by 113 teacher educators, teachers and administrators in 27 teacher education institutions and 21 schools and kindergartens in Denmark, Iceland, Finland, Norway and Sweden. All of the local projects were described in a publication intended to 'facilitate the exchange of experiences and co-operation among local projects and across national borders' (Arnesen 1994). Some results were published in all the Nordic languages: the original version with chapters in Swedish/Norwegian/Danish (languages that are related) and translations in Finnish and Icelandic (e.g. Arnesen 1998).

In Finland the project was implemented in schools and one kindergarten, as well as with a few teacher educators in some universities. Not a single university or department of teacher education formally accepted the invitation to join the project. Nord-Lilia in Finland was mostly carried out as a continuum of the experimental work initiated by the Commission of Gender Equality in Education in the 1980s (Ministry of Education 1988), and most of the Finnish projects took place in schools, instead of in departments of teacher education. Nord-Lilia produced valuable know-how for teaching equality in Finnish schools, know-how that would also be valuable in teacher education. The pioneering work by Vappu Sunnari at the University of Oulu (e.g. Sunnari 1997) had some sustainable effects on teacher training at this university, even if the small steps forward have had to be renegotiated every academic year; an experience shared by activists in gender studies who were interviewed in the context of the TASUKO project (Lehtonen 2011).

The Nord-Lilia project strengthened Nordic co-operation among gender researchers perhaps more than among teacher educators. For example, Nord-Lilia activists participated in the Gender and Education network of the Nordic Educational Research Association (NERA), which was established in the 1980s and has been active since. Nordic co-operation also widened into the European context, through the ATEE network mentioned above. As a whole, Nord-Lilia provided methods and material for development work, but it was not strong enough to provide a visible change in teacher education in any of the participating countries. As Kristiina Brunila (2009) has suggested in her study on gender equality projects, sustainable change is difficult, and the results and enthusiasm achieved during projects tend to vanish after the extra resources have been used (see also Brunila & Lahelma 2011).

## Gender awareness in Finnish teacher education in the new millennium

At the time writing this article, in 2012, the authors have finished joint work on still another national gender equality project, Gender Awareness in Teacher Education, known by the acronym TASUKO (2008-2011).[2] When Elina was invited to act as a responsible leader on the project, she soon realised how little had changed in teacher education in terms of gender equality or gender sensitivity since she had been working at the Commission on Equality in Education two decades earlier (Lahelma 2011).

The TASUKO project started by examining the curriculum of each teacher education department in Finland [3] in order to obtain a picture of where things stood as to materials and courses on gender issues. The examination suggested that the teaching curricula included hardly any gender courses, textbooks or other material that drew on the theoretical and empirical results of Finnish and international gender studies. Knowledge of good teaching practices available in numerous projects on equality (Brunila, Heikkinen & Hynninen 2005; Brunila 2009) had not been incorporated into teacher education. Small-scale studies suggested that stereotypical dichotomous understandings of gender were repeated in courses and course materials (e.g. Vidén & Naskali 2010; Norema, Pietilä & Purhonen 2011; Lehtonen 2011). Yet, at some universities, there were lectures and course literature offered that provided gender perspectives and that were integrated into the curriculum. These cases were typically the result of the persistent efforts of feminist teacher educators, and the achievements were constantly challenged (Lehtonen 2011).

It was obvious that it was not only possible, but even usual, to qualify as a teacher without ever having heard of the requirements of the Act on Equality between Women and Men (1986/2005), not to speak of learning what those requirements would mean in terms of pedagogy or school practices and processes (Lahelma 2011).

---

[2] TASUKO was a project funded by the Ministry of Education, led by Elina Lahelma and co-ordinated by Pirkko Hynninen. Liisa Tainio (2008-2009) and Jukka Lehtonen (2009-2011) acted as research coordinators. Elina Ikävalko, Jenni Helakorpi and Johanna Snellman worked as assistants for various periods.

[3] In Finland, of teachers are required to have academic education and hold on M.A. (master of education degree).

This situation might be partly due to the fact that teachers and teacher education has not been a trendy area for feminist researchers, and feminists working in teacher education were relatively few; for example, there were not many teacher educators active in the national network on feminist studies in education, which is a standing interest group of the Finnish Educational Research Association (with the acronym KAFE). Teacher education does not have a feminist view on didactics. University pedagogy is currently very powerful and resourceful in Finnish universities, but feminist pedagogy has remained on the margin, if not completely outside, of the theoretical and practical foci of the main stream university pedagogy. The results of Finnish gender studies in education or international feminist research have not found their way into the curricula. Gender equality has not generally been included in the assignments on the national developmental projects in education by the school administration. (Lehtonen 2011; Hynninen 2011).

Gender perspective, even when it has been written into the textbooks or introduced in teaching, has often remained a theme apart. Gender awareness was reduced to a kind of a new subject, and it was not easily taken up in reflective, everyday practice. Still more interesting is the inclination to combine gender perspective with multicultural studies. Gender inequality was seen in the cultural 'other', Finnnishness being equated with equality (e.g. Rajander 2010; Lahelma & Öhrn 2003).

## *Small steps forward: A Finnish project on gender awareness in teacher education, TASUKO*

We have discussed the situation in Finnish universities when the TASUKO project was established. Now we describe further the working methods and the outcome of this project.

In 2008, the Ministry of Education and Culture provided 600,000 € for the University of Helsinki for co-ordinating a project on gender awareness in teacher education. With this project, the Ministry expected a profound change within each programme in teacher education at nine universities in Finland. Based on our long history as activists in the field of gender equality in education, our expectations about room for change were more limited. We were aware that institutions of teacher education are not very open to changes initiated from outside the profession or above (e.g. Erixon Arreman 2007). The Ministry, however, gave the task to the Department of Education, which does not provide teacher education. Elina was invited to be the leader of the project; she is neither a teacher nor a teacher educator. We were aware that it is not easy to integrate theoretical and critical analysis into teacher education (e.g. Carlson 2008; Erixon Arreman & Weiner 2007); gender awareness, however, is a theme that needs theoretical and critical reflection (see also Gudbjornsdottir 2011) and is also regarded as political. This has been well known among gender researchers in other countries too; for example, Gaby Weiner (2000) suggested in her critical review on gender in European teacher education that there is a 'fear of feminism' in teacher education. Focusing on gender is interpreted as anti-male and divisive, despite the evident influence of gender factors in school and university classrooms (Weiner 2000, 11).

We therefore planned a new strategy. Instead of acting as experts given a mandate by the Ministry of Education and the Gender Equality Act, and trying to persuade the deans and other administrators and suggesting changes from the outside, we decided to carry out the project from within the teacher education departments. We addressed the teacher educators who were already engaged in gender equality work, organised an unofficial group of feminist teacher educators from different universities and developed the project plan collaboratively. For example, Vappu Sunnari, who was active in Nord-Lilia and in the ATEE network, participated in TASUKO with her research group at the University of Oulu.

The theoretical starting points were built jointly. Gender awareness was defined as awareness of the gender differences constructed in educational practices and an awareness that the practices can be changed. The principle of intersectionality (e.g. Yuval-Davies 2006) was taken as another basic principle in the work. Intersectionality means that students are not just two oppositional groups, girls and boys, but rather gender is interlinked and must be analysed in relation to other dimensions of difference, such as social and ethnic background, sexuality, age, locality or (dis)abilities. In some contexts and situations, gender is an important dimension, but not always. The aim was based on the idea that it should not be 'an impossible mission' (Lahelma 2011) but instead, 'difficult but doable' (Brunila, Heikkinen & Hynninen 2005). There should be space for at least some agency and small steps towards gender-aware teaching within teacher educational institutions.

The teacher education departments of the universities were invited to join the project only after the funding was clear. They were offered small amounts of money to organise the work at the local level, and resources were allocated for conducting small-scale studies. Unlike the earlier Nord-Lilia project, all departments now accepted the invitation.

As mentioned before, the project started out by analysing the curricula of teacher education from a gender perspective, with rather hopeless results. The action plans of the universities for promoting gender equality were also examined in order to see if and how they could be depended on in the process.[4] The plans turned out to be relatively superficial. The TASUKO group undertook to support the universities in making more concrete plans. Some departments set up a working party for gender equality, and a few teacher training schools worked out an equality plan. We succeeded in getting some feedback and support from student organisations, which also organised some seminars, and members of the network in all universities received requests for help from students who had been inspired to explore the issue of gender in their Master's theses.

In the context of TASUKO, some small studies were conducted to support the activities (e.g. Vidén & Naskali 2010; Lehtonen 2011). For example, three student teachers conducted a small ethnographic project during the period of their own pedagogical studies. During their earlier studies, they had not come across research on gender patterns in schools; however, their observations repeated the same findings found again and again in gender studies during the previous thirty years; for example, teachers' essentialist understandings of gender. The young ethnographers felt that their questioning of gendering practices was not heard or was heard as disturbing (Norema, Pietilä & Purtonen 2010). Even if their critical conclusion was that they were not provided with tools for promoting gender equality during their teacher education, their report found an enthusiastic audience in their own department, and it has been distributed to other universities as well. The explorations conducted in other universities suggest similar patterns (see also Lehtonen 2011).

[4] The Act on Equality between Women and Men (1986/2005) reguires universities to make action plans for gender equality.

The ambition in TASUKO was to do something new or different from what had been carried out in earlier projects. The idea was that each department would and could engage in the development work and carry on the project by drawing from its own expertise and on its own terms. There was the hope that the mission of twenty years and more would, step by step, turn into normal conduct in teacher education. When the curricula of teacher education in all universities were revamped in 2010 and 2011, at least some courses, lectures or elements of gender studies and gender awareness were included. It seemed to be difficult to find the right place for addressing gender, however. The idea of integrating the theme into the daily routine of education has so far evoked little response. Gender awareness remains the responsibility of those teacher educators who are committed to it, but with somewhat more leeway, legitimacy and resources than before.

The TASUKO project took place at the same time as a huge structural reform was undertaken in Finnish universities as a whole, and people working in teacher education departments were overloaded. They were also concerned about the future, because some of the teacher education units were in danger of being shut down. The first unit to be closed was Kajaani, which had been active in gender equality work already in the Nord-Lilia project. Thus, attempts to get the work of TASUKO on the agenda more comprehensively turned out to be difficult.

It remains to be seen whether any of the changes described above will be sustainable. As is characteristic of projects, after it is over, no resources are available for following up on the developments (e.g. Brunila 2009). The home pages of TASUKO, which were constructed as a resource for continuing the work of gender equality, are updated and orders for publications received by activists in TASUKO unofficially, by a mere devotion. The planning group that has since grown into a nationwide network continues to function, but now in the context of the feminist network in the FERA, mentioned above, yet without the resources that were allocated for TASUKO during the project period.

## *Has anything changed in twenty years?*

In this paper we examined what has changed in Finnish educational policies, practices and teacher education in relation to gender equality during the more than twenty years that we have been active in the field. Public policies are the same: to promote gender equality through education. Working methods are very much the same: to provide opportunities for recognizing inequalities and the know-how to avoid reproducing them. The recommendations both nationally and internationally are, generally speaking, the same (see e.g. Ministry of Education 1988; Parliamentary Assembly 1995; CIDA 2010). Gender research in education has increased and strengthened its position, at least in the Western universities. In every Finnish university with a department of education there is an increasing amount of feminist research, especially in the last fifteen years. In Finland as well as in other Nordic countries, there are dozens of doctoral theses, large research projects, units of gender studies and sustainable international connections (Nyström 2009, Lehtonen 2011). Students' interest in doing doctoral and master's theses with a gender perspective is growing.

Whilst a gender and feminist perspective on education is regarded as one of the most important paradigm changes in education (e.g. Ball 2003), the theories and concepts have changed. Understanding gender as a dichotomy has been troubled (Butler 1990), and gender has been analysed more and more at the intersection with other dimensions of difference (e.g. Yuval-Davies 2006). The more nuanced understanding of gender and equality has not, however, been able to challenge the political discourses. Equality of outcome, which was the aim of the comprehensive school reform in Finland in the 1970s, has faded, replaced by the rhetoric of sufficient equal opportunity and individual choice. At the same time the school is, in the public discourses (see e.g. Epstein & al. 1998; Lahelma 2005), seen as offering better opportunities for girls than for boys. Whereas the gender equality projects of the 1990s sought girl-friendly pedagogy in order to improve girls' educational position, school is now seen as favouring girls at the expense of boys. This trend has recently been repeated in the Finnish Government´s Development Plan for Education and Research (2012) whose aim is to even out gender differences. The juxtaposition of the two genders is not over (e.g. Lahelma 2005).

In 2010 the Finnish Government gave the first report on gender equality politics to the Parliament (Ministry of Social Affairs and Health 2010). This report, even if partly based on concern about the future labour supply, seems to signal a strengthening of political will for change. It might result in gender equality remaining on the political agenda, not just in the political rhetoric, but only if the outlines of the report reach educational authorities. In the last two or three decades a store of knowledge and good practices has been gathered and is waiting for an opportunity to be used. There is also an internationally developed and fully-tested toolkit available.

Yet in international politics there are more and more reasons for concern. What impact will the economic crisis and financial volatility have on institutional reforms such as gender-sensitizing teacher education or the struggle for equality on more general terms? As to promoting gender equality, the neoliberal, market-orientated policies and practices might enforce gendering, a hierarchical gender order and sexualisation while feminizing global employment (see e.g. Braunstein 2012; Brunila & Lahelma 2011).

Long-standing gender equality workers as we are, we try to be patient. We have, for instance, heard two international rounds of 'what about boys' talk, which breaks out during social and economic changes and is a legacy of the traditional gender order (e.g. Arnesen, Lahelma & Öhrn 2008). Even if no great changes in gender equality in educational systems have occurred, we have observed several small moves and fissures in gender order. Having given courses for students at our own university for many years, we have seen more and more young people who break gender boundaries and who want to discuss gender issues and demand to be taught equality. Perhaps the prevailing discussion on the meanings of sexuality and the relation between gender(s) and sexuality step by step frees the discussion from the pitfall of 'which of the two has it worse'.

The group called together to plan TASUKO is now a nationwide network with international connections. Within the network it is possible to discuss and disseminate ideas and experiences in gender-aware training and what literature to recommend to students who want to do their master's theses from a gender perspective. The network is even a site for mutual support for those who have encountered resistance or hostility. It helps all of us to remember that gender awareness is not a personal characteristic that a person does or does not have. It is learned and consequently can be learned – and taught. And it appears that, once one's eyes have been opened to see and recognise gender injustice – how painful and even shocking it can be – one becomes sensitized to inequalities based on other categorisations as well. We hope this is happening – both in Finland and internationally.

## *References*

Act on Equality between Women and Men (609/1986, amendments 2005). Statutes of Finland.

Allen, K. R., & Piercy, F. P. (2005). Feminist autoethnography. In D. Sprenkle & F. P. Piercy (Eds.) *Research methods in family therapy* (2nd ed., 155-169). New York: Guilford.

Arnesen, A-L. (Red.) (1994). *NORD-LILIA GUIDE. Likestilling i lærerutdanningens innhold og arbeidsmetoder [NORD-LILIA GUIDE. Gender equality in teacher education curricula]*. Apostrof, Bislet høgskolesenters skriftserie, Særnummer A/1994. Oslo: Bislet høgskolesenter.

Arnesen, A-L. (Ed.). (1995). *Gender and Equality as Quality in School and Teacher Education. Final report from the 3-year Nordic project on gender and equal opportunities in teacher education.* Oslo: Nordic Council of Ministers/Oslo University College.

Arnesen, A-L. (Ed.). (1998). *Likt og ulikt. Kjønnsdimensjonen i pedagogisk tenkning og praksis*. HiO-rapport 1998 nr. 2. Oslo: Høgskolen i Oslo.

Arnesen, A-L., Lahelma, E. & Öhrn, E. (2008). Travelling discourses of gender and education: The case of boys' underachievement. *Nordisk Pedagogik*, 28(1), 1–14.

Arnesen, A-L. & Ní Chártheigh, D. (1992.). *Pathways to Change: Gender and Curriculum in Teacher Education.* Series on Equal Opportunities and Teacher Education in Europe, Vol. 1. Sheffield: Association for Teacher Education in Europe and PAVIC publications.

Arnesen, A-L. & Ní Chártheigh, D. (Eds.). (1987). *Equal opportunities for girls and boys. A curriculum framework for teacher education and guidelines for action.* Brussels: ATEE.

Ball, S. (2003). *Politics and Policymaking in Education: Explorations in Policy Sociology.* London: Routledge / Normal University Press.

Beijing Platform for Action (1995). United Nations.

Braunstein, E. (2012). *Neoliberal Development Macroeconomics. A Consideration of its Gendered Employment Effects.* United Nations Research Institute for Social Development. Gender and Development, Programme paper number 14, February 2012.

Boulton, P., Cohen, L., Coldron, J. & Povey, H. (Eds.) (1992). *Ways and Meanings: Gender, Process and Teacher Education.* Series on Equal

Opportunities and Teacher Education in Europe, Vol. 2. Sheffield: Association for Teacher Education in Europe and PAVIC publications.

Brunila, K., Heikkinen, M. & Hynninen, P. (2005). *Difficult but doable. Good practices for equality work.* Kajaani: Oulu University, Kajaani University Consortium.

Brunila, K. (2009). *Parasta ennen. Tasa-arvotyön projektitapaistuminen.* [Best before. Projectisation of equality work]. Helsinki: Helsingin yliopisto. Kasvatustieteen laitoksen tutkimuksia 222.

Brunila, K. & Lahelma, E. (2011). *Gender equality work in education: project after project after project* ... Paper presented at the ECER Conference in Berlin, 14 September 2011.

Butler, J. (1990). *Gender Trouble: Feminism and the Subversion of Identity.* New York: Routledge.

CIDA (2010). Canadian International Development Agency: *Education, Gender equality: Tip sheets 2010.* Canada: CIDA.

Carlson, M. (2008). Kampen om kurser och perspektiv – en mångfald tolkningar och en heterogen praktik.[Struggling about courses and perspectives – manifold interpretations and heterogenous practices] In *Uppdrag mångfald. Lärarutbildning i omvandling*, eds. M. Carlson & A. Rabo, 185-225. Umeå: Boréa Bokförlag.

Council of Europe (2007). Recommendation CM/Rec(2007)13 of the Committee of Ministers to member states on gender mainstreaming in education.

Council of Europe. Retrieved from http://www.coe.int/what-we-do/democracy/gender-equality.

Dolle-Willemsen, D. & Rodenburg-Smit, H. (Eds.) (1993). *Gender and Classroom Interaction: Implications for Teacher Education.* Series on Equal Opportunities and Teacher Education in Europe, Vol. 3. Sheffield: Association for Teacher Education in Europe and PAVIC publications.

Education International (2011). Retrieved from http://download.ei-ie.org/Docs/WebDepot/WorldTeachersDay2011_PressRelease_EN.pdf

EIGE. European Institute for Gender Equality. http://www.eige.europa.eu/content/about-eige

Epstein, D., Elwood, J., Hey, V. & Maw, J. (Eds.) (1998). *Failing Boys? Issues in Gender and Education.* Buckingham: Open University Press.

Erixon Arreman, I. & Weiner, G. (2007). Gender, research and change in teacher education: a Swedish dimension. *Gender and Education,* 19(3), 317-337.

EU (2003). *Plan for action on gender equality.*

EU (2010). *Strategy for Equality between women and men 2010-2015.* Retrieved from http://eurlex.europa.eu/LexUriServ/LexUriServ.do?uri=CELEX:52010DC0491:EN:NOT

European Commission (2010). *EU Plan of Action on Gender Equality and Women's Empowerment in Development 2010-2015.* Retrieved from http://ec.europa.eu/development/icenter/repository/SEC_2010_265_gender_action_plan_EN.pdf

Fraser, N. & Honneth, A. (2003). *Redistribution or recognition? A political-philosophical exchange.* London, New York: Verso.

*Gender Differences in Educational Outcomes: Study on the Measures Taken and the Current Situation in Europe* (2010). Retrieved from http://eacea.ec.europa.eu/education/eurydice/thematic_studies_en.php

Husén, T. (1977). *Jämlikhet genom utbildning* [Education for equality]. Stockholm: Natur och Kultur.

Hynninen, P. (2011). *Tasa-arvo- ja sukupuolitietoisuus opettajankoulutuksessa. Raportti TASUKO-hankkeesta 2008-2011.* Helsinki: Helsingin yliopisto. Käyttäytymistieteiden laitos.

IIEP (2011). International Institute for Educational Planning. Policy Forum on Gender Equality in Education 3-4 October 2011. Retrieved from http://genderpolicyforum.wordpress.com/

Julkunen, R. (2010). *Sukupuolen järjestykset ja tasa-arvon paradoksit* [Gender Order and Paradoxes of Equality]. Tampere: Vastapaino.

Lahelma, E. (1992). *Sukupuolten eriytyminen peruskoulun opetussuunnitelmassa* (Gender segregation in the curriculum of comprehensive School) Helsinki: Yliopistopaino.

Lahelma, E. (2005). School Grades and Other Resources: The 'Failing Boys' discourse revisited. *NORA, Nordic Journal of Women's Studies* 13(2), 78-89.

Lahelma, E. (2011). Gender Awareness in Finnish Teacher Education: an Impossible Mission? *Education Inquiry,* 2 (2), 263-276.

Lahelma, E. & Öhrn, E. (2003). 'Strong Nordic Women' in the Making? Educational Politics and Classroom Practices. In D. Beach, T. Gordon & E.

Lahelma (Eds.), *Democratic Education: Ethnographic Challenges (39-51)*. London: Tufnell Press.

Lehtonen, J. (Ed.) (2011). *Sukupuolinäkökulmia tutkimusperustaiseen opettajankoulutukseen [Gender perspectives on research-based teacher education]*. Helsinki: University of Helsinki.

Ministry of Education (1988). *Tasa-arvokokeilutoimikunnan mietintö [Report of the Commission of Equal Opportunities in Education]*. Komiteanmietintö 1988:17. Helsinki: Valtion Painatuskeskus.

Ministry of Education and Culture (2012). *Education and Research 2011–2016. A development plan.* Reports of the Ministry of Education and Culture, Finland 2012:3.

Ministry of Social Affairs and Health (2010). *Valtioneuvoston selonteko naisten ja miesten välisestä tasa-arvosta [Government report on gender equality]*. Sosiaali- ja terveysministeriö. Julkaisuja 2010:8.

Norema, A., Pietilä, P. & Purtonen, T. (2010). *Pipot tiedon tiellä. Sukupuolihuomioita opettajankoulutuksessa [Caps on the way to knowledge. Gendered observations in teacher education]*. Helsinki: Yliopistopaino.

Nyström, E. (2009). *Nordisk forskning om genus och jämställdhet i skola och utbildning: 2005-2009. [Nordic research on gender and equality in school and education]*. Oslo: NIKK.

Parliamentary Assembly (1995). *Recommendation 1281 on gender equality in education. Council of Europe.* Retrieved from http://assembly.coe.int/mainf.asp?Link=/documents/adoptedtext/ta95/erec1281.htm.

Rajander, S. (2010). *School and choice: An ethnography of a primary school with bilingual classes.* Jyväskylä: Finnish Educational Research Association.

Ruotonen, H., Boysen, L., Krogh-Jespersen, K. & Lahelma, E. (Eds.) (1995). *Content and Gender: Transforming the Curriculum in Teacher Education.* Series on Equal Opportunities and Teacher Education in Europe, Vol. 4. Sheffield: Association for Teacher Education in Europe and PAVIC publications.

Statistics of Finland (2010).

Sunnari V. (1997). *Gendered structures and processes in primary teacher education - challenge for gender-sensitive pedagogy.* Northern Gender Studies 4. Oulu: University of Oulu.

UN Millennium development goals (2001). United Nations.

Vidén, S. & Naskali, P. (2010). *Sukupuolitietoisuus Lapin yliopiston opettajankoulutuksessa [Gender awareness in teacher education at the University of Lapland]*. Lapin yliopiston kasvatustieteellisiä julkaisuja 22. Rovaniemi.

Yuval-Davies, N. (2006). Intersectionality and Feminist Politics. *European Journal of Women's Studies*, 13(3), 193-209.

Weiner, G. (2000). A critical review of gender and teacher education in Europe, *Pedagogy, Culture & Society*, 8(2), 233-247.

Wollstonecraft, M. (1792/1983). *Vindication of the Rights of Women*. London: Penguin Books.

AUTHORS: Elina Lahelma is Professor of education at the University of Helsinki. Her fields of interest are sociology of education, gender studies in education and ethnographic methodologies. She has acted as responsible leader in several research projects, e.g. of the Academy of Finland. She learned to know Anne-Lise Arnesen in 1984, in a Nordic conference on gender equality and education. Since then they have met regularly, written together and collaborated various contexts: gender equality networks and projects, networks of ethnographic research and, currently, in the Nordic Research Network on Critical Perspectives on Young People, Children, Welfare and Education.
Correspondence: elina.lahelma@helsinki.fi

Pirkko Hynninen is an educationalist (M.A.) with special interests in feminist studies and sociology of education. She has since 1997 taught feminist studies of education at the University of Helsinki. Her precarious working career consists mainly of gender equality projects, the latest having been TASUKO, gender awareness in teacher education (2008-2011). She has two adult children and one grandchild and she has recently retired. She had a great and unforgettable pleasure to work with Anne-Lise Arnesen in the Nord-Lilia project (1992-1994) in which Anne-Lise acted as the Nordic leader.
Correspondence: pirkko.hynninen@gmail.com

# *Rethinking special education*

## CHALLENGES FOR TEACHERS AND TEACHER EDUCATION IN A TIME OF CHANGE: A NORWEGIAN PERSPECTIVE

KJELL-ARNE SOLLI
Østfold University College, Norway

ABSTRACT: *There is a strong emphasis on inclusion in kindergartens and schools in Norwegian policy documents. The question is whether this is an ideal rather than the actual practice. This article describes trends in special education in Norway. Data are sourced from official statistical data, policy documents and reviews of educational research. It could seem like a paradox that more pupils than ever receive special education in primary and lower secondary school. The traditional view of special education as something concerning children or pupils who are "special" or "different" seems difficult to change. The Norwegian example shows that special education in many cases act in favour of a non-inclusive trend. I will discuss the need for rethinking special education and some of the challenges in preparing teachers for inclusive education.*

### *Introduction*

Education for all is a basic precept of Norwegian educational policy. Children and young people must have an equal right to education, regardless of where they live, gender, social and cultural background or any special needs. In Norway the principle of inclusive education was introduced with the implementation of new laws in compulsory and upper secondary education in 1976, and further developed in the 1980s and 1990s.

Compulsory primary and lower secondary schooling in Norway lasts for ten years and children start school the year they become six. Primary and lower secondary education is founded on the principle of equity and adapted education for all pupils in a school system based on the same National Curriculum. Compulsory school is comprehensive and with no streaming or tracking. All children and young people are to share a common foundation of knowledge, culture and values. Compulsory education is divided into two main stages: Primary school (grades 1–7) and lower secondary school (grades 8–10).

Education in school is to be adapted to the individual pupil's abilities and capabilities. Pupils who do not, or cannot, achieve a satisfactory learning yield from the ordinary teaching, has a right to special needs education.

The aim of the article is to discuss the role of special education in an inclusive school. Does special education in its actual practices support the principle of inclusion or does it lead to marginalization and exclusion of children? Which patterns emerge in the field of special education, and what challenges does this bring to teacher and teacher education? I will discuss these issues against the backdrop of trends in special education in primary and lower secondary schools in Norway.

Special education was designed to provide education for children, youth and adults with disabilities (Befring, 2006).The history of special education has been a site of quite different paradigms and models (Mitchell, 2010). How education for children with disabilities has been organized has depended on how disability has been defined and understood. Tøssebro (2010) points to three basic perspectives on disability that coexist in the field of disability research. *The medical model* is based on an individual perspective that disability is caused by individual characteristics. *The social model* claims that difficulties in participation and learning are created by contextual barriers and influences. *The relational model* stresses the complex and situated interaction between the conditions of the individual and the requirement in the environment which make it possible to participate in daily life. These perspectives are reflected in the history of special education.

Persson (2003) suggests that the discourses in the special educational field can be located within one of two competing perspectives. One perspective is labelled *the categorical perspective* and the other *the relational perspective*. The categorical perspective is seen similar to the medical model described above, while the relational perspective shares aspects with both both the social model and the relational model. Table 1 illustrates approaches and implications of the two models.

| | Categorical perspective | Relational perspective |
|---|---|---|
| ***Ontology of special needs*** | Special needs refer to actual characteristics of individuals | Special needs are socially constructed |
| ***Approach to difference*** | Differentiating and categorizing | Unifying |
| ***Major contribution*** | Mapping and systematizing the field | Problematizing and deconstructing the field |
| ***Implications for provision*** | Special provisions | Integrated/inclusive provisions |
| ***Understanding of special educational competence*** | Superior support directly related to diagnosed difficulties among students | Superior support for incorporating differentiation into instruction and content |
| ***Reasons for special educational needs*** | Students *with* difficulties; difficulties are innate and located in the individual | Students *in* difficulties; difficulties arise from different phenomena in educational settings and processes |

Table 1 Perspectives on special education (Source: Persson 2003, p. 277).

Tisdall and Riddell (2006) refer three policy approaches:

1. Supporting or changing the child – an individualized approach
2. Making schools inclusive for all – a system approach
3. Challenging the mainstream – an anti-discrimination, civil rights approach

The Salamanca declaration (UNESCO/IBE, 1994) adopted by representatives of 92 governments and 25 international organizations called for a new thinking in special needs education in favour of inclusive education where all children should learn together. Assignment to special schools – or special classes or sections within school on a permanent basis, should be the exception.

> Regular schools with this inclusive orientation are the most effective means of combating discri minatory attitude, creating welcoming communities, building an inclusive society and achieving education for all; more over, they provide an effective education to the majority of children and improve the efficiency and ultimately the cost-effeciveess of the entire education system (Salamanca Statement, 1994, p.x).

The world report on disability (2011) describes how disabilities and special educational needs should be understood and also provides an explanation for how disabilities and special educational needs relate to difficulties children experience in learning. These descriptions and explanations are much debated among policy makers, researchers and those interested in the education field, and the debates illustrate that no universally agreed-upon definition of special needs education and inclusive education exist.

Thomas & Loxley (2007) finds that despite the policies and legislation that advocate the idea of "one school for all" there seems to be re- emergence of the kind of thinking which leads to ever newer forms of segregative and exclusionary practices. The categorical perspective seems very much alive, and I will discuss the persistence of this perspective focusing on trends in special education in Norway.

## *Special education in Norway- a short history*

The first special school for the deaf was established in Norway in 1827. In the next fifty years special schools for children with disabilities consisted of schools for the deaf and partially hearing, schools for the blind and partially sighted, schools for the defective speakers, education for the mentally disabled and education for the maladjusted. The schools were regulated by the special education act of 1881, which was revised in 1915 and again in 1951. In the 1960s critical voices spoke out against the system of segregation that these schools brought into being. These voices were critical of the ideology of exclusion, but also of the schools practices, both in terms of educational content and in terms of the living conditions of the pupils. These critics were heard and gained political approval for their demands to change the system.

A legal committee was established in 1969 and it proposed one common law for all compulsory education, which included the law of special schools. The school system should bear responsibility for all children. To make this possible, the law adopted a principle of *adapted education*, which related to all pupils.All children, regardless of ability, social factors, ethnicity or special needs, had the right to live and grow up with their families and attend their local classes during compulsory schooling. The law still made separate provisions for special education and allowed for various organizational solutions, inside and outside the ordinary school. But - the long-lasting legal division between 'educable' and 'not educable' children was abolished.

Equality, integration and normalisation are basic principles and the new Education Act of 1975 ("the integration Act"). The legal committee that proposed the integration laws defined integration in a broad sense as

- Belongingness in a social community
- Participation in the benefits of the community
- Joint responsibility for task and obligations

Although the separate laws of the special school were abolished when the"the integration Act" was implemented in 1975, special schools and special classes remained and there was a continuum of special education provisions available from pupils attending special schools and - special classes, to pupils participating part-time or full-time in ordinary classes. But the movement towards inclusion had now started, formulated as a policy of gradual integration Every individual should be provided optimal learning conditions in the regular learning context – *as far as possible* (Vislie, 2006, p. 405).

Compared to other countries, Norway (and other Scandinavian countries) has come a long way when it comes to inclusive education (Vislie, 2003, Meijer, 2010). Since 1998 – a passage in the Educational Act has specified that pupils, who are incapable of obtaining a satisfactory outcome from regular instruction, are entitled to receive special needs education (Section 5 – 1 of the Educational Act of 1998). This right is invoked when the educational and psychological counselling services carryout an expert assessment, which in turn forms the basis for an individual decision on special needs education. The assessment shall determine whether the pupil needs special education, and what kind of instruction should be provided. The expert assessment shall also consider and determine whether it is possible to provide help for the pupil's difficulties within the ordinary educational provisions (Section 5 – 3 of the Educational Act). The municipality has the formal responsibility for making such a decision. The principle of inclusion forms a basic tenet of the Government's educational policies. The Education Act stipulates that the educational system must be of equal quality and adapted to the abilities and aptitudes of each pupil. Special education is meant to work as a safety net for pupils who don't benefit from their education. Unlike many other Western countries the right to special education in Norway is not dependent on the individual pupil's diagnosis or categorization into a specific category. In stead, the right to receive special education is determined by the degree to which the pupils benefit from their schooling. All children in Norway have a right to attend kindergarten, to attend their neighbouring school and to receive special educational assistance and special needs education when this is required.

The 1990s saw the emphasis of inclusion. Influenced by the Salamanca Declaration (UNESCO/IBE, 1994) the term inclusion was introduced in the Norwegian curriculum revision of 1997 "The school has room for everybody and the teacher must therefore have an eye for each individual learner. The mode of teaching must not only be adapted to subject and content, but also to age and maturity, the individual learner and the mixed abilities of the entire class" (Ministry of Education Reaearch and Church Affairs, 1996, p. 29).

The latest reform in the 10-year compulsory school in Norway is called "The knowledge promotion" and took effect in 2006.The reform confirms the principle of the inclusive school.

In a recent white paper on special education (Ministry of Education and Research , 2012 ) called "Learning together", the Government states that inclusion forms a basic tenet on Norway's educational policy.

> The inclusive kindergarten and school is based on values and a view of humanity with a fundamental respect for human rights and equality. These values are deeply embedded in our society and laid down in the purpose clause for our school and kindergarten legislation.This provides the statutory basis for ensuring that schools and kindergartens are inclusive (Meld.nr.18 (2010-11) Report to the Storting (White Paper).Summary, p. 5).

It may consequently be seen as a paradox that in times of inclusive policy, more pupils than before receive special education.

## *Trends in special education in Norway*

The formal rights and policy documents are not always followed in practice. Formal rights are not sufficient to make schools and kindergarten inclusive. An evaluation of how children with special educational needs have fared with the new curriculum, Knowledge Promotion, was carried out in the period 2007-2008 (Nordahl & Sarromaa Hausstätter, 2009). The evaluation shows that the number of pupils receiving special education is increasing both in segregated and in integrated settings. Quantitative data shows that pupils receiving special education perform significantly worse on a number of variables compared to those who do not receive special education. In addition, there are a significant number of pupils who, from the teachers' perspective, need special education, but do not receive it. A closer examination of academic performance shows that there is a great variation between schools. This variance also influences who does and who does not receive special education. There are many pupils whose academic performance is poor but who nevertheless are not offered special education.

Official data sources confirm the trends found in the evaluation of special education. I will refer to data from The Primary and Lower Secondary School Information System (GSI statistics) and recent reports from research projects that illustrate and document the trends.

In the period from 1997 to 2006, 5 – 6 % of all pupils in Norwegian schools received special education determined by an assessment of the individual by experts. Figure 1 shows that this proportion has grown extensively over the last four years. In the school year 2011 – 12, the number of pupils receiving special education is increased to 8, 6 % of all pupils. In effect this means just over 66 000 children receive special education. About 17 % of the educational cost of education in Norway is connected to special education.

Figure 2 shows the percentage of pupils receiving special education for the years 2008, 2010 and 2011 distributed along grade levels 1 – 4, 5 – 7 and 8 – 10. The last grade level is part of the lower secondary school in Norway's educational system. The number of pupils who receive special education is three times higher in 10$^{th}$ grade than in first grade. In Norway, as in most other Western countries, the gender distribution is disproportional; about 70 % of the pupils who receive special education are boys.

In Norway very few pupils get all of their education in special schools or other separate institutions, but the number of pupils attending separate institution is increasing, especially in the big cities. In all, 3400 pupils attend special institutions (0,65 % of pupils in comprehensive school) and about 4000 pupils attend permanent special classes (0,55 %).

Although pupils have access to ordinary school and classes, special education in many cases are physically located in rooms outside ordinary classes, or the pupils work outside of class individually or in small groups. The use of teacher assistants in special education is prevalent, and this has lead to a discussion concerning the quality of special education that these assistants are able to provide. The location of special education are shown in figure 3.

The organization of special education is explored in a longitudinal study (Wendelborg & Tøssebro, 2010, Wendelborg , 2010) based on data assembled from interviews and questionaires given to parents of children with different disabilities (sensory impairments are not included). As pupils grow older they spend more and more of their time in school outside their ordinary class. Figure 4 is based on the reported study.

The findings in this study (Wendelborg & Tøssebro 2010) then show that children with disabilities become less often involved in regular classroom activities as they grow older (figure 5).

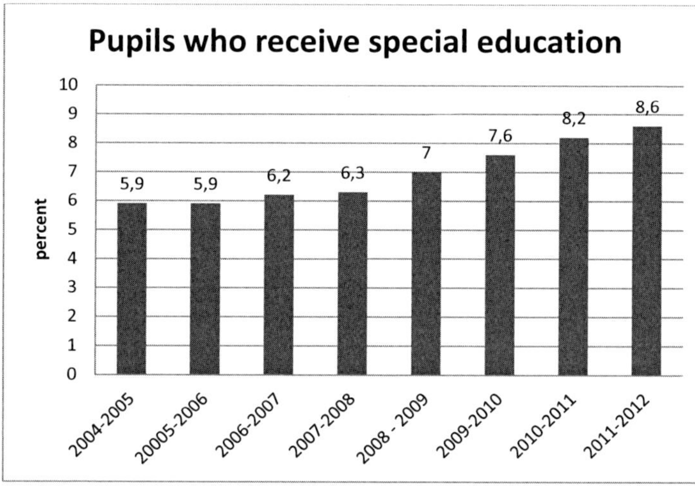


Figure 1 Percent of pupils receiving special education in primary and lower secondary schools in Norway 2004 - 2012 (Source: The Primary and Lower Secondary School Information System).

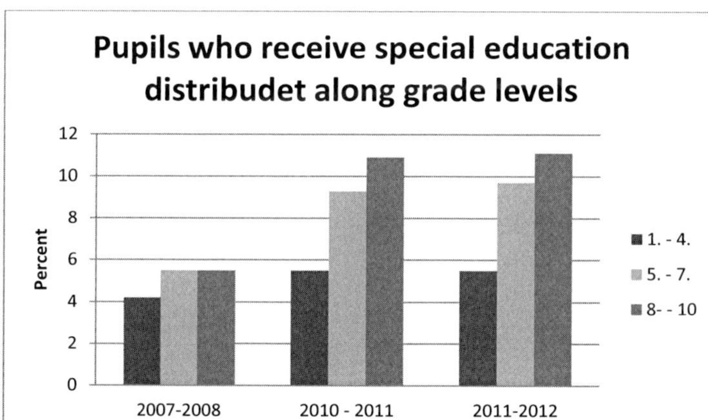


Figure 2 Pupils receiving special education in Norway distributed along grade levels (Source: The Primary and Lower Secondary School Information System).

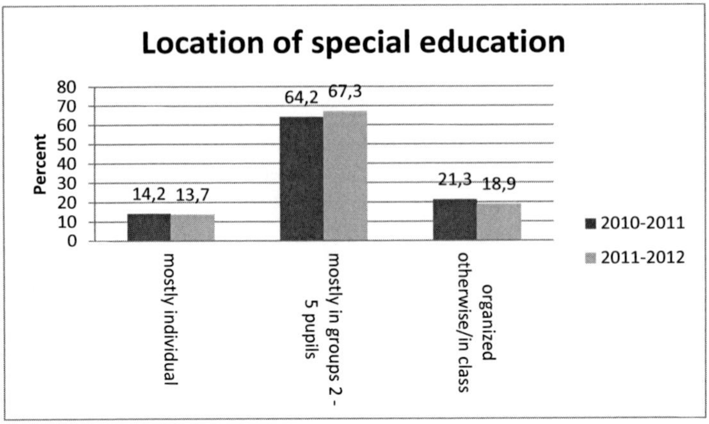


Figure 3 Location of special education in primary and lower secondary education in Norway (Source: The Primary and Lower Secondary School Information System).

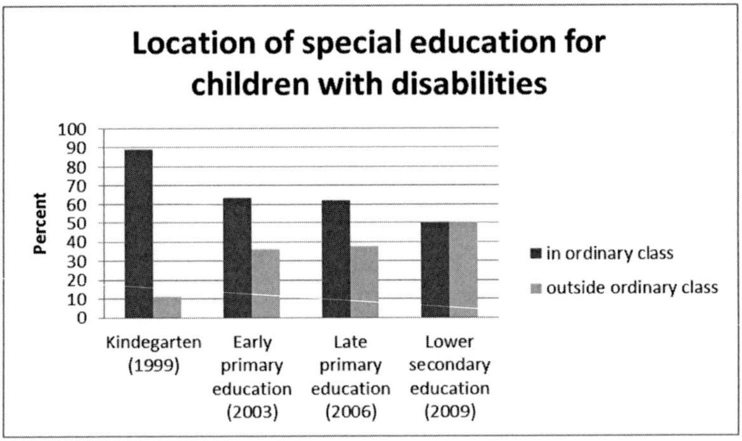


Figure 4 Location of special education for children with disability (Source: Wendelborg & Tøssebro, 2010).

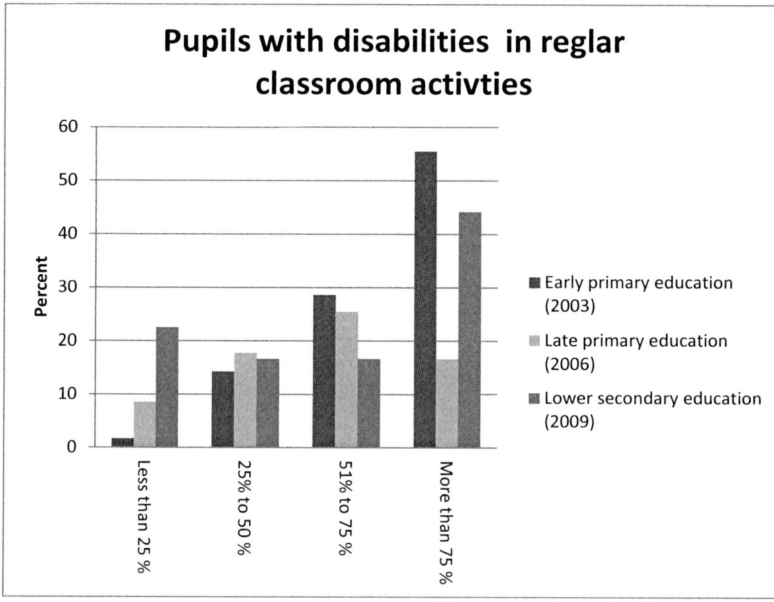


Figure 5 Pupils with disabilty in regular classroom activities (Source: Wendelborg & Tøssebro, 2010).

Wendelborg and Tøssebro (2010) concludes that despite the fact that public policies on education in Norway are based on a relational understanding of disability, and are thus in line with a perspective on learning problems as a combination of a relationship between educational factors on the one hand and environmental demands and support on the other, the results show that schools adopt an individual approach to dealing with children with disabilities and special educational needs, which reflects a medical understanding of disability.

Haug (2011) concludes that little seems to be done to create a school for all and too much seems to be done to separate ordinary education from special education. The schools are using working methods that exclude many pupils. Some students get access to special education, but far from everyone.

Presence and participation are vital parts of the principle of inclusion. The practice of special education could be seen as an obstacle to these principles. In sum the example from Norway shows a trend where:

- more pupils get special education
- more special education measures are established out of ordinary classes
- the medical or individual tradition of special education is prevalent in schools and municipalities

## *Rethinking special education*

The Norwegian example shows that despite that inclusion is an explicit goal in educational policy; special education seems to act in favor of the non-inclusive trend.These are complex issues, but to rethink the function of special education is necessary.

In order to rethink the discrepancy between ideals expressed in policy and actual teaching practices, we need to keep in mind that several levels of the school system are involved. How the discrepancy is addressed might vary depending on what level we look at. The impact of policy on learning and teaching might be addressed at the state and governmental level. The implementation of local policies and resources for education and special education must be approached at the level of the municipality. A third level pertains to each individual school's learning environment, school culture, and strategies and practices for adapting the school's education to each indvidiual pupil's abilities and capacaties. Varying understandings and definitions of special education and inclusion may operate at all levels, and contribute to the complexity of the situation.

> Mitchell (2010) point out that inclusive education affects not just the conceptualization of special education "... but it calls into question the broader aims of education, the purpose of schools, the nature of the curriculum, approaches to assessment, and schools´ accommodation to diversity" (Mitchell, 2010, p. 121).

In a commentary on the state of inclusive education research Nind (2010) points to some dimensions that were strongly evident in the research in the 1990s and are still prevalent today – the attitudinal (teachers and parents attitudes to inclusion), the organizational (the role of the special schools and school leaders), the social (around participation, culture and community) and inclusion as a stategy for education for all. Some areas, such as research into the relationships between inclusion and achievement, pedagogical approaches and teacher development for inclusive education seem to be growing in momentum, and some keep linking inclusive education back to the broader agendas of rights and social justice.

The turn to "neo liberal marked solutions" as the answer to educational problems is a global phenomenon (Apple, 2010, Allan, 2010,Arnesen, 2011). The neo-liberal wave or the standard agenda (Ainscow, Booth & Dyson, 2006) focuses on competition, tests and test scores (national and international league tables) and the curriculum focuses on attainment of academic skills. The neo-liberal wave in the 1980s and 1990s has also had an impact on Scandinavian countries which traditionally have been characterised by strong, universal welfare systems and socio-inclusive policies. There has been a change from a focus on "being, learning and working together" to a focus on differences and individual abilities and needs .The emphasis on differences and individualisation rather than social community and inclusive learning environments, has been strengthened by the institutional mechanisms operating within the system of quality assessment (Arnesen & Lundahl, 2006). In many European countries including Norway, the following tendencies can be observed:

- An increasing use of standards and manuals
- A use of narrow intermediate aims and indicators to measure children's achievements
- A variety of evaluation and test methods
- An implementation of quality reports, which make preschool teachers/school teachers responsible for their work – so-called accountability

Runswick-Cole (2011) emphasises that the standard agenda and the inclusion agenda make uneasy bedfellows, and when these agendas meets in school, the competing policy demands all too often result in exclusion of children.

> Indeed, students who demand high levels of teacher support and other resources, along with students who fail to meet behavioural and cultural norms in the classroom become unattractive clientele for schools struggling to improve standards (Runswick Cole 2011, p. 116).

This brings forward a must for rethinking not only of the purpose of special education, but the purpose of school. Biesta (2010) has questioned the educational agenda in the article (and book) "Good education in an age of measurement: on the need to reconnect the question on purpose in education". Providing students with knowledge, competence and skills are important in every way. The qualification outcome is necessary. But there are other major functions of education which have an equally important impact on student outcome of education. Biesta (2010) refers to the socialisation function and a subjectification function. These functions have to do with becoming members of and part of a particular society or "culture" and becoming autonomous and independent individuals in thought and action. Both these functions are central for an inclusive school. As Biesta highlighets in his article, it is important that we engage in discussions about what constitutes good education. With regard to the issue of rethinking special education, the "one-eyed" cognitive understanding of the purpose of school is a danger to pupils in vulnerable situations. More focus on students' academic competencies and performance implies greater risks of marginalisation and exclusion of vulnerable students, which may account for the recent increase in the number of children being reported as needing special help and for the tendency to increasingly cater for these children in segregated settings.

In Norway the municipalities are responsible for operating and administering primary and lower secondary schools, whereas the county authorities are responsible for upper secondary education and training. Legislation and regulations, including the National Curriculum, form a coherent framework, but within this framework the municipal and county authorities, schools and teachers can influence the implementation of the education and training. Each school has a head teacher and various boards, councils and committees. Some municipalities have decentralized many decisions to the level of individual schools, among other things, deciding which pupils are eligible for receiving special education.

The variation between the municipalities in the number of pupils that receive special education has the last few decades been stable. In some municipalities under 2 percent of the pupils receive special education, while in other municipalities over 15 percent of the pupils are enrolled in various special education measures.

There are no simple explanations for these variations. The use of ressources is one factor. In their evaluation Nordahl & Hausstätter (2009) find that

> There is no common understanding among school owners about what counts as an inclusive or segregated school system. The Knowledge Promotion reform sets standards for an inclusive school, but these standards are interpreted very differently from municipality to municipality. It seems in some

> cases that the reform is used to legitimize a segregated school setting for pupils with special needs (Nordahl & Hausstätter, 2009 p. 8).

At the municipality level, the increase in pupils entitled to special education means more resources to special education and less resources to adapted education which in due turn cause more pupils eligible to special education.

In the classroom ideals and good intentions meet reality. The schools as organizations play a vital part in whether the result of special education is a success, a failure or something in the middle. This dimension concerns how the purpose of the school in the form of curriculum or principles, such as inclusion and adapted education, are translated and understood at the organizational level and at various levels within the organization. The interpretation of the curriculum and principles at the organizational level are then re-translated and acted upon by teachers in their classroom practices. Bakken & Danielsen (2011) finds considerable variation between schools and between classes in terms of how well a learning culture is developed.

> On the one hand, we have observed many lessons completely in line with what international research describes as characteristics of good schools and teaching, where teachers are tight on to their students, having a clear focus on learning goals and where the teaching time is utilized in effective ways. On the other hand, we have observed lessons not working particularly well and where the learning outcomes for the students probably have been very low. These lessons are characterised by poor classroom management, noise, low commitment to learning and non-efficient teaching. Some of this variation has to do with what kind of school culture that has evolved locally and is partly related to the directly involvement of school management in pedagogical issues and what goes on in the class rooms (Bakken & Danielsen, 2011, p. 200).

The understanding of inclusion and special education on all levels is crucial when it comes to inclusion and exclusion processes. Both Scandinavian and international research (Avramides & Norwich, 2002, Nes,Strømstad & Skogen, 2004, Danmarks Evalueringsinstitut, 2011, Wilde & Avramadis, 2011) find that teachers agree with the principle of inclusion, but that they do not have the skills to do it and/or that they do not find that the schools have resources (time, money) to make this happen.

The focus on inclusion does not mean that special education should be removed. Special education has a proud tradition in establishing a life worth living for people in excluded and marginal positions in society. But that's only one side of the story. Giota, Lundborg and Emanuelson (2009) describe the dual nature of the rationale for special education

> In part there are individuals who have difficulties but, additionally, there is also the school's need to identify pupils who do not meet the context-dependent teaching demand and expectations that differ between schools. The latter fact is a real – but often not clearly expressed – motive for special needs identification and support allocation, and especially so for the more segregated" form of support given (Giota, Lundborg and Emanuelson, 2009, p. 576).

Rethinking special education means to discuss this dual nature. Arnesen (2004) points to the tensions which she finds in social relations between inclusion and exclusion. These tensions seem to works simultaneous. Pupils who are excluded in one context may be included in another. Theoretically, inclusion therefore involves two processes, inclusion and exclusion, that analytically must be seen in conjunction and in relation to the educators' understanding and emphasis on inclusive social community (affiliation, participation and contribution).

Norwich (2008) builds on a dilemmatic approach to inclusion. A dilemmatic approach recognizes tensions and conflicts and "involving accepting some crucial losses". He identifies three dilemmas that concern the inclusion of students with special educational needs:

1. The identification dilemma – whether to identify children with special educational needs/disabilities or not;
2. The curriculum dilemma – whether children with special educational needs/disabilities should learn the same common curriculum or not
3. The location dilemma – whether children with special educational needs/disabilities should learn in ordinary classrooms or not.

Special education in a time of change must recognize dilemmas concerning the tensions between

- The resources of the child versus the problems of the child
- A child with a problem versus a child in a problematic setting
- Individualization versus context

- Individuell rights versus the needs of all children (within economic constraints)
- Education versus special education
- The child as "nature" versus the child as "culture"
- Assessment versus documentation

## *Challenges for the teacher and the teacher education*

The rethinking of special education is not a challenge only to teacher and teacher education. It's easy to see that in the world of special education teachers are trapped by a disability discourse. Most teachers seek to bring out their best in their students, but they work in a system that in many ways require that their pupils be treated as disabled. But teachers play a central part in developing a school's culture and in forming teacher-pupil relations. Both these aspects can make a vital difference for a given pupil's social and academic experience of schooling. Education and schooling are crucial for children and young people in society, not least because they are gate-keepers- or openers to other social arenas, especially working life. School is also important because it is one of the few common references between people across differences. For some pupils, school may be a positive arena, for others is a place associated with failure, marginalization and exclusion.

The World report on disability (2011) emphasizes the importance of building teacher capacity:

> The appropriate training of mainstream teachers is crucial if they are to be confident and competent in teaching children with diverse educational needs. The principles of inclusive education should be built into teacher training programs, which should be about attitudes and values, not just knowledge and skills (World Report on disability, 2011, p. 22).

The understanding of inclusion and special education may operate on many levels, political, institutional, relational and ethical. Arnesen and Sollie (2003) have identified three main areas of work in which these levels are intertwined

1. Work against structural barriers that prevent active participation and access to social and societal resources and goods for individuals and groups (political, institutional)

2. Work towards recognition of social and cultural values and resources of minority groups for the benefit of the social community and for the empowerment of individuals and groups who belong to and are identifying with these groups/cultures, promoting recognition, positive identity and self-respect (institutional, relational, ethical)
3. Work towards making space for individual diversity by focusing on the uniqueness of the individual with his or hers resources and way of learning, communicating and expressing themselves, and acknowledging different notions of the "good life" (relational, ethical)

The Salamanca declaration (UNESCO 1994) highlighted that inclusive education is about all learners, not only those who have disabilities or school related difficulties

> An inclusive education system can only be created if ordinary schools become more inclusive – in other words, if they become better at educating all children in their communities (UNESCO/IBE, 1994, p. 8)

To meet the challenge for teacher and teacher education Skidmore (2004) draws attention to the differences between pedagogy of deviance and one of inclusion (table 2).

The transition to a pedagogy of inclusion must be supported by teachers who have knowledge, skills, and an appropriate positive attitude to sustain such a shift of paradigm.

Florian (2007) identifies three areas that deserve attention if teachers are to re-think questions of special education and inclusion. These are: clearer thinking about the right to education, the need to challenge deterministic views about ability, and a shift in focus from differences between learners, to learning for all.

| | A pedagogy of deviance | A pedagogy of inclusion |
|---|---|---|
| ***Educability of students*** | There is a hierarchy of cognitive skills to measure the ability of each student | Learning potentials of each student |
| ***Explanation of school failure*** | Related to the deficiencies of the students capacities | Inadequate responses generated by the curriculum |
| ***School response*** | Support for learning should seek to remediate the weaknesses of individual students | Support for learning should seek to reform curriculum and develop pedagogy across school |
| ***Theory of teachers' expertise*** | Specialized discipline knowledge | Active participation of the student in the learning process |
| ***The curriculum model*** | Designing an alternative curriculum for the less able | A common curriculum should be provided for all students |

Table 2 A pedagogy of deviance and a pedagogy of inclusion (Skidmore, 2004, p. 113).

There is a strong international focus on teacher education for inclusion. The Council of Europe, UNESCO and the European Agency for development in Special needs Education (EADSE) are some of the agencies that have formulated an agenda for teacher education for inclusion. As the chair of the Council of Europe project Policies and Practices for Teaching Socioculturel Diversity, Arnesen (2010) see the following main challenges for teacher education:

- recognising reality as plural, complex and dynamic;
- starting from within: building understanding among teacher students about themselves, their circumstances and position in a world of diversity;recognizing that teachers are part of that reality;
- shifting the focus from the differences between individuals to the factors which maintain differentiation and discrimination in social life;
- emphasising the promotion of inclusive environments for all children and young people with a focus on access and quality, equity and social

justice, democratic values and participation, balancing unity and diversity and belonging;
- developing "engaged pluralism" (Greene 1995): recognizing that some pupils are particularly vulnerable and at risk of marginalization or exclusion;
- developing a sensitivity towards tensions between diversity and unity in teacher students (Arnesen, 2010, p. 31)

Both UNESCO (UNECO/IBE 2011) and EADSNE (2011) view a broadened concept of inclusive education as a general guiding principle to strengthen education for sustainable development, lifelong learning for all and equal access for all level for society to learning opportunities.

The initial and continuous training and support of teachers are key strategies for the realization of an inclusive and right-based education system. The EADSNE project "Teacher Education for inclusion" has explored how all teachers are prepared via their initial education to be "inclusive" and the project report (EASDNE 2011, Donelly, Watkins, 2011) makes recommandations for teacher education and recommendations for wider policiey that will support the development of teachers. The question of how differences in the classroom can be dealt with need to have more room in the teacher education. Four core values relating to teaching and learning has been identified:

- Valuing learner diversity – learner difference is considered as a resource and an asset to education. The areas of competence within this core value relate to conceptions of inclusive education and the teacher's view of learner difference
- Supporting all learners – teachers have high expectations for all learners' achievements. The areas of competence within this core value relate to promoting the academic, social and emotional learning of all learners and effective teaching approaches in heterogeneous classes
- Working with others – collaboration an teamwork are essential approaches for all teachers. The areas of competence within this core value relate to working with parents and families and working with a range of other educational professionals
- Personal professional developmemt – teaching is a learning activity and teachers taking responsibility for their lifelong learning. The areas of competence within this core value relate to teachers as relective practioners and initial teacher education as a foundation for ongoing professional learning and development. (EASDNE: Teacher

Education for inclusion. Presentations from Round Table Meeting held at the European Parliament in Brussels on 24 April 2012)

Inclusive education needs teachers who in their attitudes welcome the wide range of pupils in his or her classroom, who have the competence to adapt the education within the framework of an inclusive classroom working collaboratively with others, knowing when, why and how to respond when pupils experience difficulties in learning and social relations. Teacher needs to have a professional competence when it comes to analysing and changing their class-room practices and when it comes to reflecting on meeting the dilemmas of dealing with inclusive education.

The University of Aberdeen has through a Post Graduate diploma of Education worked with the Inclusive Practice Project. Rouse (2006), Florian (2007) and Florian & Rouse (2010) have discussed and described inclusion both at philosophical and practical level. They refer to Shulman's three "apprenticeships" (Shulman 2005). The "apprenticeship of the head" means the teacher's abilities in relation to "knowing that and knowing what". In other words this refers to preparing teachers to know when, why and how to respond when pupils experience difficulties in learning, and advocatingreflective practice. "The apprenticeship of the hand" includes how to do it, that is the teacher's actions and abilities to work collaboratively with others. "The apprenticeship of the heart" denotes the ethical and moral dimensions of a profession which includes attitudes and beliefs about children and schooling that make a difference in children's lives. This dimention includes the ability to deal with difference as part of the human condition.

Teachers play a vital part in making a more inclusive school, but the teachers are entangled in an ecological net which is complex and dynamic. To handle processes of exclusion and inclusion requires more than competence in subjects and ready-made methods. First and foremost it is a question of wisdom and the ability to exercise good professional judgement. The outcomes of teacher education have to be teachers who are ready to move forward in an inclusive way. Certain conditions will facilitate the disposition of professionalism and other will hinder or obstruct it. Biesta (2010) identified time to reflect – individually and collectively the most important condition for fostering this disposition.

## Summary

There is no universal standard for what it means to be included, and what it means to participate in a satisfactory way. This is true whether we see it from the individual or from the society's point of view. Processes of social exclusions or inclusion are in themselves not inherently good or bad.

Inclusion is a term which is associated with diversity, human rights, equity and democratic participation (Arnesen & Lundahl, 2006). It could be argued that inclusion is one, if not the core value of democracy (Biesta, 2007).

As Bennett & Moss (Children in Scotland, 2010) argue, it is not possible to tackle exclusion within the educational system without addressing the underlying societal issue of inequality. Inclusive schools and kindergarten do not exist in a vacuum; they will only develop in an inclusive education system which is dependent upon an inclusive social system.

The current limitation in the capacity of mainstream school to engage the diversity of learners can be seen as a product of the social organization of education within our society. The limits to inclusion are socially constructed, defined and developed, and reflected in complex layers of exclusionary pressures, operating at the levels of school systems, schools and classroom.

The very concepts inclusion and exclusion imply a social context that involves power relations and tensions between inclusive and exclusive processes. Disabled, normal or deviant are not fixed positions, something a person is or is not. They are positions are negotiated, interpreted, defined and transformed in a complex mix of meaning, tradition, culture, history, social- and health policy, professionals and parents, policy and society, among other things.

Special education plays an ambiguous role in an inclusive school. Despite the good intensions of helping pupils participate and achieve in their ordinary environments the result is often marginalization in school and life.

This calls for rethinking special education and for critically reflectiing on the purpose of education within a broad context of issues. Educating all children more inclusively, means reducing underachievement and marginalization while striving to ensure a better life in school and society for all vulnerable children.

OFSTED (2010) recently reviewed special educational needs and disability in England. One of their key conclusions was that we must find a way of "ensuring that schools do not identify pupils as having special educational needs when they simply need better teaching".

From my point of view we cannot review or understand special education apart from the context of the ordinary school. Special education and ordinary education are embedded in ordinary education practices. The development of inclusive education depends on an "inclusive culture" where ordinary and special education work together in an inclusive direction. The challenge for teachers and teacher education is to support the inclusive values and bring about and sustain inclusive change.

## References

Ainscow, M., Booth, T. & Dyson, A. (2006).Inclusion and the standards agenda: negotiating policy pressures in England. *International journal of inclusive education,* 10 (4-5), 295 – 308.

Apple, M.(2010).Democratic education in neoliberal and neoconservative times. *International Studies in Sociology of Education,* 21(1), 21 -31.

Arnesen, A.L (2011). International politics and national reforms: The dynamics between "competence" and the "inclusive school" in Norwegian education policies. *Education Inquiry* (2), 193–206.

Arnesen, A.L. (2010). The complexity of diversity – challenges for teacher education. In Council of Europe. *Policies and practices for teaching sociocultural diversity. Concepts, principles and challenges in teacher education.* Strasbourg: Council of Europe Publishing Editions.

Arnesen, A.L. (2004). *Det pedagogiske nærvær. Inkludering i møte med elevmangfold [The Pedagogical Presence. Inclusion in meeting with a diversity of children],* Oslo: Abstrakt forlag.

Arnesen, A.L. & Lundahl, L. (2006) Still social and democratic? Inclusive education in the Nordic Welfare States, *The Scandinavian Journal of Educational Research*, 50(3), 285-300.

Arnesen, A.L. & Sollie, U. (2003). *Differensiering og tilpasset opplæring. [Differensiation and adapted and inclusive education]* HiO Report 11/2003. Oslo: Oslo university college Press.

Avramides, E. & Norwich, B. (2002) Teachers´ attitudes towards integration/inclusion: a review of the literature. *European Journal of Special Needs Education,* 17(2), 129-147.

Bakken, A. & Danielsen, K.(2011). *Gode skoler – gode for alle? En casestudie av prestasjonsforskjeller på seks ungdomsskoler [Good schools – good for all?]* Oslo: NOVA Rapport nr. 10/11.

Befring, E.(2006/1997).From Normalization to Enrichment.A retrospective Analysis of the Transformation of Special Education Principles. In R.Tangen,.(ed). *Edvard Befring: Spesialpedagigisk utsyn – læring og oppvekst. Artiklar i utvalg.* Oslo: Cappelen Akademisk forlag.

Biesta, G.J.J. (2010). *Good education in an age of measurement: Ethics, politics, democracy.* Boulder, Co: Paradigm Publishers.

Biesta, G.J.J. (2007). "Don't count me in." Democracy, education and the question of inclusion. *Nordisk Pedagogik* 27(1), 18-31.

Children in Scotland. (2010). *Working for inclusion: an overview of European early years services and their workforce,* Children in Scotland, Edinburgh.

Danmarks Evalueringsinstitut (2011). *Indsatser for inklusion i folkeskolen. [Efforts for inclusion in primary and lower secondary schools in Denmark]* København: Danmarks evalueringsinstitut.

Donnelly,V., Watkins,A. (2011). Teacher education for inclusion in Europe. *PROSPECTS,* 41 (3), 341 – 353.

Education Act. *Act relating to primary and Secondary Education.* Last amended 15 sept 2010.

EASDNE (2012).Teacher education for inclusion. *Presentation at at round table meeting held at the European Parliament in Brussels on 24 April.* Retrieved from http://www.european-agency.org/news/news-files/round-table-files/Teacher-Education-for-Inclusion-EP.pdf

Florian, L.& Rouse, M. (2009). 'The inclusive practice project in Scotland: Teacher Education for inclusion'. *Teaching and Teacher Education*, 25 (4), 594-601.

Florian,L.,Young, K.S.& Rouse, M.(2010). 'Preparing teachers for inclusive and diverse educational environments: Studying curricular reform in an initial teacher education course'. *International Journal of Inclusive Education*, 14 (7), 709-722.

Florian, L.(2007).Reimagining special education.In Florian, L.(ed) *The SAGE Handbook of Special Education.* London: Sage publication Ltd.

Giota, J., Lundborg, O. & Emanuelsson, I. (2009) Special education in Comprehensive Schools: Extent, Forms and Effects" *Scandinavian Journal of Educational Research,* 53(6), 557 – 578.

GSI statistics 2011-12. *GSI statictics. Information from primary and lower secondary school.* https://www.wis.no/gsi/

Haug, P.(2011) God opplæring for alle – eit felles ansvar [ Good education for all – a common responsibility ] *Norsk Pedagogisk tidsskrift*, 98 (2), 129 – 140.

Meijer, C. (2010). Special Needs Education in Europe: Inclusive Policies and Practices. *Zeitschrift FüR Inklusion,* 4(2). Retrieved from http://www.inklusiononline.net/index.php/inklusion/article/view/56/60

Ministry of Church and Education (1970). *Innstilling om lovregler for spesialundervisning m.v, (Blom komiteen) [Recommendation about statutory provision relating to special education etc].* Oslo: Ministry of Church and Education.

Ministry of Education Research and Church Affairs (1996). *Curriculum for the 10-year compulsory school.* Oslo:Ministry of Education Research and Church Affairs.

Minisry of Education and Research (2011). *Meld. St.18 (2010-2011). Report to the Storting (white paper) Summary. Learning together*. Oslo: Ministry of Education and Research.

Mitchell, D. (2010). *Education that fits: Review of international trends in the the education of students with special educational needs.* Final report.College of Education, University of Canterbury, for the Ministry of Education New Zealand. Retrieved from http://www.educationcounts.govt.nz/publications/special_education/education-that-fits-review-of-international-trends-in-the-education-of-students-with-special-educational-needs/executive-summary

Nes, K., Strømstad,M. & Skogen, K. (2004). *En spørreundersøkelse om inkludering i skolen. [A survey about incusion in education].* Elverum: Høgskolen i Hedmark.Rapport nr.3.

Nind, M. (2011). Inclusive Education Research. Research Intelligence, *BERA,* 115, Summer Issue, 18. Retrieved from http://www.bera.ac.uk/publications/research-intelligence/2011

Nordahl, T og Hausstätter, R. (2009). *Spesialundervisningens forutsetninger, innsatser og resultater.[Assumptions, content and learning outcome in special education]* Hamar:Høgskolen i Hedmark. Rapport 9-2009

Norwich, B. (2008). *Dilemmas of difference, inclusion and disability. International perspectives and future directions.*London: Routledge.

OFSTED (2010). *The Special educational needs and disability review.* http://www.ofsted.gov.uk/resources/special-educational-needs-and-disability-review

Persson, B. (2003). Exclusive and inclusive discourses in special education research amnd policy in Sweden. *International Journal of Inclusive Education,* 7 (3), 271 – 280.

Runswick-Cole, K. (2011).Time to end bias towards inclusive education? *British Journal of Special Education,* 38 (3), 112 – 119.

Shulman,L.S.(2005). Signature pedagogies in professions. *Daedalus,* 134 (3), 52 – 59.

Skidmore, D. (2004) *Inclusion: the dynamic of school development.* Berkshire: Open University Press.

Tisdall, E.K.M. & Riddell, S. (2006). Policies on special needs education: competing strategies and discourses. *European Journal of Special Needs Education*, 21 (4), 363 – 379.

Thomas, G. & Loxley, A. (2007). *Deconstructing Special Education and Constructing Inclusion.* 2nd edition. Berkshire: Open University Press.

Tøssebro, J. (2010). *Hva er funksjonshemming [What is disability*?] Oslo: Universitetsforlaget

UNESCO/IBE (1994) *The Salamanca Statement and Framework for Action on Special Needs Education,* Paris, UNESCO

UNESCO/IBE.(2011). Interregional and Regional Perspectives on Inclusive Education: *Follow-up of the 48th session of the International Conference on EducationInclusive education: The way of the future.* Geneva: UNESCO: International Bureau of Education. Retrieved from http://www.ibe.unesco.org/fileadmin/user_upload/Policy_Dialogue/48th_ICE/Perspectives_inclusiv_education_2011.pdf

Vislie, L. (2006). Special education under the modernity. From restricted liberty, through organized modernity, to extended liberty and a plurality of practices *European journal of special needs education* (21), 395 – 414.

Vislie, L. (2003).From integration to inclusion: focusing global trends and changes in the Western European societies. *European Journal of Special Needs Education*, (18), 17-35.

Wendelborg, C. & Tøssebro, J. (2010) Marginalisation processes in inclusive education in Norway – a longitudinal study of classroom participation, *Disability & Society*, 25(6):701-714

Wendelborg, C. (2010) *Barrierer mot deltakelse. Familier med barn og unge med nedsatt funksjonsevne [Barrier to participation Families with children and youth with impairments]* Trondheim: NTNU Samfunnsforskning.

Wilde, A. & Avramidis, E. (2011). Mixed feelings: towards a continuum of inclusive pedagogies. Education 3:13: *International Journal of Primary, Elemantary and Early Years Education,* 39 (1), 83-101.

World Health Organization.(2011).*World report on disability 2011.* Retrieved from http://whqlibdoc.who.int/publications/2011/9789240685215_eng.pdf

AUTHOR: Kjell-Arne Solli is Assistant Professor in Special Education at University College of Østfold, department of Teacher Education. He has directed the master program of special education. His academic interest includes school and pre-school development, inclusion, adaptive education and special education; focusing on students in social and emotional difficulties. He is the author of the book "Pupils in conflict" and has written articles and reviews of research in special education. The last three years he has cooperated with Anne- Lise Arnesen in the project "The work in kindergarten to enhance inclusion for children with special needs, viewed from a profession perspective". They have also cooperated in establishing the master program "Diversity and Inclusion in Pedagogical work".
Correspondence: kjell.a.solli@hiof.no

# *Beyond the pale*

## INTERSECTIONS AND OTHERNESS IN A MULTICULTURAL SCHOOL

TRINE ANKER
Østfold University College, Norway

ABSTRACT: *The article addresses how respect is enacted, and how boundaries between "we" and "others" are constructed in a Norwegian multicultural school. The main analysis is based on material constructed through fieldwork at a primary school. The article is situated theoretically within critical cultural studies, leaning on the analytical concepts of intersectionality (Crenshaw, 1989) and positioning (Davies & Harré, 1990). The material for the article shows how students enact and discuss respect according to the categories "Norwegians" and "foreigners." However, Norwegians and foreigners are not totally distinct categories. Rather, boundaries between the two groups are constructed as a mix of ethnicity, Norwegian language skills, color, religion, interests, and peer relations. I here argue that the National Curriculum's (LK06's) outline of respect for "the others" is not mirrored in the pupils' practices. However, the pupil's practices carry possibilities for new and interesting discussions of respect and otherness in curriculum and in schools.*

### *Introduction*

In her book about pedagogy as presence, Anne-Lise Arnesen (2004) highlights the importance of recognition and respect. Arnesen claims that these concepts cover several aspects of cooperation in schools, including the ability to listen and to understand. In this article, I go further into the concept of respect and analyze how respect is practiced and conceptualized among students in a primary school. The Norwegian national curriculum's presentation of respect in relation to "the others" is a point of departure for the article, which aims to answer the research question: *How is respect for "the others" enacted at East Primary, and who are these "others"?*

I will shortly comment on East Primary, a Norwegian multicultural school, before turning to the article's main issues of respect and otherness. East Primary is situated in a small town in the eastern part of Norway. I define East Primary as multicultural due to how the school is profiled on its home page. Schools are often defined as multicultural in a descriptive way based on the amount of students with non-Norwegian backgrounds. In such a descriptive understanding of a multicultural school, differences between students according to their cultural backgrounds are implicitly emphasized.

However, "multicultural" is a problematic concept because it highlights certain differences while hiding others, increasing the risk of stereotyping. Therefore, "multicultural" has been extended to include groups linked to gender, sexuality, and ability. New understandings of multicultural pedagogy include the rights of these different groups (Vedøy, 2008, p. 28).[1] Nevertheless, schools, including East Primary, usually make descriptive definitions of themselves as multicultural according to the amount of students with minority backgrounds. The main reason for selecting such a multicultural school for the inquiry was to look into possible conflicts between multicultural ideals of respect for the others in the curriculum and in pupils' practices.

A curriculum reform for primary and secondary education took place in Norway in 2006. In the new and revised curriculum (LK06), which is common and mandatory for all primary and secondary schools in Norway, learning to respect the others' cultures is identified as one purpose of education. The students are supposed to learn respect for food traditions of other cultures, for different music traditions, for the Samis' and other indigenous people's knowledge of nature, and for other cultures in general. To respect and to have knowledge about these traditions and cultures are presented as two sides of the same coin. Hence, the tool for gaining respect is knowledge, and respect appears mainly as an epistemic virtue. LK06 implicitly states that knowledge and understanding are cognitive skills which will promote respect towards the others. However, what respect is and who the others are is neither questioned nor defined in LK06. I will not go further into an analysis of possible definitions of respect and otherness as they

[1] Hovdelien (2011) does not take cultural and group rights into account in his definition of a multicultural school. Rather, he defines the whole Norwegian state school as multicultural. Because the school system is part of the Norwegian multicultural society, the schools do not have the option of defining multiculturalism away. This view is pedagogically founded.

apply to[2] I will instead address respect from a moral philosophical point of view, before introducing analytical concepts and methods and material for the analyses.

## *Respect*

Respect is a central concept in numerous theories of ethics. Some theories treat respect as the very essence of morality and the foundation of all other moral duties and obligations (Dillon, 2003). Axel Honneth (2007), situated in the German critical tradition, has made a comprehensive theory of respect (recognition) with the aim of describing the present Western society as well as contributing to a better one. Honneth (2007) uses the concept of recognition as an overarching category. Respect is limited to respect for rules and rights, and placed as a subcategory of recognition. Love and solidarity comprise the two other sub-categories of recognition. At East Primary, however, they use the concept of respect to cover Honneth's different understandings of recognition. Hence, I likewise prefer to use respect synonymously to recognition. For Honneth, the three realms or categories of recognition are essential for humans to develop healthy subjectivity. This article emphasizes the category of respect which Honneth (2007) names "loyalty" and "solidarity". This is a communitarian form of respect which highlights minority groups' rights to be recognized for their practices and ideas when differing from the majority. A communitarian understanding of respect is mirrored in LK06's aims of learning to respect other cultures.

In post-colonial theory, "the others" are identified by their difference from the center, marginalized through an imperial discourse (Ashcroft, Griffiths, & Tiffin, 1998, p. 170; Kameniar, 2005). When there are others to respect, there is also a "we." In LK06, the other is explicit, though not defined, while the "we" is implicit. A problematic aspect of a communitarian form of respect exemplified with the implicit differentiation between "we" and "other" in LK06 is that group boundaries might be considered as more fixed and obvious than they are. Furthermore, the emphasis on differences between groups leads to the neglect of the differences within groups. Hence, relevant questions to ask are who the central we is, and who fits into the peripheral other? Addressing LK06 as a starting point for this

[2] For an interesting discussion of how texts regulate people's lives and activities in institutional settings, see Arnesen and Lundahl (2010).

discussion about respect and otherness, the analytical approach is critical culture studies with the concepts of "intersectionality" and "positioning" as analytical tools. These concepts are founded in empirical studies and augment opening up the communitarian concept of respect for a more ambiguous discussion.

## *Intersectionality and positioning*

Intersectionality and positioning are used as two different lenses, with adjacent but slightly different perspectives. "Intersectionality" is the main concept structuring the empirical material, making categories, such as religion, color, language, gender, and youth, visible. Criticizing feministic research for its narrow focus on gender, Crenshaw (1989) introduced "intersectionality" to highlight the mutual constructions and hierarchies of social categories. The social position of a woman depends also on color, sexuality, nationality, and ability (Crenshaw, 1989; de los Reyes & Mulinari, 2005, p. 27; Svalfors, 2008, p. 14). Crenshaw (1989) emphasized the difference that differences make for a person. However, she warns against the use of "intersectionality" as an additive model, where different categories are added to one another, leading to hierarchies of oppression. Different categorizations intersect, and the boundaries between different groups are not fixed. What difference is, and who the others are, will change according to situations.

Nevertheless, "intersectionality," as an analytical tool, might favor structures and group-relations before human agency. To avoid a simplistic image of these students driven by pre-existing structures in terms of group affiliations, and rather emphasize their agency, I lean on Davies and Harré's (1990) concept of "positioning." Davies and Harré (1990) introduced positioning as an alternative to the use of roles. Positioning highlights the dynamic aspects of encounters in contrast to the more static and formal aspects of roles (Davies & Harré, 1990, p. 43). Arnot and Mac anGaill (2006) claimed that research conducted in schools often implicitly leans on simple categorizations of gender. A similar uncritical view on other broad categories, such as minority students, might be a part of common-sense explanations. In contrast, positioning opens up such categories and highlights pupils' agency.

## *Methods*

To focus on the students' agency and study how they enact respect for "the others" and construct group boundaries, I conducted ethnographic fieldwork in 6th and 7th grades at East Primary, presented above, from January to June 2009. The material for the analyses consists of notes from observations in classrooms and the schoolyard, together with video-taped group interviews with the students.[3] The topics for the group interviews followed up situations and talks from earlier observations. Hence, the interview material is often used to shed light on what appeared to be important topics of the classroom and schoolyard practices, and the interviews and observations appear complementary, rather than contrasting.

In the following section, the material is used to discuss how the students at East Primary divide each other into categories of Norwegians and foreigners, but also how they open up these categories, focusing on other divides. The material from East Primary gives an interesting contribution to a communitarian understanding of respect mirrored in the curriculum.

## *Norwegians and foreigners at East Primary*

At East Primary, the pupils use "Norwegians" and "foreigners" to categorize each other. These categories might correspond with "we" and "others" in LK06. The others are the ones from other cultures, implicitly making a boundary to Norwegian culture – the true "we" of LK06.[4] However, even though the pupils divide each other into two main groups, their definitions show how blurred the boundaries are and question a simple center-periphery distinction related to Norwegians and foreigners. I asked the students to define the difference between these two categories in the group interviews. Luigi explains that foreigners are those who are from another country.[5] This seems to be a simple and good answer, but when Luigi is pushed a bit further, he starts to become insecure about his definition. Madeleine, for instance, was born in Poland, and her father is from

---

[3] The material was constructed for my Ph.D. thesis about social practices of respect in a multicultural school (see Anker, 2011). In this article, I make use of small parts of this material.

[4] For a wider discussion of the concept of culture and Norwegian-ness in the core curriculum of LK06, see Eriksen (2010).

[5] The anonymous names were picked by the students. Therefore, some of them have names from TV shows, artists, and in Luigi's case, a video game.

Denmark. Luigi says that he is not sure about her nationality: "what would she call herself, Polish or Danish or..." Because of her mixed background, Luigi leaves it up to Madeleine to decide her own nationality. While Luigi initially claims that a foreigner is someone born outside of Norway, he finds that it is not that simple.

Aishwaryaa and Lisa from $6^{th}$ grade start to define "foreigner" in a similar mode as Luigi: "Foreigners are those who come from another country." When Aishwaryaa gives herself as an example of a foreigner, I ask her where she was born. She laughs and tells me that she was born in Horten, a small city in Norway. Nevertheless, she defines herself as a foreigner, explaining that this classification is based on her parents' country of origin and the traditions she therefore has grown up with. These traditions are, according to Aishwaryaa, grounded in religion (Islam), and in the fact that foreigners have stricter rules than Norwegians.

## *Stricter rules*

Aishwaryaa states that the foreigners' rules are different and stricter than the Norwegians'. Some of these rules concern Muslim practices, such as the rules of what to eat and, to a certain extent, how to behave. Aishwaryaa reports that she has had many discussions and conflicts about rules with her parents. She claims that the Albanian rules are much stricter than the Norwegian rules, especially when it comes to relations with boys. Aishwaryaa is not adapting to her parents' rules. She states that she constantly gets new boyfriends and that she is worried about what her father will do if he finds out.

From Aishwaryaa's point of view, the varied groups of foreigners have similar rules, even if they practice these rules differently. The similarity in their rules seems to be more an opposition the similarity in their rules is more an opposition to Norwegian rules than agreement among this varied group of non-Norwegians. While several students claim that Norwegian pupils can do whatever they like, the foreigners are restricted by their parents and are not free to attend parties or to hang out in the street in the evenings. Aishwaryaa discusses and reflects on the differences of rules. She positions herself as partly Norwegian in opposition to her parents' rules, and partly foreigner because she experiences a tighter family relation than her Norwegian friends. Aishwaryaa points to what immigrant youth can experience as a pressure to follow their parents' traditions. However, not all students describe these experiences as negative. Several students talk about close family relations in contrast to what they find as less tight relations to family among the Norwegians. The pupils identified as foreigners do not assimilate to what they describe as Norwegians rules (or lack of rules), or to their parents' rules. Even though they section rules in two main categories, most of the foreigners position themselves in between.[6]

## *A small little accent*

The pupils at East Primary emphasize the ability to speak fluent Norwegian as a sign of Norwegianness, while speaking flawed Norwegian is a marker of foreignness. The idea of a perfect language is questionable, and while Lisa regards Aishwaryaa's Norwegian as perfect, June can hear "a small little accent". Carridee, on the other hand, speaks perfect Norwegian, according to June. Carridee was born in Kongo, but June considers her a Norwegian. Carridee has lived some years in the northern part of Norway, and this seems to neutralize her place of birth. "When you come from northern Norway, you are totally Norwegian," June states.

While Carridee is Norwegian when she speaks, Natalia is more Norwegian when she keeps quiet. June states that they almost forget that Natalia, born in Poland, is a foreigner. When she speaks, however, they remember it. Speaking as a foreigner is not just about grammar or phonetics; it is also about the content of the conversation. For instance, June regards Vanessa as a foreigner because she often talks about her cousins in Germany. The foreigners chat with their cousins, and they visit relatives during their holidays. A close connection to the extended family is reflected by most students as a marker of foreignness.

In discussions about foreignness, June takes a very strong position. It seems natural for her to be the one deciding and defining her classmates' Norwegianness and foreignness. She possesses what Ghassan Hage (1998) calls spatial power, the power to set boundaries for insiders and outsiders.

---

[6] Hence, they practice the role of bricoleurs, or cultural navigators (see Jacobsen, 2002, p. 32; Runfors, 2003; Prieur, 2004).

## *Religious practices*

The students are well aware of the different religions present at their school, and they usually address religion in a positive way. Religion as a belief system is not explicitly mentioned as a marker for foreignness among the students. However, Aishwaryaa emphasizes the difference between foreigners and Norwegians when it comes to the rules they follow. Some of these rules are about how to dress and what to eat, which relates to Muslim practices of dress codes and halal food. Arne mentions that Buddhists are "nothing." When I try to find out what he means by this "nothing," it seems that he points to the practices of different religions. "In Buddhism, you do not have to do things," Arne states. There are few Buddhists at East Primary, and they do not claim special rights. Hence, they are invisible as a religious minority. Muslims, on the other hand, represent a large religious minority group at the school, leading to an increasing awareness of Muslim practices. In the subject Food and Health, pork is usually replaced with chicken for every student (even though it is not halal-prepared). The Muslim girls in 6th and 7th grade highlight practices of how to dress and when to pray when they talk about their religion. Some of them wear a hijab, while others do not. Muslims are quite visible in the Norwegian media context, where Islam is depicted as the other and often as a source of conflict (Eide & Simonsen, 2009; Eriksen, 2010; von der Lippe, 2010). This national discourse may contribute to making the practice of Islam a marker of foreignness to a greater extent than the practice of Buddhism.

## *To be perfect*

To be perfect is an ideal for the girls at East Primary. Perfectness is a combination of looks, clothes, and different skills. Religious practices might conflict with such an ideal of being perfect. Nelly, for instance, gets comments for wearing a hijab. These comments do not concern religion or question the obligation from her parents. Rather, the other girls think it is a shame that she hides her beautiful hair. Similarly, students ask Miley to take her long skirt off because she looks so good in the tight jeans she wears underneath.

In these examples, certain looks are considered better than others. To hide beautiful hair or to refuse to show long, thin legs is not understandable in the image of perfectness. Paris formulates how respect is seen in relation both to broad categories such as ethnicity and, at the same time, to personal characteristics: "Respect is also not to judge others due to their skin color, look, whether they use glasses or not, and that one doesn't call others a dwarf." To respect different looks is not just about skin color, but about respecting variations from "the perfect." Konrafael also includes looks into what respect is: "Respect is to have a good reputation. How you look, I also find valuable in gangs. Well I am not the most respected in class but I think I will manage well. I am also a little bit disappointed about my look." Konrafael portrays respect as a possession owned by those who have a good reputation, which in turn is tied to looking good. Konrafael is not respected, and he is not satisfied with his appearance. Another boy in 6$^{th}$ grade states that "respect is not to judge anyone according to sexuality, body appearance, gender, looks, religion, and culture." In his statement, sociological categories intersect with personal characteristics.

## *She is not that brown*

One of the markers of foreignness is, according to Aishwaryaa, the color of a person's skin. She states that she is darker than Norwegians and that her skin color is a sign of her foreignness. Lisa, on the other side, questions Aishwaryaa's self-perception of being brown. She states that Aishwaryaa is not very brown, and that she can at least be regarded as half-Norwegian. Aishwaryaa laughs about this, concluding that she is a quarter or maybe a third Norwegian. This is not according to her light brown color, but because she hangs out with Norwegian friends.

Being blonde is a sign of being Norwegian, while brown hair is a marker for foreignness. Nevertheless, being blonde can also have the subtext of stupidity. In Norway, plenty of jokes about dumb blonde women exist. Such jokes are gendered; jokes about stupid blond men are, to my knowledge, non-existent. Furthermore, jokes about stupid, blonde girls are often connected to sexuality. A dumb blonde girl might be seen as an "easy" girl, lacking the ability to set limits concerning her body and sexuality, or being too naive. Hence, dumbness and sexual availability are connected in the stereotyped image of blondeness. Such stereotypes lead to phrases like "being blonde" to describe the non-intelligent. For instance June describes Beyonce as being an "inside blonde" when she fails to understand a joke June tells. June also uses the category of wannabe-blonde.

This might refer to a wish for concrete blondness and a traditional Norwegian appearance, but it may also mean to make oneself stupid or sexually available. In a discussion about the risks of publishing nude photos, Lisa states, "I am not that blonde." Hence, blondness is used to describe stupidity, especially connected to body and sexuality. June and Lisa would probably never have used the expression "inside blond" about a boy. Blondness is linked to girls and especially to Norwegian girls.

## *To be small down there*

To have the right look is a topic for boys and for girls, but the focus on heterosexuality is much more apparent in boys' conversations than in girls'. A story several pupils tell is about the day a teacher pointed out Ali as a possible homosexual. Ali felt this was an insult. It did not matter to him that the teacher probably tried to teach respect for different forms of sexuality. "Homo" is one of the insulting words most used in Norwegian schools today, especially among boys, according to a research report on sexual bullying (Helseth, 2007, p. 15). Heterosexuality as a norm makes borders for the category of "man."

Heterosexuality is clearly the norm at East Primary. In the spring of 2009, most of the boys in 6th grade participate in the "homo-test." The "homo-test" follows a certain pattern: The participant takes an eraser and rubs the upper part of his hand very hard. If the participant is able to continue until he starts to bleed, without screaming or crying, he passes the test. He is then defined as heterosexual. None of the girls take part in the test. Some of the boys find the test to be childish and do not want to participate. Such an explanation makes their lack of involvement mature rather than "girlish." Although homonegativity is often conceptualized as an immigrant attitude, Staunæs (2004, p. 228) describes that, in her empirical material from Denmark, white ethnic Danish youths are also taking part in homophobic discourse in school (see also Eliasson, 2007; Thorne, 1993). My material reflects the same tendency in that Norwegians and foreigners participated to the same degree in the homo-test.

Among the adult Norwegian middle class, respecting different sexualities is highly valued and can be considered as taking part in limiting the tolerant we from the intolerant other. In this context, the intolerant others are often identified as the Muslims, and Muslim homophobia is one of the ongoing debates of moral panic in the Norwegian mass media. Røthing and Svendsen (2008, p. 32) claim that gender equality as a Norwegian value has a little sister in homopositivity. Homopositivity seems to take part in the constitution of a Norwegian we. That makes homotolerance a test of how well migrant minorities are integrated. The teacher's reaction to Ali can be read with such debates in mind. To be homotolerant is a positive value, something to be learned in school and part of being integrated. Even though homopositivity becomes a marker of Norwegianness, Norwegianness remains firmly heteronormative (Eriksen, 2010, p. 55; Gressgård & Jacobsen, 2008). Røthing and Svendsen (2008) ask whether homotolerance is just a part of Norwegian heterosexuality (i.e., that it is good to be homotolerant, but not to live as a homosexual).

After one of the gymnastic classes, Batista and Peter refuse to go into the boys' dressing room to shower. They say that the other boys make fun of them for being "small down there," pointing towards their penises. To be ridiculed for the size or the shape of the penis is connected to the ideal of masculinity or being a "real man." The boys fight for the girls' attention, and the girls sometimes complain about harassment from boys trying to touch them and run after them. Sometimes the girls join the game; other times they seek refuge. According to Mac an Ghaill (1994, p. 9) learning to act like men consists of contradictory forms of compulsory heterosexuality, misogyny, and homophobia. Being "small" and not masculine is something you can be teased about to the extent that these two boys refuse to take a shower.

## *The foreign boys*

The issue of ethnocentricity and racism is an explicit topic at East Primary. It is a common understanding among the students that boys with African backgrounds are the ones who usually get the blame when rules are broken. Ethnic background, color and gender seem to intersect, making boys with darker skin hypervisible in the school context. Cornelia underpins that the boys with black skin get most of the reprimands and are frequently punished. She adds that they do a lot of stupid things, but even when they are innocent, they are still blamed.

To illustrate how teachers treat these boys unfairly, Ali tells me a story. At East Primary, they have a special refrigerator room to store milk. One day, some boxes of chocolate milk were stolen. One of the teachers said that some pupils were seen in the room, and they were all “svartinger”. When Ali quotes the teacher, he uses the word “svartinger,” which is a racist word similar to the American word “niggers.” Jonas was there as well, Ali states, and he is white. Jonas disrupts Ali, saying that the teacher did not say “svartinger” but “Africans,” and he confirms that he had been there as well. I ask the rest of the class if they agree that the boys usually get the blame for broken rules. Mie nods her head and adds, “Especially the foreign boys.”

Ali and Jonas do not agree upon which word was used when the teacher referred to the rule-breakers. In a school context, the importance of truth is often pointed out as essential. Ali’s story risks being disqualified because he uses the very strong word “svartinger,” which is a word that the teacher probably did not use. If we rather listen to the underlying story, Ali, as one of the “Africans,” explains his experienced racism with the chosen word.

In the pupils’ talks about racist and ethnocentric actions, they usually delimit their stories to that of teachers. The pupils seldom describe racism among themselves. Zarah, however, states that it is different at other schools and that she changed schools to East Primary some years ago. There are more of “her people” at East Primary compared to her former school. She states, “When I was at the other school, there was only one Muslim; not all showed respect to me. If you are the only one, it is difficult, but where there are others, it feels better.” In this case, “her people” refers to Muslims. At East Primary, Zarah experiences more respect for her religion because there are more Muslim students in the school.

Cornelia’s parents are from Somalia, and Cornelia talks about how happy she was the day Dina, also with a Somali background, arrived at East Primary. It was important for Cornelia because there was suddenly someone who could understand her. Before Dina came, the only other Somali students at East Primary were boys, and Cornelia claims that is not the same. Meeting a person with the same background, meaning a combination of ethnicity, religion, and gender, was important. Cornelia appreciates having good friends with different backgrounds, but there is something special with Dina. In Dina, she found someone with whom she could share ideas and thoughts about culture and religion. Klara joins the discussion, telling about her experience moving to East Primary from northern Norway. She felt like an outsider when she came to East Primary, but it helped her to have one friend who had also lived in northern Norway. Klara explains the difference between how popularity works in the north and at East Primary. In the north, everyone was friends. Popularity, insiders, and outsiders seem to be categories operating differently in different contexts.

## *The Norwegians own*

Being Norwegian or being a foreigner is part of how these students position themselves and others. The first time I became aware of this dichotomist categorization was when I heard Aishwaryaa say, "The Norwegians 'own'" (*eier*). The Norwegian word *eier/eid* is equivalent to the English own/owned. Traditionally, *eier* cannot be used without an object. Among the youth, however, the words *eier/eid* (without an object) are used in the meaning of having control or being admired. "Jeg eier" is used in the sense of "I own the situation" or "I am in power." One of the students explained to me that the word *eier* is taken from the game *World of Warcraft* (WoW). In the English version, the words "owned" or, more informally, "pwned" are used. The term basically means to dominate ("I owned you") or to be dominated by an opponent or situation ("I got owned"), especially by some god-like or computer-like force. WoW is the favorite game of many of the boys, especially in 6th grade. It is an online game that they play together in the evenings. Almost a year later, the game is still very popular, although some of the boys have stopped playing it. The girls do not seem to have interest in this game, and when I ask the boys, they state that none of the girls ever play it. However, a couple of mothers play WoW, and Arne first started to play it with his mother.

I ask Aishwaryaa later about what she meant by her statement "the Norwegians 'eier'." She explains that she used to think bad about Norwegians, but now she thinks that they "eier," that they are cool. Zarah confirms Aishwaryaa's changed position toward Norwegians. Zarah states that Aishwaryaa thought there were differences between the foreigners and the Norwegians: "she used to talk bad about the Norwegians a lot, and then I said to her that I might color my hair blonde, and then she got really crazy and said then I don't want to be with you and I said that the blondes are really kind, beautiful, not all of them are like they don't like foreigners and such." Aishwaryaa and Zarah are both girls with strong positions in this class. How they define their relation to the Norwegians will probably be significant for the other girls. It seems as though Zarah interprets Aishwaryaa's opposition to Norwegians as feelings built on experiences of stigmatization. Zarah emphasizes the existence of different attitudes among Norwegians. While Zara characterized being blonde as something nice, in thinking about bleaching her hair, Aishwaryaa had quite different connotations of blondness. Blondness is a sign of being Norwegian, and because of Aishwaryaa's negative attitude toward Norwegians at that time, a blonde Zarah would possibly have been interpreted as a kind of betrayal.

The girls positioning is in transition. Aishwaryaa gives dating a Norwegian boy as the reason for her changed feelings toward Norwegians. Both Zarah and Aishwaryaa highlight relationships when they talk about respect. Zarah writes, "respect cute boys, respect teachers, children, parents and the people close to you," while Aishwaryaa underpins that respect means not to "date your former boyfriends." At this time, Zarah and Aishwaryaa are talking a lot about their different boyfriends. A year later, Zarah has taken another position and is staying away from the discos and parties the other girls attend. After one of these discos, Zarah comments that "it is just for the ones that know they have fun all the time, and who like to date many boys" ("det er bare for de som har det gøy hele tiden og som liker å være sammen med mange gutter"). Zarah continues, lifting her eyebrows, "and we know how they will be when they become adults" ("vi vet hvordan de blir når de blir voksne") (fieldnotes 2010-06-08). At this point in time, Zarah seems to have gotten some distance from the girls who attend parties and have many boyfriends. She also comments on how nice it is to go on holiday to visit the family in Kosovo. In Kosovo, they are surrounded by family; they eat dinner together, and they laugh a lot.

An ideal for the pupils at East Primary is to make one's own decision, not caring too much about what parents, teachers, and other students say. Before going to a school camp, Aishwaryaa said that no one could stop her from using mascara at the camp, even if using make-up was not allowed: "I am me, and if they want to send me home, they can do it." Another girl comments that the boys do not like girls with mascara. Aishwaryaa says with disgust in her voice, "I am not making myself pretty for boys, especially not these boys." Aishwaryaa takes part in a discourse of "being oneself." She wants to choose. No one else is doing it for her, not the boys and not the rules. In another conversation, Aishwaryaa and Vanessa, both with Albanian backgrounds, are talking about how much make-up the girls use in Albania. They explain and demonstrate to me how the Albanian girls exaggerate the use of make-up, in their point of view. There seems to be a limit as to how much make-up they can wear, still to be reckoned as normal. In Albania, they use too much. Ambjörnsson (2004, p. 290) discusses the topic of being unique in a study among high school girls. She finds how being unique and being the same are part of fitting in. Paradoxically, individual freedom fits into the norm (Ambjörnsson, 2004, p. 290).

A part of the youth culture for the pupils at East Primary is to hang around in the town after school, which some do without their parents' permission. This life in the town includes dating, "dissing", and shopping. [7] In the words of Aishwaryaa, those who do not take part in this activity "are not part of this age; they are more back in 1787 or so." This characteristic is first and foremost aimed at some of the Norwegian boys who like mathematics and stay at home in front of the computer more than out in the street. "Who would ever like maths?" Aishwaryaa asks rhetorically. The boys who like "math" and spend much of their time in front of their computers are considered the nerds. Arne, one of these boys, complains about this label the girls give them. Janne states that being a nerd is not positive, but at least it means that you know something. To be described as a loser is worse. According to Janne a loser is someone that does not take part in any group and always refuses invitations to parties. To be a loser is the loser's own fault. Janne finishes the description of a loser by stating that they should try, but not too hard. A loser trying too hard to fit in will be called a "wannabe." In this conversation, my comment is that it must be very difficult to know whether one tries enough, or too much. Janne does not comment back.

Country of origin, language, color, and religion are markers of foreignness at East Primary. However, these markers seem to be neutralized when the students talk about their friends. Carridee states that the definition of being a foreigner has to do with whom you hang out with. Carridee hangs out with both Norwegians and foreigners. Hence, she is a mix.

## *Norwegianness and foreignness*

Norwegianness is not a fixed category. Eriksen (2010) introduced viscosity as a metaphor in discussing how the group boundaries of Muslims and Norwegians

---

[7] "Dissing" is an English slang word to diss, originally from disrespect, and refers to the activity of making insults. Sometimes "dissing" is used as a competition and the person with the most creative insult will win (see Anker 2011, p. 158).

change. Viscosity is a technical term referring to a fluid's resistance to flow. Whereas water is "thin" and has low viscosity, honey is "thick" and has high viscosity. Using viscosity as a metaphor emphasizes how the solidity of a group with identity claims varies with different circumstances (Eriksen, 2010, p. 104). Playing further with the viscosity metaphor, we can see the borders as being permeable. Characteristics with high viscosity (thick) will not enter, while characteristics with low viscosity (thin) can enter into the category of Norwegians. The more foreign the accent is, the higher the viscosity, and so on. Some characteristics (brown) are made thinner because of other characteristics (living for a certain number of years in northern Norway). Some are in the category of Norwegians by birth, while others can strive to become members, defining themselves as half or quarter Norwegian. At times, those striving to become members are considered more Norwegian by their Norwegian friends than by themselves. An interesting point to mention is that the girls seem to cross the borders between foreignness and Norwegianness to a greater extent than the boys. What this has to do with is difficult to determine. It could be a coincidence. On the other hand, it may reveal that the combination of a non-Norwegian background and male gender is a combination of high viscosity. A third possibility is that the girls, to a greater extent, use their ability to position others, and that they are more concerned about positioning the other girls than are the boys.

The popular girls with non-Norwegian backgrounds are included in the group of Norwegians to a greater extent than are the not-so-popular, and the arguments for inclusion vary. The Norwegians seem to possess spatial power in order to set up boundaries and define insiders and outsiders.[8] Some Norwegians have the power to discuss the Norwegianness of their peers. When Lisa discusses respect, she writes, "the Somalis can't show their hair and we must respect that. We can't take off the scarf." Lisa, with a Norwegian background, uses the personal "we" (vi) here in contrast to the Somalis. Lisa shows how she sees herself taking part in a "we" that is in the position to respect (or not respect) the others (here, the Somalis). The same can be found in Dina's statement when she describes how she respects someone from Somalia: "…I respect where he or she comes from, what her belief is, which skin color and which kind of clothes he or she wears." Both Lisa's and Dina's statements can be interpreted as expressions of spatial

[8] For a discussion of the concept of spatial power, see Hage (1998).

power. They find themselves in a position to include or exclude others and to hand out respect.

## Conclusion

To answer the research questions: *How is respect for "the others" enacted at East Primary, and who are these "others"?* I started by referring to how LK06 attaches the aim of respect to otherness, mainly in a cultural and religious perspective; that is, learning to respect other cultures and religions. Such an understanding of respect is linked to the communitarian form of respect for groups with identity claims. The pupils at East Primary use "Norwegians" and "foreigners" to categorize each other. While students initially draw on an explanation founded in ethnic background to explain the boundaries between Norwegians and foreigners, they challenge their own explanation when questioned. The findings show that boundaries between Norwegians and foreigners exist but are not fixed; the boundaries are rather blurred and permeable. Some students with non-Norwegian backgrounds can be defined as partly Norwegian because they share interests which are defined as Norwegian interests.

In the discussions of foreigners and Norwegians at East Primary, it becomes distinct how different categories intersect, i.e., overlap and strengthen each other. Foreignness is increased by being a boy and by factors that intersect with ethnicity, such as speaking broken Norwegian, having a dark skin color, wearing a hijab, and eating halal food, while foreignness is decreased by being friends with Norwegians and hanging out in the street in the evenings. Student-constructed categories such as a half or a quarter Norwegian emerge from such intersections.

Respect and popularity are sometimes used interchangeably. The division between the popular students and the unpopular is not the same as the division between foreigners and Norwegians. Popularity is a mixed genre. At East Primary, the most popular students seem to be the ones crossing borders between Norwegians and foreigners. Their interests and friendships are of more importance than color or country of origin. The students with religious and cultural backgrounds from countries other than Norway are sometimes treated as "the other," while other times they are not. Who the others are depends on situations and relationships between the students, as well as the determination of the students who possess the power to define. Hence, the others at East Primary can be the old-fashioned, the ones who are obedient to teachers, the ones that follow the religious rules of their parents, and the ones defined as the losers. LK06 probably does not refer to the culture of nerds and losers when respect is the aim. Challenges regarding respect at East Primary seem to be found in how students position themselves and how they are positioned by others. It can be argued that the others at East Primary are those furthest away from the center of popularity. Different practices, looks, and friendships are of more importance than belief systems and parents' cultural backgrounds. Hence, I find an implicit critique of the curriculum's use of otherness in the students' practices, and a possible new start in defining what constitutes respect for differences in these students' thoughts and actions.

## References

Ambjörnsson, F. (2004). *I en klass för sig. Genus, klass och sexualitet bland gymnasietjejer* [Gender, class and sexuality among girls in secondary school]. Stocholm: Ordfront.

Anker, T. (2011). *Respect and disrespect: Social practices in a Norwegian multicultural school.* (Doctoral dissertation). Oslo: MF Norwegian School of Theology.

Arnesen, A. (2004). *Det pedagogiske nærvær. Inkludering i møte med elevmangfold* [The pedagogical presence. Inclusion in meeting diversity]. Oslo: Abstrakt forlag.

Arnesen, A., & Lundahl, L. (2010). Standarized individualisation: Text-mediated relations of governance in two Nordic welfare institutions. In S. Kvam, K. P. Knutsen, & P. Langemeyer (Eds.), *Textsorten und kulturelle Kompetenz. Interdisziplinäre Beiträge zur Textwissenschaft*,147–173. Münster: Waxmann.

Arnot, M., and Mac an Ghaill, M. (2006). "(Re)contextualising gender studies in education:schooling in late modernity." In Madeleine Arnot and Mairtin Mac an Ghaill (eds.). *The RoutledgeFalmer Reader in Gender and Education.* London: Routledge.

Ashcroft, B., Griffiths, G., & Tiffin, H. (1998). *Key concepts in Post-colonial studies*. London: Routledge.

Crenshaw, K. (1989). Demarginalizing the intersection of race and sex: A Black feminist critique of antidiscrimination doctrine, feminist theory and anti-racist politics. *University of Chicago Legal Forum,* 139-167.

Crenshaw, K. (1995). Mapping the margins: Intersectionality, identity politics and violence against women of color. In K. Crenshaw, G. Pellner, & K. Thomas (Eds.), *Critical race theory: The key writings that formed the movement.* New York: The New Press.

Davies, B., & Harré, R. (1990). Positioning: The discursive production of selves. *Journal for the Theory of Social Behaviour*, 20(I), 43-63.

De los Reyes, Paulina and Mulinari, Diana (2005). *Intersektionalitet. Teoretiska reflektioner över ojämlikhetens landskap* [Intersectionality. Theoretical reflections over differences]. Malmö: Liber.

Dillon, R.S. (2003). "Respect." In *Stanford Encyclopedia of Philosophy*. Retrieved July 21, 2010 from http://plato.stanford.edu/entries/respect/

Eide, E., & Simonsen, A. H. (2009). Fallen angels: The end of a colourful community? In S. Alghasi, T. H. Eriksen, & H. Ghorashi (Eds.), *Paradoxes of cultural recognition: Perspectives from Northern Europe*. Farnham: Ashgate.

Eliasson, M. A. (2007). *Verbal abuse in school. Constructing gender and age in social interaction.* (Ph.D. thesis). Stockholm: Karolinska Institutet.

Eriksen, L. L. (2010). Learning to be Norwegian: a case study of identity management in religious education in Norway. (Ph.D. thesis). Coventry: University of Warwick.

Gressgård, R., & Jacobsen, C. M. (2008). Krevende toleranse. Islam og homoseksualitet. Tidsskrift for kjønnsforskning, 2, 22-39.

Hage, G. (1998). White nation: F*antasies of white supremacy in a multicultural society.* Annandale: Pluto Press.

Helseth, H. (2007). Kunnskapsstatus om kjønnsrelatert mobbing blant barn og unge [Sexual bullying – status of knowledge]. Retrieved September 11, 2011 from http://www.udir.no/Upload/Satsningsomraader/5/Kunnskapsstatus_kjonnsrelatert_mobbing.pdf

Honneth, A. (2007). *Disrespect: The normative foundations of critical theory.* Cambridge: Polity Press.

Hovdelien, O. (2010). *Den multikulturelle skolen hva mener rektorene? Grunnskolerektorer, skolens verdiforankring og religions- og livssynsundervisningen* [The multicultural school – what do the principals think? School principals, values in school and education in religion and life philosophy]. (Ph.D. thesis). Kristiansand: University of Agder.

Kameniar, B. (2005). *Seeing invisibility: Whiteness in religious education.* (Ph.D. thesis). University of Melbourne, Melbourne.

Kunnskapsdepartementet. (2006). Læreplanverket for Kunnskapsløftet i grunnskolen og i videregående opplæring (LK06). / The National Curriculum for Knowledge Promotion in Primary and Secondary Education and Training (LK06). Retrieved April 20, 2011 from http://www.udir.no

Mac an Gaill, Mairtin (1994). *The making of men: masculinities, sexualities and schooling.* Buckingham: Open University Press.

Røthing, Å., & Svendsen, S. H. (2008). Norske verdier. Homotoleranse og heteroseksualitet [Norwegian values. Homotolerance and Heterosexuality]. In O. Leirvik & Å. Røthing (Eds.), *Verdier.* Oslo: Universitetsforlaget.

Staunæs, D. (2004). *Køn, etnicitet og skoleliv.* [Gender, ethnicity and school life]. Fredriksberg: Samfundslitteratur.

Svalfors, U. (2008). *Andlighetens ordning. en diskursiv läsning av tidskriften Pilgrim* [The order of spirituality. A discursive reading of the journal Pilgrim]. (Ph.D. thesis). Uppsala: University of Uppsala.

Thorne, B. (1993). *Gender play. Girls and boys in school.* New Brunswick: Rutgers UP.

Vedøy, G. (2008). *"En elev er en elev," "barn er barn" og "folk er folk" – Ledelse i flerkulturelle skoler* [Children are children, people are people - Leaderships in multicultural schools]. (Ph.D. thesis). Oslo: University of Oslo.

von der Lippe, M. (2010). *Youth, religion and diversity. A qualitative study of young people's talk about religion in a secular and plural society. A Norwegian case.* (Ph.D. thesis). Stavanger: University of Stavanger.

AUTHOR: Trine Anker is Associate Professor at Østfold University College, Norway. The author's main focus of research is in the field of education, with a special interest in education as a moral practice. She has written her Ph.D. thesis about respect in school, and has a practical-theoretical perspective on processes of inclusion and exclusion. She is currently affiliated with the research network NORDCRIT (Nordic Research Network: Critical Perspectives on Young People, Welfare and Education), initiated by Professor Anne-Lise Arnesen and others. The author will take part in an upcoming NORDCRIT project on students who drop out from school and face possible social exclusion. Correspondence: trine.anker@hiof.no.

# *Concepts of gender equality in Norwegian textbooks and classrooms*

## DEPOLITIZATION, RACIALIZED EXCLUSION AND HETERO-NORMATIVE STEREOTYPES

ÅSE RØTHING
Østfold University College, Norway

ABSTRACT: *This article is based on classrooms observations from 8th and 9th grade in three Norwegian public schools, on interviews with teachers, as well as analyses of national curriculum plans and textbooks. Drawing on an understanding of "Norwegian gender equality" as already achieved and depoliticized, the text focuses on how gender is addressed in Norwegian secondary schools. The purpose is not to discuss gender equality in the school context as such, but to elaborate on certain possible interpretations that become available as a result of this specific understanding of "Norwegian gender equality". I argue that gender equality has come to "belong" collectively to majority Norwegians in ways that lead to racialized exclusion and in ways that tends to veil discrepancies in the field of gender and sexuality in Norway, both related to politics and cultural norms.*

### *Introduction*

Over the last decade gender equality has been portrayed as one of the "core symbols of what "we" stand for in "our" modernization project", as the Norwegian anthropologist Marianne Gullestad expressed in her book *Norwegianness seen in a different light* (2002, p. 32). Gender equality is seen to characterize individual Norwegians as well as the Norwegian society as such and this image is continuously presented in public media as well as in the school context (Berg, Flemmen and Gullikstad (ed.), 2010; Mühleisen and Røthing (ed.), 2009; Røthing and Svendsen,

2011; Røthing, 2011; Støren, Waagene, Arnesen and Hovdhaugen, 2010). This conceptualization of gender equality depicts equality as something "we" in Norway already have achieved and thus no longer need to pay political attention to. At the same time equality is perceived as a marker of differentiation that characterizes "us Norwegians" *as opposed to* "the others".

In this article I argue that the concept of "Norwegian gender equality" influences heavily on how gender is being addressed, performed and interpreted in the Norwegian school context. Firstly I will briefly discuss how "gender equality" is being addressed in Norwegian curriculum plans and textbooks for secondary schools. Secondly I will elaborate on how (1) privileged Norwegian-ness, (2) culturalized disrespect for women and (3) Norwegian gender stereo-types, seem to "pass" as acceptable and/or not problematic or paradoxical in Norwegian classrooms, due to the discourse of Norwegian gender equality that implicates that gender equality has come to belong collectively to Norwegians (Brown, 2006, p. 16). I will propose that Wendy Brown's concept of "depoliticization" (Brown, 2006) offers a valuable key to understanding the current Norwegian situation when it comes to gender equality in the school context.

## Material and Method

This paper springs from a research project on "Norwegianness in schools", which has been conducted between 2007 and 2010 in affiliation with the research program *Cultural complexity in the new Norway* at University of Oslo[1]. The project involves classroom observations from 8th and 9th grade (13-15 year olds), interviews with teachers and analyses of curriculum plans and new textbooks. I have conducted observations at two secondary schools in Oslo; one downtown/ West End with around 70 % students of ethnic majority background and one school in the East End with around 75 % students of ethnic minority backgrounds.[2] The students at the first school had primarily middleclass background while the second school was dominated by students with working class background. The observations lasted for six weeks in both schools and I observed all classes of the same grade level (in the spring of 8th grade at one school,

[1] Through out this project I worked closely together with Stine H. Bang Svendsen. I want to thank her for theoretical inspiration that has informed this article.

[2] Arnfinn Haagensen Midtbøen was my research assistant at the first school and took part in observations and did of six out of eight interviews with teachers at this school.

in the fall of $9^{th}$ grade at the other), primarily in Social sciences and the subjet called Religion, philosophies of life and ethics (RPE). In addition to my observations at these two schools I spent three days observing classes in Social Science and RPE in $8^{th}$ grade at a small town school in Western Norway. I have interviewed 14 teachers from these three schools, 7 males and 7 females, whereas all the males were in their thirties while the females aged from early thirties till late fifties.

The empirical material I possess is obviously not representative of Norwegian schools and cannot be used to make generalizations. However, my assertion is that the interviews and classroom observations I discuss in this paper could have been taken from any school in Norway today. There is nothing special with the schools where I observed, that indicates that the practices at these schools should be any different from practices at other Norwegian schools. Furthermore, the discourse on Norwegian gender equality is very prevalent and shapes both public discourse in general *and* teaching methods and practices more specifically (see also Iversenn 2012; Nielsen, 2009). The teachers' practices and understandings may therefore be seen as reflecting an established gender equality discourse that shapes teaching practice and understandings on a more general basis. In that sense I believe the analyses are relevant on a broader level.

National curriculum plans, textbooks, teaching practices and teachers' reflections on their work, as expressed in the interviews, are in various and multiple ways related, which makes it relevant to combine these four different kinds of material. When curriculum plans and newly published textbooks are briefly discussed in the following it provides a presentation of the Norwegian context as well as a backdrop for the following discussions. Curriculum plans and textbooks cannot be said, however, to have certain or predictable effects on teaching practices and classrooms interactions, as the educators continuously do their own priorities and interpretations. The second part of the article is based on classroom observations and interviews. The aim is not to interpret or "understand" the teachers that appear in my discussions, and it is not my intention to criticize these teachers. It is the preconceived notions on gender equality and what opportunities and conditions they offer in the school context that the analysis will focus on.

## *Theoretical perspectives*

Several researchers, both nationally and internationally, have over the last years argued that gender equality and gay and lesbian rights, both in the United States and in a number of European countries, are used to emphasize and create differences between the white population and non-Western immigrants. Hence, a feminist, equality-oriented and gay positive policy may act as a national boundary marker which leads to exclusion[3]. Gullestad's work, as mentioned in the introduction, follows the same line of argument, as I will in this article.

Analyses and theories on national boundary markers is usually somehow inspired by postcolonial perspectives. To put it simply, postcolonial theory states that the Western view on "the others" creates and maintains certain stereotypical ideas of these others (cf Said, 1978). *Furthermore,* the Western viewer's perception of himself/herself as free and modern is strengthened because the Western ideals contrast the others as unenlightened and suppressed, as Chandra Mohanty points out in her classic paper *Under Western Eyes: Feminist Scholarship and Colonial Discourses* from 1984.

As part of the research project on Norwegianness in schools as this paper springs from, Stine H. Bang Svendsen and I have conducted analyses on how a "Norwegian sexuality" appears when new, Norwegian textbooks in social sciences for secondary school, according to the current curriculum plan from 2006, discuss sexuality and cultural norms. The "Norwegian sexuality" is, according to the textbooks, characterized by freedom of choice, gender equality and "gay tolerance", and is thus perceived to be "modern" (cf Gullestad, 2002. See also Gressgård and Jacobsen, 2008). At the same time the Norwegian past, other cultures and other places are portrayed as representatives of the suppressed, the non-egalitarian, the old-fashioned and the primitive. However, our analyses shows that there is a selective culturalization taking place, as it is only sexual practices that live up to the ideals of freedom of choice and equality that are culturalized as "Norwegian". Practices like sexual harassment, sexual assault and gay negativism, all of which are relatively widespread among Norwegian youths, are not considered "Norwegian culture". When speaking of ethnic, cultural or

[3] See for instance Berg, Flemmen and Gullikstad (ed.), 2010; Brown, 2006; Butler, 2009; Gressgård and Jacobsen, 2008; Haritaworn, 2010, Mühleisen and Røthing (ed.), 2009; Mühleisen, Røthing and Svendsen, 2012; Puar, 2007; Røthing and Svendsen, 2011. See also Mohanty 1984; Narayan 1997.

religious "others", however, problematic practices like forced marriage and parents controlling their daughters' sexuality, are culturalized and portrayed as characteristics of "them" (Røthing and Svendsen, 2009a; 2009b; 2011)

The analyses in this paper are inspired by postcolonial perspectives on privileges and "othering", in line with the discussions on "Norwegian sexuality" presented above. I am, as mentioned in the introduction, particularly inspired by the American political scientist Wendy Brown's analyses of *depoliticization*. In her book *Regulating Aversion. Tolerance in the Age of Identity and Empire* (2006), Brown claims:

> Depoliticization involves construing inequality, subordination, marginalization, and social conflict, which all require political analysis and political solutions, as personal and individual, on the one hand, and as natural, religious or cultural on the other (Brown, 2006, p. 15).

Inspired by Brown, Svendsen and I have earlier asserted that the question of gender equality has undergone a *process of depoliticization* in Norway over the past two decades (Røthing and Svendsen, 2011). This is because "gender equality" today is something that "everyone" "supports", but it does not seem to require political analysis or action as it is already achieved. "Gender equality" as a political challenge is thus perceived as "solved" and "dealt with" and relocated from the political sphere to the moral sphere, where it largely becomes a question of personal support and good will (Røthing and Svendsen, 2011; Røthing, 2011). Whilst Svendsen and I have earlier related Brown's concept of depolitization to discourses on sexuality, this paper focuses on gender equality and on how gender is being addressed, interpreted and performed in the school context.

## Gender equality and depoliticization in curriculum plans

The national curriculum plans for primary education represent formal, public guidelines for schools. Gender equality was first mentioned in a Norwegian curriculum plan in 1974. Before this, the curriculums to some degree required gender differentiated teaching in accordance with the current ideology of gender complementarity (Røthing, 2004). Gender equality as a subject was in 1974 included in the general instructions. That way, it became a comprehensive guideline for the schools' tasks and goals. The focus on gender equality was politically motivated and Norwegian schools were told to encourage young women to take higher education that might help them become economically independent (from their future husband). The following curriculum plan came in 1987 and included the same perspectives on gender equality as the previous plan.

In 1997 gender equality was still mentioned in the general part of the curriculum, but the politically-rooted argument why schools ought to promote gender equality was radically weakened and the subject was mentioned in just a short paragraph. At the same time focus shifted from "gender equality" to "equal worth". In line with Brown's analyses this may on one hand indicate that "gender equality" was considered an achieved goal and therefore no longer needed to be focused on. On the other hand, this shift in focus may be interpreted as an implicit support for "natural" gender differences of equal worth instead of a political focus on discrimination, distribution of power and equal opportunities (Røthing, 2004).

The current curriculum plan from 2006, pursued the general part from 1997, including the paragraph mentioning gender equality, while the specific guidelines for each subject were new. Gender equality is mentioned twice in these guidelines: In the general instructions for Social studies it says that the subject shall "promote the understanding of and support for basic human rights, democratic values and gender equality…". This phrasing supports the idea discussed earlier, that schools no longer need to help *create* gender equality because it already exists. "Gender equality" is portrayed as a *value* schools must encourage students to support, a kind of "inner virtue" and "good personality" (Brown, 2006, p. 12; Røthing and Svendsen, 2011; Røthing, 2011).

The second reference to "gender equality" – and the only one in the curriculum plan's specific competency goals – is a goal for what students should know by the end of 10$^{th}$ grade[4] in the subject of RPE, regarding the topic of "philosophy and ethics". Here it is stated that "the students should be able to discuss ethical questions concerning human worth and human rights, equal worth and gender equality based on for instance well-known role models". When "equality" and "human rights" get tied in with "ethical questions" they are placed in the moral sphere instead of in the political sphere and are depicted as

[4] The goals reflect what students should learn in 8th-10th grade and thereby what they should know by the end of 10$^{th}$ grade. The same goes for the rest of the curriculum: goals for 4$^{th}$ grade reflect what the students should learn 1.-4. grade while goals for 7$^{th}$ grade reflect what they should learn in 5$^{th}$-7$^{th}$ grade.

questions that call for moral reflections and personal opinions rather than political analyses and political solutions.

As already mentioned the general instructions for Social science states that this subject should promote gender equality. However, the competency goals do not contain any specific instructions as to how this will or shall be done. True, one of the goals state that "the students should be able to discuss human worth, racism and discrimination in a historical and modern perspective", but it is not given that "discrimination" is related to questions regarding gender related discrimination. The only goals for Social science that mention gender are two goals for 4th grade that bring up (assumed) differences between girls and boys concerning "different expectations" and "spending"(money). These goals may invite the teachers to accentuate diversity and to problematize stereotypical notions of differences between girls and boys. They are, however, just as likely to contribute to reproducing stereotypical notions of gender differences (Røthing and Svendsen, 2009, pp. 99-101).

It is worth noticing that two competency goals for 7th grade, one for RPE and one for Natural Science, state that students should be able to discuss "different gender identities". It is not specified further what the students actually should be able to discuss, but given discourses on gender and identity in current Norway, most teachers will take it to mean that they should encourage a discussion on what "being a girl" and (as opposed to) "being a boy" entails, stressing supposed *differences* between girls and boys (Røthing and Svendsen, 2009, pp. 46-51). In other words, the competency goals in the current curriculum plan from 2006 contain few guidelines for teaching related to gender equality. However, some competency goals implicitly encourage the teaching of gender differences, as will briefly be demonstrate in the following.

## *Gender equality and depoliticization in textbooks*

Textbooks can be seen as normative interpretations of the curriculum plan's specific instructions, and teaching in Norwegian schools is usually more or less shaped by the textbooks. RPE is, as mentioned, the only subject that is explicitly required to discuss gender equality. Due to changes in the curriculum plan for RPE in 2008, there are only two sets of textbooks for $8^{th}$-$10^{th}$ grade that are currently used extensively. In addition, publishers seem to be hesitant to produce new books for RPE since the subject has generated heated public debates since it was implemented in 1997.

One of the sets of books, called *Horizons (Horisonter),* brings up the topic of gender equality in the book for 8$^{th}$ grade under the headline "Living together" (Holth and Deschington, 2006 p. 98-121). This chapter deals with issues like "Identity – who are you?", "Family life", "Heterosexuality and homosexuality" and "Friends and friendship". Gender equality is hereby placed in the private sphere and as a depoliticized issue. Under the headline "Equal worth and equality" there is half a page on "What do we mean by equal worth and equality?". Then there is a section on "We are not the same!", which lists a number of (supposed) differences between girls and boys (p. 113-114). Finally there is a section with the headline "Gender identity and gender roles". Half of it deals with differences between "Norway today" and "those who come from non-Western countries". It ends with the statement "In a multicultural society there will be differing views on gender roles" (p. 115). This suggests that there would not be any disagreement in an imagined, monocultural Norwegian society and that it is "the others" who cause "disagreement on gender roles". Implicitly, "the others" disagree with "us" whereas "we" agree on gender equality.

The second textbook for RPE, *Under the same heaven* (*Under samme himmel*), brings up both human worth, equal worth and gender equality under the headline "Choices and values" in the 9$^{th}$ grade textbook (Wiik and Waale, 2006 p. 12-51). The headline refers to the moral and private sphere, but the chapter has a somewhat broader perspective than *Horizons*, as one of the sections is called "The World and Norway". The section on "equal worth and gender equality" in particular is more wide-reaching and more political than in *Horizons.* It mentions both the Equality and Anti-Discrimination Ombud, violence against women, women's shelters, freedom of expression, and racism, as well as racialized housing and job discrimination. The portrayal of ethnic discrimination entails a critical perspective on the Norwegian society. This book too, however, finds it relevant to point out in the section on equal worth and equality that "there are differences between boys and girls" (p. 26). Under the headline "Equality between the sexes" a long list of numbers is presented to illustrate that "there are still many areas where total gender equality is not achieved" (p. 27). But the book does not present any political or ethic (cf competency goals) analyses of what the numbers may represent and what may cause them. After the list of differences follows a question for reflection directed at the students: "What is your opinion on equality between men and women?" (p. 27). This supports the impression that gender equality (and implicitly gender discrimination) is a personal question that the individual can be "for" (or "against".) As indicated above, ethnic discrimination is to a larger degree treated as a political question in this book, which indicates that this is not yet depoliticized and seen as "solved".

As mentioned earlier, Social science is supposed to "promote the understanding of and support for […] gender equality" but none of the competency goals specify how this is to be done. Authors have responded to this requirement in various ways. Some books on Social science pay some attention to the issue, while other books do not mention gender equality at all, which can be seen as an illustration of depolitization. One of the books states that "Norway is proud of being a society that has come fare when it comes to equality between women and men" (Borge and Berner, 2006 p. 45), and thus establishes a nationalistic collective that may *feel* proud of its own success in this area, implicitly contrasted to those who have come "shorter" (Røthing, 2011, p. 75).

A recent report on gender equality efforts in Norwegian primary and secondary schools called "Equality isn't really "in" anymore…" (Støren et al., 2010), supports the impression that the question of gender equality currently is *depoliticizated* in the Norwegian school context. The report states that Norwegian schools in 2009 rank "aims for gender equality" below all other aims and that the action plan for equality in preschools and primary education 2008-2010 (from the Ministry of Education and Research) is not well known. Furthermore, the discourse of gender equality as a marker of Norway and "Norwegian culture", as opposed to "other cultures", is clearly present, as illustrated in the conclusion of the report:

> The most common position we encountered is that gender equality is so obvious that it is not an issue. Gender equality is something we to a large degree have in Norway today. Thus, teachers usually approach the subject from a historical perspective rather than from a modern-day perspective. This is also the case with regard to other cultures; the focus is on how other groups and cultures lack the Norwegian level of gender equality (Støren et al., 2010, p. 98).

However, while "most people" think that "equality" is important and the report states that equality is a value that "undoubtedly has a strong position in Norwegian schools", the report also documents that "the gender equality perspective rarely is concretized as a goal within the school system" (Støren et al., 2006, p. 13). In other words, gender equality is depicted as a value that students, teachers and the school as an institution support, but is not regarded as a matter that requires continued political analyses and action.

It is worth noticing, however, that in the school context, two matters related to "gender equality" have attracted political and media interest over the last few years and both have to do with boys and men: Boys as "school losers" and better recruitment of men to jobs in preschools and primary schools. According to the report "Gender equality isn't really "in" anymore" "*More interest in reading/improved reading skills among boys* is the single measure that seems to be the top focus, especially for the municipalities as school owners (89 per cent)" (Støren et al., 2010, p. 11). In comparison, only 28 % of primary schools have focused on *"promoting the natural sciences, especially among girls*" (same). Furthermore, the report shows that around one third of the municipalities have made use of the instructions to favor men when hiring teachers (p. 13). Thus, it may appear that schools apply political analyses and tools in order to create changes with regard to gender equality efforts directed at boys and men. In other words, the process of depoliticizing gender equality in the school context is not unambiguous. On the contrary, certain issues seem to have received more political attention over the past years. This shift in focus, however, may illustrate the notion that equality *for women* already is achieved in Norway today.

## *Privileged Norwegianness*

"Norwegianness" and "the Norwegian" is by and large a preconceived starting point in textbooks and teaching. Statements like "We get more and more used to foreign cultural expressions" – as found in one social studies textbook for secondary schools, published in 2008 (Henriksen, p. 93) – imply the idea of a Norwegian "we" who become increasingly used to the others' "unfamiliar" culture. This type of "we talk" is usually not emphasized or discussed either in school or in public in general. Consequently, "the Norwegian" is privileged both as the obvious starting point but also by being so taken for granted that it requires no form of argument, thus becoming invisible (cf Foucault, 1980/1995)[5]. This was clearly demonstrated during one of my classroom observations when the teacher – in honor of the researchers – encouraged the students to say "where they were from". The students said that they "were from" countries like Turkey, Pakistan, Morocco, Bosnia and Afghanistan, even though the vast majority were born and raised in Norway. But the students were apparently familiar with this type of exercise and stated their parents' or grandparents' native country without hesitation. When the first ethnic Norwegian student was to respond he simply turned to the student behind him and nodded that it was his turn. Evidently it was completely unnecessary for him to state that he "was from" Norway. His Norwegianness was obvious (to him) and needed no clarification.

"Coming from" Norway or *being* (ethnic/white) Norwegian offers certain privileges also when gender and sexuality is discussed in schools. Wendy Brown points out that "tolerance", which is her object of analysis, to a large degree "has come to belong collectively, rather than selectively to westerners", and that "intolerance has become a code word for a fundamentalism identified with the non-west, with barbarism and with anti-western violence" (2006, p. 16). In line with this, whiteness and ethnicity seems to offer certain privileges of collective belonging. According to my observations, ethnic Norwegian boys who express gay negativism are considered likely to "grow out of" such "immature" ideas and are expected to become gay tolerant when they get older. They seem to be incorporated into a Norwegian collective "gay tolerance" since this currently is a central marker of Norwegianness and a boundary marker toward "the others". Boys of ethnic minority origin, however, who express similar gay negativism, are considered less likely to change their attitude. On the contrary, their gay negativism is often culturalized and thus appears as something fixed. Similarly I have observed ethnic majority boys who make discriminating statements regarding gender equality and women or girls as a group, who clearly expect teachers and class mates to take this as a joke and not as something they "truly" mean. Ethnic minority boys cannot expect the same. As in the example with gay negativism they risk being taken "seriously" and literally if they try to "joke" by making discriminating remarks about girls and/or women. Gender equality as a

[5] For more on Heteronormativity in Norwegian sexual education, see Røthing, 2008, Røthing and Svendsen, 2009.

core symbol of "Norwegianness" seems to belong collectively and exclusively to white/ethnic Norwegians.

Not only students benefit from Norwegian privileges. My observations indicate that teachers may do that as well. In one of the lessons I observed, the class was going to discuss gender equality. The male teacher in his early thirties – called "David" – started by writing on the blackboard: "Gender equality is about women and men having equal rights and equal duties and opportunities". He then exclaimed, seemingly out of the blue:

> Who is the stronger sex? Who was created first? What sex is God? Don't you remember how it is? David at the top, then God, then the Pope, and Peter [a colleague of David, my comment] way further down…

The teacher's question "don't you remember how it is?" indicates that the students were familiar with this "joke". I got the clear impression that David expected the students to understand that he was merely joking because he – implicitly – *of course* is "for" gender equality and don't "really" believe that man is the stronger sex. Due to his position as ethnic Norwegian, young and "modern" he is part of a collective that is assumed to support gender equality. Hence, he is not required to explicitly state his opinion. The majority of the students in David's class belonged to the same ethnic Norwegian collective as him. This is probably why he could take for granted that he would be interpreted "correctly". At the same time he becomes a representative of the class' Norwegian "we". That way he includes the (majority) students in his own joke whether they want to be included or not.

According to my observations this type of statements is quite typical of how some students joke about gender and gender equality but not as common among teachers. However, I find it reasonable to assume that *similar* statements regularly occur within the school context. This is because gender equality today is depoliticized and therefore is not perceived as a political issue that requires political analysis and action. That way it becomes something that teachers and students can joke about in various ways – if they can certify that they are part of the Norwegian collective that gender equality belongs to. However, teachers joking about these things support the idea that gender equality no longer is seen as an important issue (cf Støren et al., 2010).

## *Culturalized disrespect for women*

Several of the teachers I interviewed argued that "equal gender roles" was the biggest difference between ethnic Norwegian students and students with an ethnic minority background. While "the ethnic Norwegians to a larger extent have equal gender roles ingrained", as one male teacher put it, the ethnic minority boys were said to have "difficulties" respecting female teachers and/or represented values that go against "Norwegian gender equality". When gender equality is seen as a marker for "Norwegianness", gender *in*equality is implicitly seen as a marker for "the others". Furthermore, since ethnic majority Norwegians are continuously positioned as a contrast to minority Norwegians, *and* as "owners" of gender equality, a "lack of respect for women" cannot be seen a *cultural trait* of ethnic Norwegian males. Recent Swedish research has to some degree challenged this culturalized dichotomy. They have argued that Swedish youth, both ethnic majority and minority, in areas with a high number of immigrants tends to portray ethnic minority boys as those who respect women whereas ethnic Swedish boys are considered disrespectful to women (Bäckman, 2009; Hammarén, 2009[6]). My interest in the following is not to discuss notions that minority boys of non-Western origin lack respect for women in general and female authority figures in particular. What I want to focus on is what is drawn to the foreground and what is left unnoticed when this point of view gets to dominate how actors in the school context are interpreted.

I interviewed eight teachers at the school with 75 % students of minority backgrounds. All of them expressed, in one way or another, that "minority boys" represented a challenge at their school and that many of them were noisy and seemed to lack respect for several of the female teachers. About 10 % of the teachers at this school had minority background, including one of the ones I interviewed. One ethnic Norwegian female teacher in her thirties that was quite affected by noisy male students explained her situations like this:

> Very many boys in my class had problems having a female teacher. They mostly have two male teachers in other subjects and they behaved totally different then. I have been there and seen how differently they behave with them. But when I am alone they seem to totally lose respect. But they have developed and I think it works better now. [...] Some of them are a bit

[6] This research deals with questions of social class in relation to ethnicity, which is an obviously important perspective that I will not be able to follow up on in this paper.

> aggressive and need some extra attention, and have less respect for female teachers. It took me a long time to be accepted as a teacher.

An ethnic Norwegian male teacher in his thirties comments on the situation at the same school like this:

> Some female teachers struggle with… some of the boys in my class in particular, because they have no respect for female teachers. None whatsoever. And it must come from somewhere. It is often easy to attribute it to culture…

When discussing culturalized disrespect for women in the following, I'll take the last quote as my starting point. This male teacher had a high number of ethnic minority students in his class and the quote refers specifically to boys with a non-Western background. During the interview he emphasized contextualizing the individual students' background and learning capability and from what I understood, he displayed a thorough knowledge of each student's background. He took also care to stress the diversity among the minority students rather than to present stereotypes, and apparently wanted to avoid sustaining common culturalization. This culturalization of "the boys' lack of respect for female teachers", which he also repeated later on in the interview, thus contrasts with the general impression from the interview.

Inspired by postcolonial theory one might say that the teacher quoted above considers "a lack of respect for women" as something alien as it "must come from somewhere", implicitly a place that is unfamiliar *to him*. From his point of view disrespect for women is not understandable and is localized in an unfamiliar and implicitly non-Norwegian place. The narrative of the others' culture lacking respect for women contributes to establish a narrative of "our Norwegian culture" as one that is characterized by respect for women. But what may be left out when this argument is used to explain the interaction between minority boys of non-Western origin and "female teachers"? What may we fail to see when this "problem" is focused on, thereby overshadowing other potential "problems" within the given school context?

The teaching team that this teacher was a part of was determined to find ways to control noisy students as a way to improve the teaching and learning environment in their grade level. The minority boys' lack of respect for women was, according to this teacher and others of his colleagues, demonstrated by the fact that they were noisy and did not do as they were told. When "noise" is culturalized and used to describe an entire group of students, it is obvious that the situation is oversimplified. Let us examine this more closely.

The focus on *the others'* culture contributes to camouflage the "noise" from ethnic Norwegian boys. When noise in some situations is interpreted as a culturally-rooted lack of respect for women, ethnic Norwegian boys can hardly be included since their Norwegianness makes them part of a collective gender equality that contrasts "a lack of respect for women". My impression from these classes was, however, that both minority and majority boys were noisy. And of course, not all the boys were noisy and there were also noisy girls. Other categories, like "social background" or gender norms rather than "culture", or combined with "culture", could have given more nuanced understandings of "noisy students" (cf. Rosales, 2010)

Secondly, the focus on the problematic culture among minority boys draws the attention to the students, not to the teachers. This has several implications. First of all, the teachers do not seek an explanation for the noise within themselves or their teaching methods. However, my observations indicate that both the teachers' competency level and their teaching methods influenced the atmosphere in the classroom. The teachers with poor academic skills seemed to experience more noise and/or lack of respect. This was mainly true of two of the teachers I observed, a young man and a young woman. There were also both male and female teachers who, by disciplining the students in different ways, managed to keep the class quiet. The absence of noise, however, does not necessarily entail a good learning environment, because quiet students can also mean passive students. Stereotypical notions of gender and culture may in other words camouflage varying teaching strategies and, more importantly, they may cause possible connections between teachers' competency levels, teaching methods and learning environment to be overlooked.

Another consequence of emphasizing the students' problematic behavior may be that the teachers' behavior escapes critical attention. The teacher quoted above used a form of "male bonding strategy" to discipline the boys in the class. This entailed for instance an extensive use of football metaphors in his teaching, as well as being "buddies" with "the guys". This type of mono-gendered and gender-traditional approach may cause girls in general and perhaps minority girls in particular, to feel excluded and become passive. This is of course also true of the boys who are unable or unwilling to take part in the football/ buddy jargon. Teaching that is primarily aimed at the boys and to a little extent addresses the girls may be considered a "lack of respect for women". But the focus on disrespect for women as a "minority culture phenomenon" makes in this case such an interpretation of one's own teaching strategies unlikely. It might serve as an illustration that during one of the lessons I observed with this teacher, not one girl spoke the entire class – and that the teacher did not seem to consider silent girls "a problem".

The report "Gender equality isn't really "in" anymore…" (Støren et al., 2010) also presents a connection between "cultural differences" and "attitudes toward women". In discussions on the subject of "gender-related bullying" in schools this is presented as a problem that largely is related to minority boys. The teachers explain the boys' actions "with cultural differences in attitudes toward women" (p. 107). This way, the problems regarding "gender-related bullying" gets a one-sided and specific focus, in line with the previous discussions (see also Røthing and Svendsen, 2009b). The teachers also stress that girls and boys bully in different ways, so that "gender-related bullying" rather becomes a question of "gender-different bullying". The report, on the other hand, defines gender-related bullying as "teasing, harassment or negative characteristics of fellow students related to gender and/or sexual identity", in line with research in this field (Støren et al., 2010, p. 106). The teachers associations to gender differences rather than to harassment related to gender norms and identities may be seen as an illustration of the lack of competence in this field among educators, despite the collective ownership to "Norwegian gender equality".

## *Norwegian gender conservatism*

Research on gender and sexuality has pointed out that gender and sexuality is closely related. Questions related to gender are not, as emphasized by Eve Kosofsky Sedgwick, the same as questions related to sexuality, but they are nevertheless closely intertwined (1990, p. 30-31). In daily use, such as in classrooms, the term "gender" quite often refers to "heterogender" (Ingraham, 1996) since heterosexuality is implicit in what is said about gender, and likewise, the term "sexuality" tends to refer to "heterosexuality". In my observations I have noted several times how the interrelations between gender and sexuality appear when students freely associate from one theme to another. This calls, in my opinion, on educators to hold a certain level of theoretical competence in this field, to avoid discriminating and exclusive teaching practices. My last empirical example may illustrate this:

> *Teacher:* Are there different expectations…can boys and girls act the same way?
> *Students:* No. If Fredrik came to school wearing make-up, that would be a bit weird.
> *Teacher:* Yes, then he would be called gay, like Kahlid was before. You use it as an insult. But if guys wore skirts, that would be peculiar.
> *Student (boy):* I heard of a man who was a woman ten years ago and now he's pregnant.
> *Teacher:* Yes, but it's crazy that you can be something in between. That's really crazy!

As previously indicated, the current curriculum plan seems to promote the teaching of gender differences when dealing with the subject of "gender identity". In line with this the male teacher in this example, an ethnical Norwegian in his mid-thirties, starts out with a question on gender differences. He invites the students to focus on differences between girls and boys and may thus be said to promote the teaching of gender differences. Both students and teachers said that it is "weird" and "peculiar" if boys wear make-up and skirts, and the weird and peculiar is connected to "homosexuality". Earlier in the class the students were rebuked by the teacher for using "gay" as an insult, and he repeats this now. But he also clearly states what is considered "normal" behavior for boys, including what is "normal" for "gays". Apparently the line is drawn at wearing a skirt. Also, boys who come to school wearing make-up must be prepared to be called "gay". One of the students mentions a news story involving a picture of a person with facial hair and a baby bump (cf Dagbladet 28.04.08). The newspaper referred to this person as a pregnant man and a female-to-male trans person who had kept his female reproductive organs in order to be able to have children. The teacher's response to the student's comment is to state that this is "really crazy" and that "you can't be something in between".

In her book *Gender, Ethnicity and School Life (Køn, etnicitet og skoleliv)* (2004) the Danish educationalist Dorte Staunæs argues for the benefits of using "boundary figures" when discussing relevant issues. Boundary figures are "living pointers to where the line is at", "they live by and expose the limits of the normative" and "they are reverse mirrors that the other students can mirror themselves in with regard to what they are not and perhaps do not want to be" (2004, p. 43, my translation). In line with this, the Norwegian sociologist Randi Gressgård, with reference to Wendy Brown, claims that "the ritual management of liminal figures is a matter of incorporation and regulation of the presence of the threatening "other" within (cf. Brown, 2006, p. 27). The liminal monstrous figure is called upon to demonstrate the limits of the cultural order, to map out the contours of normality." (Gressgård, 2010, p. 548).

The pregnant man is introduced in the dialogue above as an example of the absolute limit. A pregnant man is not merely a bit strange, like "gays" wearing make-up, it is a "really crazy" example of something that should not be possible. Drawing the line this way, as both the students and the teacher do, not only demonstrates some concrete limits, but also reminds the students that they must be aware of the line between "normal" gender performances versus "weird", "crazy" or "absurd" ways of performing oneself. According to Judith Butler "trans people can produce a crisis – a productive crisis – that allows for a critical release of alternative imaginary schemas, a radical rearticulation of the symbolic horizon in which bodies come to matter at all" (Butler, 1993, p. 23 in Gressgård, 2010, p. 552). The curriculum plan for social studies states that the subject should "better enable the students to think freely, broadly, critically and tolerantly". If the teacher had used the opportunity, the dialogue above could have been a chance for the students to explore different, possible ways of doing gender and it could have given them the opportunity to reflect on their own and others' limiting practices – in line with the curriculum plan for social studies.

The purpose of presenting the last dialogue is not to spur a debate on transsexualism as such, although this might be relevant. My purpose, however, is to point out discrepancies in the field of gender and sexuality. The concept of Norwegian gender equality implies that Norway has solved any problems related to subordinating gender norms and practices. Norway's policy regarding transexualism, however, is highly heteronormative, exclusive and gender conservative (see Folgerø and Hellesund, 2009, p. 99-119). And when a male-to-female trans person is presented as a monstrous liminal figure, as in the example above, it illustrates the lack of freedom, openness and inclusiveness in this field in Norway. Mainstream Norwegian views on trans people as well as Norwegian politics in this field, do, in my opinion, collide with the Norwegian, liberal project of modernity that is said to be characterized by freedom in the field of gender and sexuality. I propose that the concept of "Norwegian gender equality", the national ownership to "gender equality" and the process of depoliticization all together seem to help Norwegian gender conservatism and discriminating norms and legislations, to slide away from critical attention.

## *Conclusion*

The discourse of "Norwegian gender equality" seems to produce two interrelated but still different sets of effects and challenges. On the one hand gender equality is seen as a marker of "Norwegianness" and a value that belongs collectively to white majority Norwegians, while non-white, ethnic minority Norwegians are contrasted and excluded from this – in double meaning – attractive and nation building collective. On the other hand, equal opportunities and equal rights regardless of gender are depicted as something Norway, as opposed to most other countries, has already achieved and thus not need to strive towards. This portrays gender equality as available for each individual Norwegian citizen and inequality or discrimination seems not to call for political attention or solutions. Lack of gender equality tends to be explained by reference to individual choice and/or nature for white Norwegians and by reference to culture and/or religion for non-white Norwegians. Thus "Norwegian gender equality" is both racialized and selective/exclusive when it comes to which issues are acknowledged as important and nation building in the field of gender and sexuality.

One effect of the process of depoliticization of gender equality in Norway seems to be that "given gender differences" are, as indicated in textbooks and the current curriculum, presented as the most relevant response to why there are still vast differences between how girls/women as a group and boys/men as a group live their lives in Norway today. This situation calls for alternative interpretations and approaches. Firstly, while the focus on "natural" gender differences draws the attention to differences between girls and boys as two exclusive and opposing groups, another option is to actively draw attention to complexity and differences between girls and between boys instead. Secondly, rather than keeping different categories apart, an alternative approach would be to look for similarities, differences and complexity by investigating how gender, social background, culture, religion, functionality, sexuality and ethnicity are interrelated and intertwined. Thirdly, critical analyses of different normative limits connected to attractive, possible and monstrous gender configurations could offer new knowledge on how and why children and students perform gender in certain ways. In the example above, the lines of demarcation concern specific aesthetic expressions. However, there is good reason to believe that similar gendered limits continually are being drawn in other fields as well, giving boys and girls a constant sense of how they best can orientate themselves in life to stay on the right side of what is "weird" or "absurd". It is highly relevant to ask which gendered connotations young people's opportunities and images of the future have. What are the gendered connotations of that which youths turn to – and turn away from?

The discussions throughout this paper indicates that gender equality, due to the process of depoliticization, is portrayed as something it is acceptable to make jokes about as long as you are part of a collective "Norwegianness" that is "for" equality. Thus gender equality seems to be more a question of personal opinion, ethnic belonging and even sense of humor. Furthermore, lack of equality, here represented by "minority boys' lack of respect for women", is relocated to the cultural and religious field, which encompasses the others' problematic cultural and religious norms and practices. Due to the notion that equality is already achieved among ethnic Norwegians, critical analyses focusing on power imbalance, processes of exclusion and discrimination and cultural gender norms that reduce the freedom of individuals, are replaced by a focus on support, virtue, values and so called "natural" gender differences.

## *References*

Bäckman, M. (2009). *Miljonsvennar. Omstridda platser och identiteter.* Göteborg & Stockholm: Makadam.

Berg, A.-J., Flemmen, A. B. & Gullikstad, B. (eds.) (2010). *Norske likestillinger. Om kjønn og etnisitet.* Trondheim: Tapir.

Brown, W. (2006). *Regulating aversion: Tolerance in the age of identity and empire.* Princeton, N.J.: Princeton University Press.

Butler, J. (2009). *Frames of War. When is Life Grievable?* London: Verso.

Foucault, M. (1980/1995). *The history of Sexuality.* New York: Vintage.

Gressgård, R. (2010). "When trans translates into tolerance – or was it monstrous? Transsexual and transgender identity in liberal humanist discourse." *Sexualities vol. 13, 5:539-561.*

Gressgård, R. & Jacobsen, C. (2008). "Krevende toleranse. Islam og homoseksualitet", *Tidsskrift for kjønnsforskning,* nr. 2:22-39.

Gullestad, M. (2002). *Det norske sett med nye øyne. Kritisk analyse av norsk innvandringsdebatt.* Oslo: Universitetsforlaget.

Hammarén, N. (2008). *Förorten i hovudet. Unga män om kön och sexualitet i det nya Sverige.* Stockholm: Atlas.

Haritaworn, J. (2010). "'Queer Injuries: The Cultural Politics of "Hate Crimes" in Germany", *Social Justice* 37, no. 1-2, (in print).

Henriksen, Alexander (2008). *ZOOM. Samfunnskunnskap 8.-10.* (2. utgave). Oslo: Gyldendal.

Holth, G. & Deschington H. (2006) *Horisonter 8 Grunnbok.* Oslo: Gyldendal Undervisning.

Ingraham, C. (1996). "The Heterosexual Imaginary: Feminist Sociology and Theories of Gender". In Steven Seidman (ed.): *Queer Theory/Sociology.* Cambridge: Blackwell Publishers.

Iversen, Lars L. (2012). *Learning to be a Norwegian. A case study of identity management in religious education in Norway.* Münster: Waxman.

Mohanty, C. T. (1984). "Under Western Eyes: Feminist Scholarship and Colonoial Discourses". In *On Humanism and the University I: The Discourse of Humanism* Vol. 12, nr 3:333-358. Durham: Duke University Press.

Mühleisen, W. & Røthing Å. (ed.) (2009). *Norske seksualiteter*. Oslo: Cappelen Akademisk Forlag.

Mühleisen, W., Svendsen, S. H. B., & Røthing, Å. (2012). "Norwegian sexualities. Assimilation and exclusion in Norwegian immigration policy". *Sexualities*. 15(2):139-155.

Narayan, U. (1997). *Dislocating Cultures. Identities, Traditions, and Third World Feminism.* New York: Routlegde.

Nielsen, H. B. (2009). *Skoletid*. Oslo: Universitetsforlaget.

Puar, J. (2007). *Terrorist Assemblages. Homonationalism in Queer Times.* Durham: Duke University Press

Rosales, R.L. (2010). *Vid framtidens hitersta gräns. Om maskulina elevposistioner i en multietnisk skola*. Tumba: Mångkulturelt centrum

Røthing, Å. (2004). "Kjønn og seksualitet i grunnskolens læreplaner. Historisk tilbakeblikk og aktuelle utfordringer." *Norsk pedagogisk tidsskrift*. Nr 5:356-368.

Røthing, Å. (2011). "'De norske har det mer i seg…' Norsk kjønnslikestilling i skolen". *Sosiologi i dag* 3-4:67-87.

Røthing, Å. & Svendsen, S. H. (2009a). "Norskhet og seksualitet i skolen". In Mühleisen, W. og Røthing, Å (eds.): *Norske seksualiteter*. Oslo: Cappelen akademisk forlag.

Røthin, Å. & Svendsen, S. H. (2009b). *Seksualitet i skolen. Perspektiver på undervisning.* Oslo: Cappelen akademisk forlag.

Røthin, Å. & Svendsen, S. H. (2011). "Sexuality in Norwegian Textbooks: Constructing and Controlling Ethnic Borders?". *Ethnic and Racial Studies*, first article April 1th, p. 1-21

Said, E. (2003/1978). *Orientalism.* London: Penguin.

Staunæs, D. (2004). *Køn, etnicitet, og skoleliv*. Fredriksberg: Forlaget Samfundsliteratur.

Støren, L. A., Waagene E., Arnesen C. Å. og Hovdhaugen, E. (2010). *Likestilling er jo ikke lenger det helt store…* NIFU STEP Rapport nr 15. Oslo.

Wiik, P. og Waale, R. B. (2006). *Under samme himmel 2.* Oslo: Cappelen.

AUTHOR: Åse Røthing is Professor at Østfold University College, Faculty of Education. Røthing was senior researcher at the strategic research program "Cultural complexity in the new Norway" at The University of Oslo, working on processes of inclusion and exclusion related how "Norwegianness", culture, gender and sexuality are being produced in Norwegian secondary schools. Since May 2012 she is a Professor at Østfold University College and will be working together with Professor Anne-Lise Arnesen in the field of diversity and inclusion. Røthing has among other works edited *Norwegian sexualities* (with Wencke Mühleisen, 2009), and written *Sexuality in Schooling. Perspectives on Teaching* (with S.H. Bang Svendsen, 2009).
Correspondence: ase.rothing@hiof.uio.no

# *Democracy and education for a new era*

## THE CASE OF NORWAY AFTER 22ND JULY[1]

TORILL STRAND
Østfold University College, Norway

ABSTRACT: *This paper explores the close link between democracy and education and argues that this link needs to be reinvigorated. Within democratic welfare societies, education is a fundamental civil, political and social right for all. A central task is to promote active citizenship. But to what degree do educational theory and practice relate to what is going on? Is it possible to prevent marginalization? And in what ways should we educate for democratic participation?*

*In the first part of this paper, I identify some processes of marginalization taking place within and beyond educational institutions. In the next part, I explore the concepts of "democracy" and "education", and their mutual interdependence. Drawing on the work of John Dewey, democracy is here seen as a way of life, an ideal and an outlook. In the third part of the paper, however, I contrast Dewey's harmonious image with the current situation while asking: In what ways should we rethink democracy and education for the new era? I here draw on Chantal Mouffe's model of agonistic democracy and Alain Badiou's ethics to examine some potential possibilities of rethinking and strengthening the link between democracy and education. In summing up, I point to some challenges meeting educational researchers today.*

---

[1] This is a polished version of the lecture I gave 6th January 2012, on acquisition of the professorial chair at Østfold University College.

## Introduction

In this paper, I perform a three-step philosophical analysis of a current event that illustrates democracy and education as a *way of life*, an *ideal,* and an *outlook*. My aim is to throw some lights on the close link between "democracy" and "education" and their mutual interdependence. Also, I set out to explore the potential possibilities of rethinking and strengthening the link between democracy and education in the present.

Within democratic welfare societies, such as the Nordic countries, education is a fundamental civil, political and social right for all. And its central task[2] is to promote active citizenship (Marshall, 1949; Kymlicka & Norman, 1994). Thus, educational institutions are crucial for building and promoting a democratic society (NOU 2011:20; Strand & Huggler, 2011). However, parallel with increasing economic, political, social and educational inequalities, new and ugly processes of marginalization emerge. One example is how the "lost generation" of European youths now experience poverty, hopelessness, and distrust in nearly all major institutions. Another example is how everyday racism and xenophobia undermine civic participation and engagement for all. But is it possible to prevent marginalization? Is it doable to educate for democratic participation? To what degree do contemporary philosophies and theories of education relate to what is going on? And what may be the potential possibilities of rethinking and strengthening the link between democracy and education in the present?

Already by now I should stress that I do not question the value of democracy. By contrast, democracy is here taken as an axiom, which means that the worth of democracy is seen as self-evidently valuable and true. This worth represents the very starting point and basis for my analysis on the link between democracy and education. My assumption is that an idea of ethical-political education cannot be separated from the idea of a vigorous democracy. Moreover, that education *within* and *towards* the democratic is a vital pre-condition for building, maintaining and justifying a vigorous democracy.

---

[2] In Norway, public schooling shall "promote democracy, equality and scientific way of thinking" (The Norwegian Act on Education, § 1-1, 4th section). In other words, the Norwegian school system shall promote democracy, inclusion and knowledge building. The democratic mission of the school comes forward in the mission statement «promote democracy», but also in the way in which the Act on Education underlines that "the pupils must have responsibility and right to participation" and how "all forms of discrimination should be counteracted".

The notion of “democracy”, however, can be given multiple interpretations (Dewey, 1985; Held, 2006; Honneth, 1998; Mouffe, 2000). The term is composed by the Greek *demos* (people) and *kratos* (government), and translates “governed by the people” or “rule of the people”. In general, “democracy” denotes a political community in which all members have an equal say in decisions that affect their lives. Social and political studies tend to explore democracy as a form of government or political system justified by the people (*demos*). But educational studies turn this notion on its head as educational researchers set out to explore democracy as lived experience[3]. Democracy is not here seen as a form of government, neither as a model of a state, or as an abstract idea that every now and then materializes into everyday experience. Democracy is rather studied as tangible forms of everyday and inclusive practices which mirrors and shapes loyalties and identification with a *polis* (body of citizens). In doing so, the focus is not so much on citizenship-as-legal-status, but rather on citizenship-as-desirable-activity.

Consequently, the identities and loyalties of citizens are drawn to our attention: The health of a democracy does not only depend on the legitimacy of its political system. A healthy democracy also depends on the citizens’ sense of belonging; “their sense of identity and how they view potentially competing forms of national, regional, ethnic and religious identities”; their “abilities to tolerate and work with others that are different from themselves”; their “desire to participate in the political processes in order to promote the public good and hold political authorities accountable”; and “their willingness to show self-restraint and exercise personal responsibilities in their economic demands and in personal choices which affect their health and the environment” (Kymlicka & Norman,

---

[3] Within education we should be able to handle more democratic concepts simultaneously. First, pupils should of course learn that "democracy" is a rule that requires that all citizens are heard in decisions concerning themselves. They should also learn about different ways to practice such a system of government and understand the normative basis and justifications of democracy. Moreover, that there is no universal accepted definition of the concept of democracy. In Norway, the national curriculum states that: "the school should be an important democratic arena for children and young people where they can experience empowerment." Thus, the pupils' council is on everybody’s work schedule. All children will be given experience of democratic participation; both in terms of formal and informal forums where decisions are made that will be binding on all members of the group. The idea is that each student will gain experience with democracy as a form of decision - albeit in a miniature version.

1994, p. 353). So, "instead of limiting the participatory activity of citizens to the function of periodically legitimating the state's exercise of power, their activity [...] should be understood as the source of all political decision-making processes" (Honneth, 1998, p. 763). Thus, in the intersection between "democracy" and "education", democratic will formation seems crucial.

When asking to what degree contemporary philosophies and theories of education relate to what is going on, the idea of active citizenship and 'democratic will formation' need to be highlighted. Consequently, when studying democracy and education as a *way of life*, an *ideal,* and an *outlook* we are also invited to question the current discourses on democracy and education in regards to the processes of marginalization now taking place within and beyond the classroom. In the first part of this paper I point to some processes of marginalization emerging within and beyond educational institutions. Next, I explore the concepts of "democracy" and "education" and their mutual interdependence through the analysis of a current event. Drawing on the work of John Dewey, I read this event to illustrate democracy and education as a way of life, an ideal and an outlook. In the third part of the paper, however, I contrast Dewey's harmonious image with the current situation while asking: In what ways should we rethink democracy and education for the new era? In doing so, I draw on Chantal Mouffe's model of agonistic democracy and Alain Badiou's ethics to examine the potential possibilities of rethinking and strengthening the link between democracy and education in the present. In summing up, I point to some challenges meeting educational researchers today. But first of all, let me briefly portray the current situation.

## *Altered realities*

Our conventional ways of thinking democracy and education seem to be challenged by the new and ugly processes of marginalization that now emerge. In a world characterized by increasing economic, political and social differences, more and larger groups of fellow citizens balance the limit between social inclusion and exclusion (Born & Jensen, 1998; OECD, 2011; Pedersen, 2010). Thus, their possibilities of self-determination and co-determination seem threatened.

## Europe's lost generation

With a youth unemployment rate close to 40%, an entire generation of young Europeans now experience poverty, hopelessness and distrust in nearly all social institutions (Eurostat, 2011; OECD, 2010). In December, 2012, OECD reported that the gap between rich and poor has reached its highest peak since fifty years (OECD, 2011). This puts the societies' social contract to a test. Current examples may be the continuous demonstrations in Athens; last summer's wild youth riots in Great Britain; and the Occupy Wall Street movement, which has now spread from the US to other countries and continents. The employment rate of Norwegian youths is much lower than the European average (Statistics Norway, 2011a). But despite this low unemployment rate, the youths are more vulnerable than other parts of the population. Financial crisis, a knowledge intensive society, and free flow of workers beyond national borders contribute to the fact that youths without formal education or training are offered fewer opportunities and are far more vulnerable than before: Workplaces earlier available for school drop-outs do not exist any longer or the positions are already occupied by skilled workers. Moreover, several studies document that youths between 15 and 24 are more negatively affected by being unemployed than others (Reneflot & Evensen, 2011).

## Everyday racism and xenophobia

Another reality is the ways in which everyday racism and xenophobia seem to undermine the possibilities of participation and active citizenship for all. Racism is systematic discrimination on the background of assumed inherited qualities. Xenophobia is based on feelings, and is a fear or dislike towards strangers. A study carried out in 2011 document an increased xenophobia in Norway. One third of the informants claimed that immigrants cause an insecure society[4]. This claim seems paradoxical since 76 percent of the informants told that they had been in contact with immigrants, and that this contact was a positive experience (Blom, 2011). All 35 percent agree in the statement that "immigrants misuse the welfare goods", which is a significant increase of four percent from the year before

[4] It may seem contradictory that everyday racism and xenophobia is so prevalent when immigrants make up only 10.2 percent of the Norwegian population and the majority come from neighboring countries in Scandinavia and Europe (SSB, 2011b).

(Blom, 2011)[5]. Another large study, however, documents that immigrant youths between 16 and 25 years old – with background from Pakistan, Vietnam and Turkey – have the same level of access to studies and employment as other Norwegian youths. However, a remarkable large percentage of these youths reported discrimination on the background of their immigrant status (38 % of the youths from Pakistan, a lesser percentage of the youths from Vietnam and Turkey). Of those who had experienced unemployment, as many as one out of three reported that discrimination from the employer was the *reason* for being unemployed (Løwe, 2008; 2010).

## *Oppositions towards multiculturalism*

A third, but less visible, reality is oppositions towards multiculturalism. "Multiculturalism" is a normative stance that celebrates cultural diversity, often substantiated by the claim that such diversity benefits the larger society. Multiculturalism as an idea should not be conflated with a multicultural society. A multicultural society is, on the one hand, a society consisting of several cultures. Multiculturalism, on the other hand, is a normative orientation that can motivate a policy of promoting cultural diversity, often justified by the right of different groups to receive recognition and respect. Multiculturalism can also justify the protection of minority cultures (Bø, 2011; Eriksen & Næss, 2011). Oppositions towards multiculturalism have many faces. (1) One way is to openly reject a policy of cultural diversity, which may be seen as naive, relativistic, and a threat to the basic values of society. The arguments may be that multiculturalism encourages parallel societies, promotes conflictual values, ignores problems, promotes ugly practices, and provides free passages for terrorists (Eriksen & Stjernfelt, 2008; Kymlicka, 2009). (2) Another way of rejecting multiculturalism is the social construction of a form of "Norwegianness" difficult or nearly impossible to access. Examples are the idea of Norway as a nation of skiers; the common distinction between "ethnic Norwegians" and others; and the communal

[5] The survey from 2011 also shows that the Norwegian population is divided roughly at the middle when it comes to accepting refugees and asylum seekers: 44 percent think it should be harder to stay, while 45 percent think the right of residence should be like today. There are only 6 percent who think it should be easier to stay in Norway. The groups that are most sympathetic towards immigrant are those with higher education, who live in urban areas and those who have most contact with immigrants (Blom, 2011).

self-satisfaction expressed in the common saying that "it is typically Norwegian to be good" (Gullestad, 2002; Røthing, 2012). The dilemma, however, is that an exclusive and excluding "Norwegianness" may turn the fear of parallel societies into a self-fulfilling prophecy (Strømmen, 2011). (3) A third way of opposing multiculturalism is to be found in the anti-Islamic political orientations now emerging on the internet. These debates often promote a strong disapproval of Islam and carry more or less the conspiracy theories related to the Eurabia thesis. Eurabia is a social-political neologism which refers to the alleged Arabization or Islamization of Europe, as a result of immigration from Arabic countries. The conspiracy theory holds that the Arabization is result of a conscious plan in which the main actors are the government, the politicians, intellectuals and journalists (Strømmen, 2011). In Norway, we experienced a completely unthinkable and cruel manifestation of this conspiracy theory 22nd of July, when a Norwegian terrorist exploded a bomb in the government quarter and also massacred 69 youths at a political summer camp to protest against what he calls the Norwegian "cultural Marxism" and the increasing number of non-European immigrants in Norway[6].

## *The event*

Just a few days after the terrorist attack, the Norwegian Broadcasting Company [NRK] initiated an online meeting with experts on violence and traumas. Here, a Norwegian teenager wrote:

> Hi. I am 13 years old and Norwegian Muslim. I feel that I am to be blamed. He says that he killed everyone because I am here. Should I move out to protect Norwegian children in the future? This is what I feel. Regards, Sophia. [7]

[6] The terrorist, Anders Behring Breivik is a so-called 'ethnically Norwegian', polite young man brought up in the affluent neighborhood of Oslo West.

[7] Sophia's letter and the interview with her in *Sommeråpent* 4th August 2011 represents moments in a public discourse that I here take to illustrate some aspects of democracy and education in a new era. To this discourse, Sophia's personal and private matters are not relevant.

Sophia's letter received much media attention. On the 4th of August, she was interviewed on a talk show on national television[8].

> Sophia Adampour. You were the one submitting this question. Welcome to "Sommeråpent"
> *Thank you*
> You should tell us what happened. You were on the Internet. And then you discovered the online meeting at NRK. And then you wrote this question. What … what did you think when writing this?
> *I have learned, through my upbringing and the fact of being Norwegian and Muslim and Iranian that we should care for each other and protect each other, no matter background or orientation ...hmm ... yes ... and appearance*
> So, you were thinking … What made you think that you were to be blamed?
> *Ehm. He was not a Muslim, but he said he did it because of us Muslims. And ... yes ...*
> What were you thinking while you wrote this? What did you want … What did you wonder?
> *No ... if ... if what we should do, then, to protect Norwegian children in the future ... yes.*

The terrorist attack in Norway 22nd July aroused a call for "more democracy, more openness and more humanity" (the prime minister's address to the nation 24th July, 2011). And there are now signs on an increased awareness of the democratic mission of the school (NOU 2011:20[9]) and a revitalization of long-established discourses on democracy and education (Steinsholt & Dobson, 2011; Hagtvedt & Ognjenovic, 2011). But to what degree do current philosophies and theories of education relate to what is going on? The example of Sophia may help to illustrate democracy and education of the present, as her letter can exemplify democracy and education as a *way of life*, an *ideal,* and an *outlook.*

[8] The interview with Sophia can be viewed at: http://nrk.no/skole/klippdetalj?topic=nrk:klipp/774789

[9] The Norwegian report on Youth, Power and Participation (NOU 2011:20) which was published December 2011 looked to public school as an important arena for citizenship education (despite the fact that public education as not included in the Committee's mandate). In doing so, the Committee pointed to how the terrorist attacks on 22 July demonstrated the necessity of a democratic education from early childhood.

### *A way of life*

First of all, it is noteworthy how Sophia is oriented towards the community. She claims to "*have learned, through my upbringing ... that we should care for each other and protect each other*". Background, orientation or appearances have lesser priorities. Caring is more important than demonstrating individual differences. Even, the norm "to care" is so precious, that Sophia conceives the norm as an imperative: "*we* should *care for each other and protect each other*". This imperative has priority over personal needs or interests. Consequently, she asks in the online meeting: "*Should I move out to protect Norwegian children in the future?*"

In this way, Sophia's letter demonstrates a solidary citizenry. When claiming that "*we should care for each other and protect each other*", she demonstrates her orientation towards the common good. Following Honneth (1998), such an orientation towards communal goods does not only demonstrate solidary citizenry. It also points to the normative basis of democracy, since the citizens' orientation towards common goods is the very source of our normative judgments and decisions (Honneth, 1998). A perspective on active citizenship can therefore not be limited to a perspective on to what degree each citizen is being included and involved in formal democratic procedures and decisions (i.e. Habermas, 1996). Active citizenship also concerns the formation and strengthening of a democratic will (Honneth, 1998, p. 763). Or in other words: a perspective on active citizenship should include the citizens' orientation towards, and their *will* to promote, communal goods (Honneth, 1998, p. 763). The generation and formation of such a will happens through formal and informal education situated in and oriented towards the democratic[10].

Such a democratic will formation is the focus of John Dewey (1859 – 1952), when he in *Democracy and Education* (1916) uses the term democracy synonymous with education[11]. Deweys' perspective does not only open for a normative concept of democracy that moves beyond other models of democracy. Dewey also opens for a perspective of democracy as based on and justified through the social. Honneth (1998) points to the fact that Dewey's model of

---

[10] Consequently, it appears as a paradox that a vital precondition of democratic education seems to be the fact that democracy already exists.

[11] However, in "*Democracy and Education*" (1916), Dewey uses no less than four different concepts of democracy.

democracy is unique since it starts and ends in the social. Moreover, he argues that Dewey's concept of democracy is "not just an alternative but is superior to the approaches predominating today" (Honneth, 1998, p. 765). Democracy and education are to Dewey reflexive cooperative and social processes played out in peoples' everyday life. This means that democracy exists only as lived experience. Next, that democracy needs to be created, recreated, upheld and justified through an open dialogue and confrontational forms of practices within and between groups.

The value of such confrontations, however, depends on to what degree the interest of the group is shared by all. And to what degree the social group participates in open and free dialogues with other social groups.

> The two points selected by which to measure the worth of a form of social life are the extent in which the interests of a group are shared by all its members, and the fullness and freedom with which it interacts with other groups (Dewey, 1916, p. 105).

Hence, the worth of democracy is based on and justified through the social:

> From the standpoint of the individual, it consists in having a responsible share according to capacity in forming and directing the activities of the groups in which one belongs and in participating according to need in the values which the groups sustain. From the standpoint of the groups, it demands liberation of the potentialities of members of a group in harmony with the interests and goods which are common (The Public and Its Problems, LW2, 327-8).

When Sophia is asked "What were you thinking while you wrote this?" she responds by pointing to her upbringing: "I have learned, through my upbringing … that we should care for each other and protect each other no matter ...". The interview with Sophia may thus be taken to illustrate how her upbringing has shaped her orientation towards some communal values to approve of and respect. And which next shapes her democratic will.

In other words, democracy starts and ends in the social. In the same way as education, democracy is to be seen as a social process characterized by participation, communication, shared interests, freedom of speech and unlimited experimentation. The value of these confrontational interactions depend, however, on to what degree the communal interests are shared by all members of the group. And to what degree the social group is free to interact with other groups.

Consequently, democracy is social processes of educational and reflexive cooperation in which the child has a vital contribution. Through these social processes, the child will adopt community values, and next use these powers to social ends. Such as in the school:

> I believe that the school is primarily a social institution. Education being a social process, the school is simply that form of community life in which all those agencies are concentrated that will be most effective in bringing the child to share in the inherited resources of the race, and to use these powers to social ends (Dewey, 1897, s. 230).

To Dewey, a democratic way of life is both the mean and the end to realizing the democratic within and beyond the classroom. Democratic education presupposes and promotes democracy. A prerequisite is that the democratic already exists. Concurrently, there is an expectation of democracy to come. But to what degree does Dewey's harmonious image of democracy and education overlook the realities of children's life within and beyond the classroom anno 2012?

## *Ideal*

A key prerequisite for democratic education is that democracy already exists. In other words; a democratic way of life presupposes the support of the democratic as an idea and an ideal. The ideal concerns, on the one hand, our *community values,* which serves as the normative basis for justifying education within and towards democracy. On the other hand, the ideal concerns our shared images of the *ideal society*, which constitutes the aim of democracy and of education. Third, the ideal concerns the relationship between the two.

Sophia may illustrate this when asking in her letter: *"Should I move out to protect Norwegian children in the future?"* Next, when responding to the question of what she was thinking while she wrote this: "*I have learned, through my upbringing and the fact of being Norwegian and Muslim and Iranian that we should care for each other and protect each other no matter background or orientation ...hmm ... yes ... and appearance"*. At first glance, this may signify Sophia's high regards of the communal values to the extent that she is willing to move out of the country in order to protect that which she sees as an ideal society.

However, contrary to what Sophia, with her more or less naïve statement; “we should care…”, seems to believe, the concept of an ideal society is not given. Values and ideals earlier regarded as shared and justified by all are continuously being questioned, challenged and renegotiated in complex societies marked by transnational flows of people, ideas, knowledge and cultures (Beck, 2006; Fine, 2007; Strand, 2010). In today’s societies, there seem to be an increased uncertainty about what ideals to hold. Chantal Mouffe (2000) thus speaks of a new symbolic order in which the communal values represent an empty space. Several authors thus point to the fact that modern, pluralistic and complex societies seem to be characterized by a radical indecision, which often materializes as ugly processes of marginalization (Benhabib, 2011; Neuman, 2001; Mouffe, 2000).

Sophia seems to articulate this kind of indecision. On the one hand, she speaks of herself as “*Norwegian and Muslim and Iranian”*. But on the other hand, she is deeply concerned by protecting Norwegian children. In this way, she portrays herself as both Norwegian and non-Norwegian. She is concurrently part of a “we” and “the other”. This is in fact the democratic paradox pointed to by Chantal Mouffe: In complex societies, *demos* (the people) are concurrently “we” and “the other”. Sophia seems to be standing just at the center of this paradox. Accordingly, she asks: “*what should we do, then…”?*

## Outlook

Sophia’s question is important. In a new world order, which has not only created a new framing of identities, loyalties and self-understanding, but also altered the ways in which our identities and loyalties are continuously negotiated according to people’s insecure nationalities, religious aspirations and struggle for recognition. People’s active and loyal citizenship is not based on nationality or cultural heritage only. Citizenship is also marked by engagement with, commitment to, and identification with a polis (Benhabib, 2011; Delanty, 2006; Kymlicka, 2009). So, who are we, and “*what should we do, then…”*?

In these regards, the interconnection between democracy and education is also about a perspective, a point of view, a normative and diagnostic outlook. It is a way of seeing the world that may justify our moral, political, and social commitments.

When this normative and diagnostic outlook presupposes what it wants to create, the perspective makes us realize that which is absent. Consequently, the formation of a democratic will is based on the paradox that the *absence* of democracy is its very prerequisite. So maybe it is her eye for that which is absent that motivates Sophia's question: "*what should we do, then, to protect Norwegian children in the future?*"

However, it seems pertinent to ask to what degree this outlook merely confirms the same world as it is a product of, - or if the outlook also carries a potential for going beyond and change the present.

## *Education para doxa*

Dewey points to democracy and education as lived experiences, while Mouffe points to the incommensurable symbolic logics that generate ugly processes of marginalization within complex societies. The problems, however, appears to be that Dewey's perspective is limited by the fact that the communal values appear as given and that Mouffe's agonistic model merely represents a perspective on the perspective. To Dewey, a prerequisite for democracy as lived experience is that democracy already exists. To Mouffe, a prerequisite of democratic will formation is the absence of an ideal democracy. The theories of Dewey and Mouffe have both great influences on educational thinking. To some extent, they also seem as fruitful tools for educational researchers. But neither Dewey nor Mouffe offer tools for analyzing the crossing of boundaries and for revealing to what extent hegemonic discourses now seems to be made insignificant.

The French philosopher Alain Badiou (1937 - ), however, offers an alternative perspective. His logic is neither based on pragmatism nor post structuralism, but rather mathematics (set theory). He argues against those who tend to conflate politics with philosophy and also truth with knowledge, and contends that there is no such thing as a philosophical truth. Philosophy cannot and will not tell what particular position to take in politics or science. Because truths are produced and continue to emerge in other, non-philosophical spheres of life: In love, art, politics and science. Here, "truths not only are, they appear" (Badiou 2001). However, philosophy – and philosophy alone – contains the resources to reveal and preserve the appearance of truths. In this way, philosophy deals with logical transformations; truths as creation. The task of philosophy is to "examine the constitution, in singular worlds, of the appearing of truths, and therefore on what grounds the evidence of their existence" (Badiou 2009, p. 9). In other words, the task of philosophy is to reveal the ways in which truth-procedures appear, emerge and develop. To Badiou, this task is vital, since truth-procedures not only change our thinking about a phenomenon, they also radically the very origin of our thinking.

So, to Badiou the object of philosophical analysis is thinking as such. Not, as for Dewey, different forms of practice, or, as for Mouffe, different discourses. In this way, Badiou's philosophy represents an unusual logic, an alternative meta-philosophy that offers new ways of performing philosophical analysis. But this meta-philosophy is never disconnected from a practical reality. Because – as Badiou states – "Philosophy is not worth an hour's effort if it is not based on the idea that true life is present" (Badiou, 2009, s. 14). Philosophy connects with reality by affirming three major dimensions of emerging truth processes: The event, the fidelity and truth.

The event is unexpected and unpredictable, something that vanishes and disappears. But it institutes a radical rupture, as it brings to pass instituted outlooks, knowledge and opinions. In this way, the event is both situated and something additional to the situation: On the one hand, it is conditioned by a situated void, around which a plenitude of outlooks, knowledge and opinions circulates. On the other hand, the event carries a radical novelty, a deep-seated change, a radical different logic that implies that it is impossible to continue to practice – let us say a field of science or arts – in the same way as earlier.

Fidelity amounts to a persistent exploration of the situation under the imperative of the event itself. Fidelity is thus the name of the processes of immanent and continuing ruptures. Truth (or truth-processes) is internal to the situation and produced by fidelity. "Truth is what the fidelity groups together and constructs, bit by bit".

But does Sophia's letter represent an event? Does Sophia's letter make it difficult to think ethical-political education within and towards the democratic in the same way as earlier? Yes, it is true that the letter received enormous media attention. Not without a reason, because the letter represents something never seen before. The letter represents something totally unexpected in the days shortly after 22$^{nd}$ July 2011, in Norway. When Sophia, as a Norwegian, Muslim and Iranian, says she considers changing her life completely on behalf of

"Norwegian children", her letter – against all odds – invites us to see that which is missing in the Norwegian society. Sophia's letter thus surprises and confuses.

The surprise is in the dislocation of meaning from one scene towards another. After 22nd July, Norwegians were taken by surprise when they learned that the terrorist was an insider, a so-called ethnic Norwegian citizen[12]. Moreover, they were surprised by the fact that the unconditional will to care for and protect Norwegian children belonged to a young girl concurrently being an outsider and an insider. The dislocation of meaning thus happened as a deviation from conventional beliefs about the citizens' different loyalties and roles in the Norwegian society. But also by the fact that there is a young Muslim teenager that appears as the accountable and vigorous caregiver, while Norwegian children are those in need of protection. This dislocation and deviation causes confusion. Because there are contrasting views between the common and widespread beliefs about immigrant children (i.e. Statistics Norway, 2011) and the way in which Sophia was eager to protect Norwegian children.

- One out of three Norwegian hold that "immigrants are a source of insecurity in society" (Blom, 2011). But on the contrary, Sophia's letter shows that she wants to do whatever possible to create a safe society
- There is also a tendency to define immigrant youths as being in need of caring. But here, there is an immigrant youth being the caregiver.
- Norwegians hold that the liberal immigrant policies are threatening the Norwegian society. But Sophia is not a threat. On the contrary, she reveals an urge to protect the Norwegians
- It is also said that immigrant youths do not participate in the larger society. But Sophia appears as an active, participating and vigorous citizen

Sophia's letter therefore appears as a surprise and confusion. The reason is that it jumbles our categories of thought by mixing ideas and realities, myths and truths. Consequently, the letter disturbs the very ground and categories of thinking about democracy and education. Sophia's letter invited the larger Norwegian society to imagine something totally new.

---

[12] See note 5.

Hence, the confusion happens by the fact that Sophia made us realize the impossible image of the normative basis of democracy. Next, the confusion happens as Sophia's letter signifies a deviation from already existing myths about "the good Norwegians" and "immigrant children". So, there is a thorough mix-up of our categories of thought, and our ideas about "truths" and "realities" (which were suddenly made insignificant by Sophia's letter and appearance in the talk show).

The most important work of this mix-up, however, is not about the deviation or displacement of meaning, but rather by the ways in which it might educate us. The education might happen because the logical mismatches and the jumbling of categories carry a potential of violating previous ways of thinking by disarranging the very categories that generates the ways we think. Sophia's letter should therefore not only be read as a testimony to Sophia's active citizenship and democratic will. Sophia's letter should also be read as a way of initiating some truth-procedures that may educate us.

In this way, the example of Sophia may challenge our perspective on democracy and education for a new era. And also the educational discourse.

## *What now?*

In sum it seems pertinent to ask once again: To what degree do educational theory and practice relate to what is going on? Do educational policies and practices help to strenghten democratic will formation of the next generation?

The philosophy of John Dewey focuses on democracy and education as a lived experience. To Dewey, the democratic life in schools are the very precondition for promoting a healthy democracy. But education is not just a mean for the formation of good citizens. Education is the very way of living and experiencing citizenship. The school should therefore not be perceived as a place to promote active citizenship for the future, but rather as a place where competent children are continuously living, experiencing, learning, justifying, strengthening and developing democratic ways of life. However, a prerequisite is that democracy already exists in the larger society. A Deweyan outlook on democracy and education may thus serve to strengthen already outdated ideals and practices of democracy and education.

Chantal Mouffe, by contrast, helps to realize the paradoxical fact that the absence of democracy is one of its vital preconditions. She also points to the impossible fact that the relationship between that which is included and excluded seem to be a central characteristic – and a vital precondition – of democracy in complex societies. In this way, Mouffe offers tools to reveal the democratic will formation in complex societies. Also, her theory may help to recognize and strengthen a democratic vision and will formation of the present. However, as Mouffe only offers a perspective on the perspective, her theory does not offer tools to move beyond the discourse.

The philosophy of Alain Badiou offers a different outlook, as it offers tools to reveal the incommensurable logics, the paradoxical situations, the events in which truth-procedures appears. Sophia's letter after 22nd July is an example of such an event. The event was totally unexpected and unpredictable. Sooner or later it will die out and disappear. But it has already instituted a radical rupture, a break with former ideas of democracy and education. Sophia's letter signifies that the event has brought to pass instituted outlooks, knowledge and opinions. On the one hand, Sophia's letter was conditioned by a situated void, a negation, something unthinkable. On the other hand, her letter carried a radical novelty, a radical different logic that implies that it is impossible to continue to practice citizenship education in the same way as earlier. In this way, a Badiouan analysis may help to extend and renew our thinking of democracy and education for the current era. A precondition, however, is that we read the situation, recognize the extraordinary, and ask new questions.

## *References*

Badiou, A. (2009). Thinking the Event. I: Badiou, A. & Zizek, S. (2009). *Philosophy of the Present* (pp. 1 – 48). Cambridge: Polity Press

Badiou, A. (2001). *Ethics*. London & New York: Verso

Beck, U. (2006). *The Cosmopolitan Vision*. Cambridge, UK: Polity Press

Benhabib, S. (2011). *Dignity in Adversity. Human Rights in Troubled Times*. Cambridge: Polity Press

Blom, S. (2011). Holdninger til innvandrere og innvandring. *Rapport 41/2011*. Oslo & Kongsvinger: Statistisk sentralbyrå

Born, A. W. & Jensen, P. H. (1998). Priviligering av perspektiver. En refleksjon over begrepskonstruktionerne inklusjon/eksklusjon og integrering/marginalisering i den sociologiske iaggtagelse. [Privileged perspectives. Reflections on the sociological constructions of inclusion/exclusion and integration/marginalization]. *Dansk Sociologi, 98* (2), 22 – 37.

Bø, B. P. (red.) (2011). *Multikulturell teori og flerkulturelle praksiser. Artikler om norsk minoritetspolitikk.* [*Multicultural theory and practice. Essays on Norwegian minority politics*]. Oslo: Abstrakt

Delanty, G. (2006). The cosmopolitan imagination: critical cosmopolitanism and social theory. *British Journal of Sociology*, *57*(1), 25 – 47.

Dewey, J. (1897). My Pedagogic Creed. I: Hickman & Alexander (red.). *The Essential Dewey, Vol. 1* (s. 229 – 235). Bloomington & Indianapolis: Indiana University Press

Dewey, J. (1985/1916). *Democracy and Education*. Carbondale & Edwardsville: Southern Illinois University Press

Eriksen, T. H. & Nøss, H. E. (red.) (2011). *Kulturell kompleksitet i det nye Norge [Cultural complexities in contemporary Norway]*. Oslo: Unipub

Eriksen, J.-M. & Stjernfelt, F. (2008). *Adskillelsens politik [The policies of Differentiations]*. København: Lindhardt og Ringhof

Eurostat (2011). *Unemployment statistics*. Retrieved December 2011 from http://epp.eurostat.ec.europa.eu/statistics_explained/index.php/Unemployment_statistics

Fine, R. (2007). *Cosmopolitanism*. London & New York: Routledge

Gullestad, M. (2002). *Det norske sett med nye øyne [Re-imagining Norwegianness]*. Oslo: Universitetsforlaget

Habermas, J. (1996). *Between Facts and Norms. Contribution to a Discourse Theory of Law and Democracy*. Cambridge: MIT Press

Hagtvedt, B. & Ognjenovic, G. (red.) (2011). *Dannelse. Tenkning, modning, refleksjon [Education. Thinking, maturing, reflecting]*. Oslo: Dreyer

Held, D. (2006). *Models of Democracy*. Cambridge: Polity Press

Honneth, A. (1998). Democracy as Reflexive Cooperation. *Political Theory, 26* (6), 763 – 783.

Kymlicka, W. & Norman, W. (1994). Return of the Citizen: A Survey of Recent Work on Citizenship Theory. *Ethics 104* (January 1994), 352 – 381.

Kymlicka, W. (2009). The Rise and Fall of Multiculturalism. New Debates on Inclusion and Accommodation in Diverse Societies. In: Verlovec, S. & Wessendorf, S. (ed.). *The Multiculturalism Backlash*. London: Routledge

Lov om grunnskolen og den videregåande opplæringa (opplæringslova). Retrieved January 2012 from http://www.lovdata.no/all/tl-19980717-061-001.html

Løwe, T. (2008). Levekår blant unge med innvandrerbakgrunn [Living conditions of youths with immigrant background]. *Rapport*. Oslo & Kongsvinger: Statistisk sentralbyrå

Løwe, T. (2010). Unge med innvandrerbakgrunn og arbeidsmarkedet [Young immigrants and employment]. *Rapport 21/2010*. Oslo & Kongsvinger: Statistisk sentralbyrå

Marshall, T. H. (1949). *Citizenship and Social Class*. Cambridge: Cambridge University Press

Mouffe, C. (2000). *The Democratic Paradox*. London & New York: Verso

Neumann, I. B. (2001). *Mening, materialitet, makt: En innføring i diskursanalyse [Meaning, materiality, power: An introduction to Discourse Analysis]*. Oslo: Fagbokforlaget

NOU 2011:20. *Ungdom, makt og medvirkning* [Youth, power and involvement]. Retrieved December 2011 from http://www.regjeringen.no/nb/dep/bld/dok/nouer/2011/nou-2011-20.html?id=666389

OECD (2010). Rising Youth Unemployment during the Crisis. How to prevent negative long-term consequences on a generation? *OECD social, employment and migration papers, no 106*. Retrieved January 2012 from http://www.oecd.org/dataoecd/10/8/44986030.pdf

OECD (2011). *Divided We Stand. Why Inequality Keeps Rising*. OECD, Dec. 2011

Pedersen, W. (2010). Sosiologi i ghettoen [Sociology in the Ghetto]. *Nytt Norsk Tidsskrift, 27* (4), 421 - 429

Reneflot, A. & Evensen, M. (2011). Arbeidsledighet og psykisk helse blant unge i Norden. En kunnskapsoversikt [Unemployment and psychic health among Nordic youths. A report on knowledge]. *NHV-Rapport 2011:1 R*. Oslo: Nordiska Högskolan för Folkhelsovetenskap

Røthing, Å. (2012). Concepts of gender equality in Norwegian textbooks and classrooms. In: Strand, T. & Roos, M. (eds.). *Education for Social Justice, Equity and Diversity*. Munster: LIT Verlag

Statistics Norway (2011a). Mange jobber, få ledige, men ungdom er utsatt [Many available positions, few unemployed, but youths are still vulnerable]. Retrieved January 2012 from http://www.ssb.no/samfunnsspeilet/utg/200705/08/index.html

Statistics Norway (2011b). Innvandring og innvandrere [Imigration and immigrants]. Retrieved January 2012 from http://www.ssb.no/innvandring/

Steinsholt, K. & Dobson, S. (red.)(2011). *Dannelse. Introduksjon til et ullent pedagogisk landskap [Education. Introduction to a diffuse landscape]*. Trondheim: Tapir

Strand, T. (2010). The Cosmopolitan Turn: Recasting 'Dialogue' and 'Difference'. *Paideusis. International Journal in Philosophy of Education, 19* (1), 49 - 58.

Strand, T. & Huggler, J. (2011). Educating the Global Village. *Nordic Studies in Education, 31* (2), 69 – 76.

Strømmen, Ø. (2011). *Det mørke nettet [The dark network]*. Oslo: Cappelen

UNESCO (2010). *Citizenship education*. Retrieved December 2011 from http://www.unesco.org/education/tlsf/mods/theme_b/mod07.html

AUTHOR:,Torill Strand is Professor at Østfold University College and Professor II at the University of Oslo. Strand teaches philosophy of education and has since August 2011 been a close colleague of Professor Anne-Lise Arnesen. Her competencies range from meta-theory to social epistemologies, educational philosophy, cosmopolitanism and semiotics. Among her most recent titles are *"The Rudeness of Lived Experience"*, *"Peirce's New Rhetoric"*, *"The Making of a New Cosmopolitanism"* and *"Metaphors on Creativity and Workplace Learning"*. Recently, Strand has guest-edited special issues on '*Educating the Global Village*', '*Cosmopolitanism in the Making*' and '*C. S. Peirce's Rhetorical Turn: Prospects for Educational Theory and Research*'. Strand is now in charge of the Master program *Diversity and Social Inclusion* at Østfold University College.
Correspondence: torill.strand@hiof.no

# *Dwelling, hesitating, but still acting*

## THE APORIA OF PEDAGOGICAL WORK

ANN SOFI LARSEN
Østfold University College, Norway

ABSTRACT: *This article focuses on professional practice and inclusion in a Norwegian kindergarten. Based on narratives from every-day life, the article examines how narratives put thinking in motion and contributes to open conditions that are not immediately easy to discover. The crux of the article is the examination of situations with apparently no possibility of «doing the right thing», while simultaneously avoiding «the wrong thing». This implies an opening up of a multitude of differentiated knowledge sources. In such situations, ethical dilemmas and questions arise. By putting Derrida's terms of «aporia» (a philosophical puzzlement) into work with empirical material taken from a kindergarten context, the article exposes the vulnerability of educational practices. Critically, the article destabilizes the assumptions regarding the ability of texts to put forward arguments in neutral and transparent ways.*

### *Introduction*

This article reports a PhD project[1] that examines processes where practitioners in kindergarten[2] reflect on pedagogical work based on children's statements and

[1] Larsen (2009-2013): Professional practice and inclusion; disruption as possible inputs to dwell on ethical actions and issues of inclusion. PhD Programme; Interdisciplinary Child Research, Norwegian Centre for Child Research (NOSEB), Faculty of Social Sciences and Technology Management (NTNU), Trondheim, Norway.

[2] «Kindergarten» is chosen as a translation of the Norwegian word « barnehage». It refers to an ECEC institution providing pedagogical settings, covering ages zero to six, containing structures of both family daycare and pre-school. Responsibility for ECEC falls under the Governmental Ministry of Education, it is regulated by the «Kindergarten Act» (Kunnskapsdepartementet 2006)

actions. One key research question in this context is: *What are the practitioners doing when discussing their pedagogical work?* The question is based on previous research, in which kindergarten staffs were criticized for their reticence regarding the use of existing theories to reflect on their own pedagogical work (Fleer, Tonyan, Mantilla & Rivalland, 2009; Olsson, 2009; Allan, 2008, 2012).

Some of the findings regarding the staff's approach to discussions of their pedagogical work were reached in two ways. The first is described here as *maintenance of the existing and already known*. In this approach, the material discussed is recognized by the staff to be something they have experienced previously, they confirm it *as the same as* they have previously experienced. In these cases, the staff's participation contributes to conserving and reproducing professional practice and kindergarten traditions. Such an approach may help to create and maintain a common reference, a common terminology and a common language. Biesta (2006) called this type of community a «rational community», where participants are considered to be representatives of rules and regulations in a rational discourse. The community provides a sense of security and contributes to predictability, clarity and continuity. However, such an approach may also contribute to excluding what lies beyond what is taken for granted and further discovery.

When something unexpected, something different and undesirable, disrupts what is taken for granted, another approach to discussions about the practitioners' pedagogical work was found. *This is described as disruptions of the existing and already known.* These two approaches, *maintenance* and *disruption*, cannot be separated from each other or be described as if a conversation is characterized by one or the other. Rather, they became intertwined in the staff's discussions as answers and responsibility in educational work.

The current study is directed towards tensions between these two approaches and to processes in which the familiar is disrupted by something unexpected. When something, or someone, disrupts what is familiar, it may be understood as *active initiatives* and *small confrontations*. It is such «lack of flow» and «vibrating impact» that most likely allows for inclusive practices (Edgoos, 2001; Allan, 2008; Biesta, 2006). However, the practitioners' challenge is the confusion that

---

and informed by the national curriculum's The Framework Plan for the Content and Tasks of Kindergartens (Kunnskapsdepartementet 2011).

arises owing to the «lack of flow». In light of this, this study focuses on how disruptions and «lack of flow» allow for inclusive practices.

To date, analyses of questions of inclusion have shed little light on its discontinuities, contradictions and complexities (Allan, 2008; Allan & Slee, 2008; Arnesen, 2012). By examining how disruption and «lack of flow» influence the practitioners' reflection, the intention of the current study is to open up multiple reflections, contradictions and discontinuities situated in the staff's re-reading of events from their practices. The attention is focused on how disruptions and «lack of flow» influence the staff's thinking and their pedagogical work, and on rethinking questions of inclusion.

One way to obtain empirical data in order to shed light on this issue is to present parts of practice as an object for thinking through narratives (Taguchi, 2006). The empirical material for this study is based on narratives from the staff in three kindergartens. The narratives were created by the staff in light of every-day events in the kindergarten, and were used as a starting point for further reflection at their regular discussion meetings. *Thinking with* narratives[3] is intended to open the concept of disturbances in pedagogical work. The narratives are regarded as a methodological tool that works in relation to the staff's thinking about and understanding of their pedagogical work. This study is not interested in how the staff's actual actions are carried out. Rather, the interest lies in how thinking with narratives allows for the unexpected and contributes to open, new, unpredictable issues and questions. Based on this interest, the findings from the empirical data are structured into two groupings: events that invite further discussion and events that include disturbances, disruption and vibrating impact.

Theoretically the narratives are contextualized in a way that offers the possibility of rethinking educational practices through *deconstruction* (Derrida, 1990). In order to conceive and engage with questions of disruption in pedagogical work, the study uses some philosophical concepts inspired by Derridas`s «philosophy of difference» (Allan 2008). Derrida and others are «recognised as philosophers of difference because of their attempt to formulate a politics of difference, which is based on an acceptance of multiplicity» (Allan, 2008, p. 57). Although much of Derrida's work has been criticized as over-complex, «...there is general acceptance that his method of deconstruction has been a key legacy for

---

[3] This idea of "thinking with" came from a seminar at MMU presented by Sabi Redwood in which she talked about thinking ethics with Levinas. (Mazzei 2009)

philosophy» (Allan, 2008, p. 71). Derrida has a pedagogical interest in questions concerning meaning making and transformation (Haaland, 2009). In his later works, he «demonstrates that deconstruction is not just about unsettling texts, but can be put to use to unsettle institutions in many different contexts» (Jackson & Mazzei, 2012, p. 15). The kind of thinking in which deconstruction is engaged is a kind of theorizing that is never finished and which therefore opens up endless approaches to pedagogy and «justice» in early childhood education. «Deconstruction has to do with what is not present; it destabilizes; it snags; it is what remains to be thought; it is excess» (Jackson & Mazzei, 2012, p. 22). Spivak (1976) described deconstruction as «A way out of the closure of knowledge» (p. 6). The use of deconstruction in this study is to look for events[4] (Jackson & Mazzei, 2012) where deconstruction happens to unsettle pedagogical order and institutions. This study highlights how narratives contribute to the development of awareness of discontinuities, undecidable moments and that which lies beyond the expected. «It is through an inclusion of difference that sources of tension and disruption signal the deconstructive event» (Jackson & Mazzei, 2012, p. 26).

The following section will present an event that emerged from a destabilization of lunchtime in a Norwegian kindergarten. A pre-school teacher wrote this narrative. She is one of the pedagogical leaders and therefore responsible for the planning, documentation and assessment of pedagogical work with this group of children. Formally, she is responsible for the following:

> Organise everyday activities in such a way that there is a planned alternation between periods of rest, activity and mealtimes, to help children to develop good habits, attitudes and knowledge regarding diet, hygiene, activity and rest (*Framework Plan for the Content and Tasks of Kindergartens*, 2011, p. 23).

The pedagogical leader is working together with Olga, who is an assistant in the kindergarten, and with Peter, another pre-school teacher. From this point, these three people are described as «the staff». Together, they are responsible for a

---

[4] The term «event» refers to an example of deconstruction at work: «It is deconstruction at work or the happening of deconstruction in the event that causes a reconstitution of that which has been constructed (fixed) and unproblematically accepted. The event is an actual happening that jars things and pushes them off balance just enough to keep things moving, thus enabling transformation» (Jackson & Mazzei, 2012, p. 19).

group of 24 children aged three to six years. Martha and Celina, mentioned below, are two of the children in this group.

## *A beginning*

> *Olga has covered three small tables. She has arranged it so that the children can make the sandwiches themselves. There are many different toppings, including meats. The children are queuing to wash their hands; then, they enter and sit down at the tables. Peter and I are waiting inside at the tables. When the children finish washing their hands, they enter the room and choose a seat at the table with some of their friends. Before we start to eat, we recite the poem of the month; at this point, something happens, and all the adults react. The same thing happens at all the tables. One or two children jump on, and eat greedily from the meats; Martha puts caviar and four pieces of turkey sausage on her sandwich, meaning that there is only one piece of turkey sausage left. Celina rushed to take this, while using her other hand to take a pork sausage. We usually recite the poem of the month first, and only afterwards may we eat, but she has managed to make her sandwich before we say the poem, and she doesn't stop. We all react, based on the display of greed and impatience that we have witnessed.*

In this narrative, we should pay attention to tensions, contradictions, omissions and moments of destabilization. Critically, the study will discuss how assumptions regarding the way in which narratives, as written or oral texts, can communicate arguments relatively clearly and the way in which application of rules and standards of behaviour can be problematic and difficult to maintain.

The information we receive through the excerpt tells us how the staff establish frames and procedures for a regular lunchtime. These provide a certain degree of predictability for both children and adults that provide a form of control for the situation. Mostly, the children keep themselves within the existing frames and routines. However, in this instance, when they are supposed to recite the poem of the month before they are going to eat, someone/something breaks through and interrupts:

> *The same thing happens at all the tables. One or two children throw themselves at the food and rush to take an unfair share.*

One of the first questions the staff asks following this event is: What do we do? This question is not asked because of their lack of experience in acting in similar situations. Rather, it is the opposite; based on many years of professional practice, the staff have a wealth of experience. They also express that this type of behaviour is something they regularly have to deal with and talk about. Yet, they discuss this narrative and ask an open question: What do we do? The very fact that the staff have to re-think constantly how to deal with the recurrent situation, leads to the question: How do this narrative and the staff's question open up discussion of the unknown? How do they reach interesting and productive discussion guided by a familiar, everyday situation and some *undecidable* moments?

## *Lineage and rupture*

In situations where something, or someone, breaks in and disrupts existing rules and routines, it is possible to discover the pedagogical order and practitioners' reasoning behind their actions (Gulløv, 2004; Sandvik, 2012). In order to recognize something as a disruption, it is assumed that there must be something to disrupt. It demands both *lineage* and *rupture*. It has to be something that has stabilizing, predictable, recognizable and calculating effects, and, at the same time, something that gives opportunities to challenge and break with these stabilizing conditions. The pre-school teacher's narrative highlights a number of such stabilizing and predictable conditions, which govern how to conduct a meal in the kindergarten: the children queue to wash their hands; then they enter and choose a seat at the tables; two adults are waiting inside at the tables; they recite the poem of the month before they start to eat… The staff's sensitivity to how these regulations and practices work and to the situation where not everything flows as planned is essential in order to teach responsibility and ensure *justice* in the situation. According to Derrida (2002), justice and responsibility require experience of the undecidable, implying that actions do not follow, nor are they controlled, by rules.

The narrative puts the lunchtime event into context: it is part of the kindergarten's routine, which is stabilizing and predictable and is organized according to prescribed rules. The system of rules enables both children and adults to recognize the situation. The children's breaking of the pedagogical order creates a temporary imbalance and uncertainty among the staff. It triggers a situation where the rules and procedures for the lunchtime behaviour have to be justified again. This is not to say that there should not be any rules, however; the situation triggers a tension between the rules and practices, and the particular, yet complex lunchtime situation; involving children, adults, turkey sausage, caviar, pork sausage, greediness and the poem of the month.

## *Aporia – undecidable moments*

Derrida (1990; 2002) described the *undecidable moment* as an «aporia». This concept implies doubt, uncertainty, anxiety and that which is overly complex, as well as that which often brings hesitation and new questions. An aporia is a paradox, "that which proposes a difficulty in logic because it presents evidence for more than one truth" (Jackson & Mazzei, 2012, p. 17). It might be described as a process in which something or someone breaks in and disrupts that with which we are familiar when we are acting according to earlier experiences (Allan, 2008). «Too often, according to Derrida, these aporias are resolved into certainty and decision about the way forward» (Allan, 2008, p. 22). Allan emphasized that pedagogical work, and work with inclusion, must be understood as a number of aporias. To actively bear or endure aporia is, according to Derrida, the very condition of responsibility and justice. «Derrida claims that justice, based upon a radical openness to alterity, can be preserved only as a result of the aporias of suspension, undecidability, and urgency» (Edgoose, 2001, p. 129).

The terms *suspension, undecidability*, and *urgency* might prove fruitful in opening up the multiple reflections situated in the staff's narratives and examining the hesitation that inhibits their reflections and decisions. So, how can we seek that which is in the aporias that destabilizes and allows for inclusive practices? This study uses the concept of aporia as a touchstone to open up new, unpredicted issues and questions about destabilization and disruption in pedagogical work. Thinking with these concepts involves searching for something other than patterns, programmes of content in kindergarten or assessment of expected outcomes. This study looks for situations where the staff suspend activity, where they put their immediate reactions and solutions on hold, and where they open up to discover new aspects of their pedagogical work. Thinking with deconstruction (Jackson & Mazzei, 2012) and the concept of aporia may open up consideration of how disruptions influence the practitioners' reflections, where deconstruction happens to unsettle pedagogical order, what is produced in the narratives and where in the narratives sentences and words lead elsewhere than expected. The concepts are also used to create new ways of seeing and thinking about inclusion.

## *The aporia of suspension—the commonly known receives a temporary dispensation*

It is this tension between the familiar, and that which breaks with the familiar, which Derrida put out as *the aporia of suspension* (Derrida, 1992):

> The law must be conserved and also destroyed or suspended, suspension being the meaning of the word «epoche». Each case is other, each decision is different and requires an absolutely unique interpretation, which no existing coded rule can or ought to guarantee. If a judge programmatically follows a code, he or she is a «calculating machine». (Derrida, 1992, pp. 22–23).

Different types of guidelines, content and tasks that control and regulate everyday life in kindergarten permit deconstruction, because they already are constructed. They are both repeatable and changeable; they are re-thinkable and allow themselves to be understood from multiple perspectives. Here, Derrida (1990) drew the question of justice away from procedures and discourses and constructed a distinction between two types of justice the French *le droit* (right, rights, law) and *juste* (justice). Justice and law are not supposed to be opposites, but to interweave. Justice demands the experience of undecidability and cannot be reached through formulas or programmes but, rather, involves a loss of fluency and understanding (Edgoos, 2001).

That which is commonly known receives a temporary dispensation to include something in addition. The narrative below shows some of the staff conversations that took place when they suspended their own solutions for a while.

> *I am thinking from a global perspective. We are talking about how we in the Western world ought to maintain an attitude of reserve towards eating so much food. We should be moderate and we should be good role models. The first thing that struck me was, I might want to eat something, but I need to keep back, to share. The idea of sharing is important. I am thinking that we*

> *have to work on attitudes towards food in general. In the long term, it is better to try to help the children to understand themselves.*

Here we notice that the pre-school teacher's narrative cannot be separated from the context and the time in which it was written. The production of the narrative constitutes an addition, or a response, to other existing chains of speech communication. This is a useful perspective, which helps to emphasize that it isn't just about the experience of the lunchtime. It is also about other texts, which in various ways influence the pre-school teacher's writing and the staff's reflections.

The staff discover how the concept of greediness is related to their understanding of *being moderate, keeping back and having a reserved attitude.* They were aware of how greediness could be seen as a disruption of keeping back and being moderate. Terms or concepts never give meaning themselves, but get their meaning by defining themselves against other words or opposing concepts. Creating meaning is also related to that which is absent. By examining the unsaid, ambiguities and contradictions may be raised, and with them openings for alternative understandings made clear (Hultman, 2011).

The discourse of children's greediness may be an example of implied understandings of existing truths. In this context, this has consequences for the staff's construction of knowledge and for broader content in their pedagogical work. The staff faces the children's disturbance and recognize it to be something decided and already known. From a critical perspective, it may be understood that they confirm their experiences as the same as they have previously experienced several times at lunchtimes and as maintenance of the existing pattern of behaviour.

## *The same as and different from…*

There are several issues that could be causative factors in what is taken for granted, what is listened to and what is passed on as truths. The staff's observation, what they have seen and paid attention to at the meal, can be one factor; their earlier experiences another; their cultural, local and global interest a third; their oral re-telling a fourth and so on. These factors contribute to focusing on and to maintaining understanding in pedagogical work. However, regulations and comprehension that help to control the staff's interpretation are not given.

Rather, they can be seen as products of a fellowship consensus on what makes a good, questionable strange or bad interpretation.

The lunchtime narrative receives institutional support through the fact that *all the adults responded* to the experience of *the children's greediness.* They confirm among themselves that this type of behaviour is something of which they have extensive experience. The staff responds to the experience from an understanding of sameness; *we all reacted, based on the kind of greediness we felt.* The documentation contributes to verifying the staff's constructed knowledge about children's greediness at the table. As such, it also contributes to maintaining and producing knowledge in the institution. The staff's experience is taken as «truths» that confirm, and adapt, that which is perceived as logically or proper to do in situations like this. Communication regarding *the same as*, leads to something that is already known. Simultaneously, it contributes to closures and precludes new opportunities. Reducing the new into the same implies a closure and a reduction (Steinsholt, 2009). Understandings, characterized by *the same as,* justify one truth, and do not reflect values such as diversity, uncertainty and contradictions. Such approaches may imply closure and reduction.

While we find meaning making characterized by *the same as*, we simultaneously notice that *the same as* is destabilized and pushed out of balance «just enough to keep things moving» (Jackson & Mazzei, 2012, p. 20). Given what is described as *the same as*, the staff discover *that which is different from.* Given what is considered to be *the same as* what they have experienced at lunchtime several times, the staff simultaneously tracks the unique and peculiar situation and exceed their understanding of it. This they do by contributing as co-authors, by challenging, disturbing and interpreting what is being said and what is already known.

> It involves a double reading, a reading with at least two layers, usually by first repeating the dominant interpretation of a text, which takes the form of a commentary; and then opening up the text to its own blind spots, which lie behind and are protected by the commentary (Allan, 2008, p. 78).

Processes that begin when something unexpected, something different and undesirable, disrupts what is taken for granted have to be managed simultaneously. Embedded in the staff's experience about *the same*, are included rules for what may apply to the new. Guided by the narrative, the practitioners explore their experiences, discover connections and examine how educational practice points back to performances that are not neutral, obvious, or which cannot be taken for granted (Hultman, 2011).

In the following section, this paper presents situations where the familiar becomes destabilized and is pushed out of balance; the commonly known receives a temporary dispensation to include something else.

## *Bending the rules slightly aside*

The staff recount that they found it relatively unproblematic to stop children in situations where they challenge regulations and routines (Larsen, 2012). In such situations, they guide the children into more acceptable activities or behaviour. Based on the kindergarten's regulations and routines, they probably act correctly, and certainly legally, but not always *justly*. To work on the children's attitudes in relation to the meal may, in this context, be seen as a pedagogical measure, where the intention is to change, divert and regulate the children's behaviour. The measures suggested by the staff may also be understood as a way to create a kind of order in the situations and in the kindergarten as an institution (Sandvik, 2012).

Based on a desire to change children's attitudes and behaviour, the staff has an implicit control, which veils the rules and implied actions. If we try to look beyond the need to divert and adapt, and beyond the understanding that similar situations have been experienced regularly by the staff at mealtimes, we will be able to see something other than what was intended. In the conversation, there were several unexpected phenomena, which opened up the possibility of discovering the complexity of the situation. One was set up when the staff became aware of how the concept of greediness works in the narrative and through their conversations:

## *We are affected by this...*

> *I describe the meal as neutral, there are no feelings there.*
> *But listen; now something happens that all the adults react to, the kids **jumped on**, and eat greedily from the meats, **greediness**. You cannot describe it as neutral. You are affected by it.*
> *[Laughter.]*
> *It's fun to see. Because I thought this here, I write «neutral».*

> *[Laughter.] This is interesting. She **rushes** to take the sausage **with both hands**.*
> *No, this is not neutral, it is not neutral. [Laughter.]*

*You know, we are learning so much about ourselves.*

Through the conversation, the staff discovers how their pedagogical practices point back at performances that they initially thought were neutral, but which it transpires are not. In a way, the narrative «turns back» and makes it possible to discover several dimensions in the text. By modifying the focus from an inter-subjective relationship between children and adults and instead exploring how the concept of greediness can have agency (Lenz Taguchi, 2010), it is possible to discover discontinuities, contradictions and complexities.

Throughout the texts we may be aware of a number of values that affect the situation at the meal. Thinking with the text, the staff's assumptions to put forward arguments in neutral and transparent ways is destabilized. They become aware of how language is working, compared to what is being focused on, and how they construct knowledge based on discourses of greediness. By recognizing and confirming «some children's greediness», they also contribute to maintaining their understanding of existing theories and truths. Thinking with the narrative and the concept of greediness, they discovered how their professional practice is based on ideals such as being neutral, showing moderation, keeping back and sharing the benefits both from a local and global perspective. By dwelling on the conversation, and by bending the rules slightly aside, they discover multiple reflections and complexities attached together, as in a kaleidoscope. When the staff, like the children, disrupts their thinking about the lunchtime behaviour, they contribute to displacing the experience from *the same*, to *something else*.

## *The aporia of undecidability; to be prepared for the unpredictable*

Derrida called the second aporia «the ghost of the undecidable» (1992). Traditionally, we may consider undecidability as something unstable; as losing a foothold in the pedagogical work. However, such an understanding is challenged by regarding undecidability as a necessary element in opening a diversity of perspectives and inclusive and just practice. The practitioners' worries about what they are teaching, or about how they are teaching, exposes the vulnerable side of those responsible for education. Professional practice requires attention, sensitivity, commitment and what Arnesen (2004, 2012) describes as «pedagogical presence».

> Pedagogical presence is based upon an understanding of people as acting and responsible ... [it] is an approach for the individual to become aware of their own resources and opportunities to create inclusive communities with their children, including those that require something extra (Arnesen 2012, p. 254).

The staff's questions deal with something other than losing control; the staff are dealing with responsibility and justice, and need to be aware of their own resources and opportunities to create inclusive communities with all the children. The question, «Is it okay to talk about this at the table?» may involve conditions for development, opportunities to rethink and to act in a responsible and just way. If the way is not «blocked», without obstacles, it may be possible to float away guided by *cruise control*, remaining within what is considered possible and acceptable in a given context. It is through disturbances and ruptures that deconstruction finds its power. It aims to highlight, and take apart, the contradictions that are hidden in what is presented as recognizable and natural. The children, who break into the routines and create obstacles to the flow of the meal, also contribute in assisting the staff to discover something beyond the behaviour of greedy children.

Interestingly, Derrida described deconstruction as a form of «affirmation». This is a different understanding of the term than that mentioned above; an affirmative, confirmed and contextual speech, where the *said* is confirmed and recognized by the staff as *the same*. Deconstruction opens us to the possibility of affirming what has not yet been said or thought. It is not about to affirm the same, or what is already intended, but to confirm something that we still have not discovered, which we have forgotten, or failed, to look for (Larsen, 2010). This has to do with an ethical acknowledgment that involves attention to the *otherness*, to the alterity of the other, to what is different, new and *something else*. «Deconstruction is not a matter of rebuilding. It is a matter of going further, displacing, changing…It is constructing something else, something other, and, in that sense, deconstruction is—if it is—an ethic» (Derrida, 2001, p. 180). The pre-school teacher's assertion that «There is something here that we do not see and to which we do not pay attention» is resistance against simplistic, preconceived performances, and allows for the re-investigation of aspects of the complexity of everyday life (Larsen, 2010; 2012). From this perspective, we can understand Derrida's statement "that deconstruction is justice", because it always has to with the other (Derrida, 2002, p. 36). For Derrida, justice is characterized by caring and openness to the other and regarding anything that may come. In this, undecidability may be seen as key and as a necessity for any decisions (Dobson & Steinsholt, 2009). This implies that, in order to make decisions beyond calculations, one must risk that which cannot be calculated, that which cannot be understood, or that which can be misunderstood. One has to deal with the incalculable and unpredictable situations that are faced.

Based on the present, in what is already available, deconstruction opens up what remains to be considered. In what is already present, lays rules for that which could apply to the new. «A new invention implies that the rules to some extent are challenged or disturbed» (Pålshaugen, 2005, p. 61). The dichotomy of moderation and greediness allows the staff to rethink and deconstruct the rules and the procedures they have constructed for the meal. This should not consist of questions about more of the same, but rather «bending the rules slightly aside» (Pålshaugen, 2005, p. 61) to create new openings.

We will now look at some examples of how the lunchtime narrative makes it possible to discover some more discontinuities and undecidability and how that which is recognizable also opens up new understandings in pedagogical work.

## *To open up to the unexpected*

When the concept of greediness is suspended for a while, uncertainty arises. It is within this process that the focus is displaced.

> *In the long term, it is better to work with the children's attitudes, trying to make them understand themselves. However, when there are five slices of turkey sausage on a table...*

There seems to be a significant reversal alluded to in this quote. That which the staff imagines as a further pedagogical approach, working with children's attitudes, such that the children themselves gradually understand values like sharing and holding back, is being disturbed by the amount of turkey sausage. It is not only the language; the amount of turkey sausage also has some kind of agency.

Gradually, the staff becomes aware that the turkey sausage has a form of agency in the meal and that this is interrupting the routines and rules of the meal.

> *The turkey sausage disappears from all the tables, because there are five slices on each, but those are thick. Since they are so small and because there are so few at the table, it looks tremendous. They are thick, right? The children takes that which there are few of. Do they have to be so thick? No. [Laughter.] You know, they are thick.*

The narrative opens up a complex diversity of new and temporary stories and a multitude of alternative actions. Rethinking is not just about putting things in place in new ways, it is also about being aware that there are lots of ways to put things in position (Reinertsen, 2009). Working with children's attitudes is not the only option, it is just one among many options.

The narrative contributes to opening up to the unexpected. Right from the beginning, the staff are concerned about what to do and how to do things justly and correctly. However; justice is *circumstantial*. The picture changes once the staff get new information. Derrida (2002) pointed out repeatedly that the importance of «distance» and «lack of linearity» could open up new ideas and opportunities in practical life. At the same time, he also problematized this; justice is impossible since it is troubled by aporias and is simultaneously determined by conditions of aporias. «The struggles with universal requirements are of an ethical nature. It is not ethical because it rejects the universalized, but just because it is a struggle» (Steinsholt, 2004, p. 179).

## *The aporia of urgency; to remain in contradiction*

The aporia of undecidability alone would bring *procrastination.* However, the *aporia of urgency* defines this as an impossible instant of hesitation (Edgoose, 2001, p. 129). A just decision is always required immediately. The staff cannot wait to make decisions until they have collected limitless knowledge or have found *the only right thing to do.*

> ...while the educator feels that there is no right choice for his/her attention, he/she understands that a decision must be made. This aporia of urgency reveals that there is no smooth path to justice. In ethical teaching, [...], there are only and necessarily frustrating hesitant steps (Egéa-Kuehne & Biesta, 2001, p. 7).

Undecidability is not only tension between two possible decisions. Undecidability also involves the experience of that which is foreign and different in relation to regulations and what is taken for granted, but which we simultaneously need to take a decision in relation to (Derrida, 2005). What is happening around the meal is a situation that the staff have to deal with without rigorous reflection or deliberation. It necessitates immediate action, «right away», where the staff will always be lacking complete knowledge about the particular context. Their interpretation goes quickly and the executive structure of the meal calls for action. The pre-school teacher considers the situation as follows;

> *One should not moralize or set boundaries in a situation when the children are hungry. Therefore, I stop; I am not saying anything more about it around the table. I'm starting to talk about something friendly.*

Still, the pre-school teacher wonders, «Am I doing right in this situation?» When the meal is over, she writes the narrative and brings it along for further reflection with her colleagues. Only in retrospect can they talk about the experience as a starting point for further critical perspectives and to develop knowledge about their professional practice. Through this, the staff show a willingness to contribute to the collective and individual evaluation and learning processes related to their common activities and professional practice. From an ethical perspective, we might see the staff participation as an answer to, and as taking responsibility for, the children, the lunchtime experience and the pedagogical contextual tradition they are a part of.

To regard the undecidability as a force in pedagogical work is by no means an easy or simple process; this perspective helps as a reminder to work through a constant openness to that which breaks in and intrudes. The practitioner describes these trials as bodily demanding and painful processes. At the same time, they also describe these processes as enjoyable and transformative (Larsen 2012).

## Conclusion

This article has shown some examples of practitioners using narratives as starting points for reflexivity on pedagogical work in a kindergarten context. The narratives usually concern situations where the staff meets resistance, or when something or someone breaks into the pedagogical order and in what is considered *normal* and *proper*. That which is commonly known receives a temporary dispensation to include something else. The tension between the familiar and that which breaks with the familiar demands both lineage and rupture. «As educators, we need to be attentive to the aporetic punctuation of the codes of morality and knowledge that we all too often sell as seamless» (Edgoos, 2001, p. 132). The notion that everyone experiences in the same way, or understands things in the same way, or that anyone else would have done the same, can be understood as an attempt to hide behind the law (*le droit)*. Here, we lean to Derrida's distinction between law and justice (2005). Justice and law are not supposed to be opposites, but to interweave. A synthesis of justice and law is not possible. Both need each other, Derrida writes, yet there is always necessarily a gap between them. Justice is what deconstruction of laws, rules and formal constraints should open up for. This is by no means an easy process. The aporia of justice requires failure, undecidability and urgency; in educational work, a decision must be made. These aporias reveal that there is no smooth path to justice, only necessarily frustrating, hesitant steps (Edgoos, 2001). This paper has shed light on situations where there are some ruptures or contradictions between different values and between law and justice. It is situations where the practitioners consider that there is no possibility of *doing the right thing* without also doing something which may not be right. In such situations, ethical dilemmas arise.

The practitioners' reflective thinking and reading strategies, offering alternative ways of doing pedagogical work and open up processes of inclusion. The staff's experiences of the contextual event are a starting point for conversation that gradually creates reflexivity about regular habits, routines and regulations in daily life. It contributes to opening up a multitude of differentiated knowledge, based on everyday stories. Derrida helps us think about the nature of early childhood education as an ethical site and he shows the importance of developing sensitivity to discontinuities in the practitioners' experience in the kindergarten. Assumptions that there is a text, or a narrative, which can communicate an argument quite clearly and logically, is, in this context, problematic and difficult to maintain. The kind of thinking that engages deconstruction is a kind of thinking that is never finished and which therefore opens up endless ways of doing justice in early childhood education.

## *References*

Allan, J. (2008). *Rethinking Inclusive Education. The Philosophers of Difference in Practice.* Stirling: Springer.

Allan, J. & Slee, R. (2008). Doing inclusive education research. Rotterdam: Sense Publishers.

Allan, J. (2012). Re-thinking inclusion. In Arnesen, A., (Ed.). *Inkludering. Perspektiver i barnehagefaglige praksiser. [Inclusion. Perspectives in professional practices of early childhood education and care].*Oslo: Universitetsforlaget.

Arnesen, A. (2004). *Det pedagogiske nærvær: inkludering i møte med elevmangfold.[The pedagogical presence: Inclusion in meeting with diversity].* Oslo: Abstrakt forlag.

Arnesen, A. (2012). Den komplekse inkluderingen og pedagogiske nærvær. [The complexity of inclusion and pedagogical presence]. In Arnesen, A. (Ed.). *Inkludering. Perspektiver i barnehagefaglige praksiser. [Inclusion Perspectives in professional practices of early childhood education and care].* Oslo:Universitetsforlaget.

Biesta, G. (2006). *Beyond learning: democratic education for a human future.* Boulder, Colo: Paradigm.

Biesta. G.. and Egéan-Kuehne, D. (2001) *Derrida & Education.* London & New York: Routledge.

Derrida, J. (1990). Force of Law: The Mystical Foundation of Authority. Trans. M.Quaintance, *Cardozo Law Review,* 11: 919–1070.

Derrida, J. (1992). *Deconstruction and the Possibility of Justice.* Ed. Drucilla Cornell, Michel Rosenfeld, David Gray Carlson. New York: Routledge, 1992.

Derrida, J. (1997). The Villanova Roundtable: A conversation with Jaques Derrida. In J.D. Caputo (Ed.). *Deconstruction in a Nutshell. A conversation with Jaques Derrida.* New York: Fordham University Press.

Derrida, J. (2001). Talking liberties. Jaques Derrida's interview with Alan Montefiore. In G. Biesta& D. Egéa-Kuehne (Eds.), *Derrida & Education.* New York: Routledge.

Derrida, J. (2002). *Lovens makt. [The force of law].* Oslo: Spartacus Publisher A/S.

Derrida, J. (2005). *Lagens Kraft. [The force of law].* Brutus Östlings Bokförlag Symposion. Stockholm;Stehag.

Dobson, S., & Steinsholt, K. (2009). *Verden satt ut av spill: postmoderne pedagogiske perspektiver. [World put out of action: postmodern pedagogical perspectives].*Trondheim: Tapir akademic publisher.

Edgoose, J. (2001). Just decide! Derrida and the ethical aporias of education. In G. Biesta& D. Egéan-Kuehne, D. (Eds.). *Derrida & Education* (pp. 133-199). Routledge.

Fleer, M., Tonyan, H.A., Mantilla, A.C. & Rivalland, C.M.P. (2009). A cultural-historical analysis of play as an activity setting in early childhood education. In M. Fleer, M. Hedegaard & J. Tudge (Eds.). *Childhood studies and the impact of globalization: Policies and practices at global and local levels* (pp. 292-312). New York: Routledge.

Gulløv, E. (2004). Institutionslogikker som forskningsobjekt. [Institutional logics as research object]. In U. Ambrosius Madsen (Ed.) *Pædagogisk antropologi: Refleksioner over feltbaseret viden (1st ed.). [Educational Anthropology: Reflections on field based knowledge (1st ed.)].*Copenhagen: Hans Reitzel.

Haaland, Ø. (2009). Pedagogikk, postmodernitet og transformasjon. Education, postmodernity and transformation]. In K. Steinsholt, & S. Dobson, S. (Eds.). *Verden satt ut av spill. Postmoderne pedagogiske perspektiver. [The world put out of action: postmodern pedagogical perspectives]* (pp.79–96). Trondheim: Tapir academic publisher.

Hultman, K. (2011). *Barn, linjaler och andra aktörer. Posthumanistiska perspektiv på subjektskapande och materialitet i förskola/skola.[Children, rulers and other actors: Posthumanist perspectives on subjectivity and materiality in pre-school and school.]* [Thesis]. Stockholm: Department of Education, Stockholm University.

*Jackson, A. & Mazzei, L. (2012). Thinking With Theory in Qualitative Research. Viewing Data Across Multiple Perspectives.* NY: Routledge.

Kunnskapsdepartementet.(2011; 2006). *Rammeplan for barnehagens innhold og oppgaver [The framework for the contest and tasks of Kindergartens, Laid down by the Ministry of Education and Research 1th of March 2006, amended by Regulation 10th of January 2011 No. 51].* Oslo: Ministry of Education.

Kunnskapsdepartementet. (2006). *Barnehageloven [The Kindergarten Act].* Oslo: Ministry of Education.

Larsen, A. S. (2010). Dokumentasjoners kraft til å skape bevegelse og oppmerksomhet. [The documentations forces to create movement and awareness].In B. Aamotsbakken (Ed.), *Læring og medvirkning. [Learning and participation]* (pp.153–165) Oslo: Universitetsforlaget.

Larsen, A. S. (2012). Hvordan stop skapte nye vilkår for praksis. [How stops creates new conditions for practice]. In Arnesen, A., (Ed.). *Inkludering. Perspektiver i barnehagefaglige praksiser. [Inclusion. Perspectives in professional practices of early childhood education and care].*Oslo: Universitetsforlaget.

Lenz Taguchi, H. (2006). *In på bara benet. En introduksjon till feministisk poststrukturalism. [In to the bone: An introduction to feminist poststructuralism].* Stockholm: HLS Publisher.

Lenz Taguchi, H. (2010). *Bortenfor skillet mellom teori og praksis: en introduksjon til intra-aktiv pedagogikk i barnehagefeltet. [Tranls. Ane Sjøbu]. [Going beyond the theory: practice divide in early childhood education: introducing an intra-active pedagogy].* Bergen: Fagbokforlaget.

Olsson, L.M. (2009). *Movement and experimentation in young children's learning: Deleuze and Guattari in early childhood education.* Abingdon/New York: Routledge.

Pålshaugen, Ø.(2005). Dekonstruksjon, en oppfinnelse av Derrida? [Deconstruction, an invention by Derrida?] Agora, *Journal for metafysisk spekulasjon,* 1–2.

Reinertsen, A.(2009). Vurdering som læring innenfor en usikkerhetspedagogikk. [Assessment as learning within a pedagogy of uncertainty]. In S. Dobson, A. Eggen & K. Smith (Eds.). *Vurdering, prinsipper og praksis. Nye perspektiver på elev- og læringsvurderinger. [Assessment, policies and practice. New perspectives on students' learning and assessment].*Oslo: Gyldendal Akademisk.

Sandvik, N. (2012). Re-thinking the idea/ideal of pedagogical control: considering de/stabilizing intensities. *Contemporary Issues in Early Childhood Education*, 13(2).

Spivak, G. C. (1976). *Transator's preface to J. Derrida, Of Grammatology,* Baltimore: Johns Hopkins University Press.

Steinsholt, K. (2004). *Steinsholt LIVE.* Trondheim: Tapir academic publisher.

Steinsholt, K. (2009). Enhver beslutning må være avsindig. Noe om det ubestemmelige grunnlaget for pedagogiske beslutninger. [Any decision must be mad. Something about the indeterminate foundation for pedagogical decisions]. In *Verden satt ut av spill.Postmoderne pedagogiske perspektiver. [The world put out of action: postmodern pedagogical perspectives]* (pp.79–96).Trondheim: Tapir academic publisher.

AUTHOR: Ann Sofi Larsen is Senior Lecturer and PhD student at Østfold University College (HiØ). She is affiliated to the PhD Programme; *Interdisciplinary Child Research at Norwegian Centre for Child Research (*NOSEB) at the Faculty of Social Sciences and Technology Management (NTNU) in Trondheim, Norway. Professor Randi Dyblie Nilsen (NTNU) and Professor Anne-Lise Arnesen (HiØ) are supervising for Ms. Larsen's PhD project: «Professional practice and inclusion; disruption as possible inputs to dwell on ethical actions and issues of inclusion». In 2008-2012, Ms. Larsen participated in the research project, «The work in kindergartens to enhance inclusion for children with special needs, viewed from a professional perspective», led by Professor Arnesen. Correspondence: ann.s.larsen@hiof.no

# *Teachers' development of practice*

## A STRUGGLE FOR VISIBILITY, INFLUENCE AND RECOGNITION

TOVE STEEN-OLSEN
The University College of Sør-Trøndelag, Norway

ABSTRACT: *The article discusses a completed research and development project aimed at finding ways to improve teachers' assessment methods and develop a Norwegian school into a learning organization. The project used a bottom-up design, in which action learning based on colleague observations and systematic sharing of knowledge and reflections was employed to enhance knowledge creation and collective learning. A further important aim was to develop a sustainable practice that would persist after the researchers had left the field. The article explores the teachers' learning experiences in a follow-up study two years after the departure of the researchers. The teachers' learning is studied in the frame of agency and discursive practices, and in this respect the influence of structural and individual factors is discussed. The results indicate that the teachers gained in terms of the work related to development. However, they struggled individually when not acting collectively in their efforts to establish a learning organization.*

### *Introduction*

This article elaborates on the outcome of a completed research and development (R&D) project based in a Norwegian combined primary school and lower secondary school,[1] where two researchers and a team of 17 teachers collaborated for

[1] In Norway, grades 1–7 (for ages 6–13 years) are taught in *barneskole* (i.e. primary school), and grades 8–10 (for ages 13–16 years) are taught in *ungdomsskole*, (i.e. lower secondary school). Some Norwegian schools teach all 10 grades within the same school.

two years (2006–2008) (Steen-Olsen & Postholm, 2009).[2] The overriding aim of the project was to develop the school into a learning organization. The school is a comprehensive elementary suburban school for grades 1–10, with 40 teachers and 500 pupils. The pupils were mainly from middle-class families and a few were immigrants. The teachers were organized into three working teams: one team for the lowest grades (hereafter referred to as Team 1), one team for the middle grades (Team 2), and one team for the highest grades (Team 3). Each team conducted an R&D project in collaboration with outside researchers. In the case of Team 1, on which our project was closely based, the aims were development of formative assessment strategies and turning the school into a learning organization.

Drawing on the knowledge that collective ambitions to develop organizations from the inside have previously given good results, the project was based on a bottom-up design (Argyris & Schön, 1978). It was set out from the start that the teachers should have a high level of autonomy in the project, and therefore they decided which areas of their practice they wanted to develop. During the development work, the teachers used planned strategies such as colleague observations and systematic sharing of experience, reflections, and knowledge to enhance collective learning. By deliberately reinforcing the teachers' ownership of the project, the aim was to generate sustainable practices that would endure after the researchers had left the school. Findings at the end of the development work indicated that the majority of the teachers had developed enthusiasm and ownership of the project, and that almost all of them wanted to continue with the development work on their own. Two years later, in a follow-up study, it was found that the number of teachers willing to continue had declined significantly.

This article studies the teachers' learning experiences two years after the development work ended, by addressing the following research questions: Did the teachers continue the development after the researchers had left the school? Did the project contribute to develop a learning organization? In what way was the teachers' knowledge disseminated throughout the school? Discussion of the research questions addresses organizational factors related to authority, priority, and resources, and individual factors related to agency, strategies, and practice. Data are discussed by contextualizing the development work to the ideas of a

[2] The project was funded by the Research Council of Norway

learning organization (Argyris & Schön, 1978; Senge, 1990; 2007; von Krogh, Ichijo, & Nonaka, 2000), and in this context the teachers' strategies are studied within the frame of agency and discursive practices (Chouliaraki & Fairclough, 1999; Fairclough, 1995; Giddens, 1984).

The article is structured in the following way. First, the research project and the methodology are introduced. Thereafter, the strategies for knowledge creation in the development work are outlined, followed by factors in organizational learning. This is followed by a presentation of the conceptual framework of the study, and then a discussion of the findings of the empirical study. The article concludes with comments on the teachers' development of practice in the frame of a learning organization.

## *Background and methodology*

When the project started in 2006, the school was already participating in five other small development studies. There was a positive attitude towards development work among the teachers and on the part of the school's principal. Nevertheless, we[3] noted that in general the teachers strived to obtain sufficient time for all tasks (Steen-Olsen & Eikseth, 2010). We also noted that there were status hierarchies connected to the teachers' positions, ranked according to their tuition levels, from higher grades to low grades. In seminars where all teachers were assembled, teachers of lower grades did not receive the best attention.

Due to retirement, a new principal joined the school in the autumn of 2007, and she carried out an evaluation to map the teachers' opinions of the usefulness of our ongoing R&D work. The teachers' answers included indications of positive experiences: '*It is useful to have allocated time and place for reflection. ... It has been helpful to share and learn from each other.*' In addition, they found it instructive to observe each other's teaching practices, and subsequently to discuss and reflect upon their experience. Regarding the question of whether the teachers would continue the development work on their own after the researchers had left the school, most teachers answered that they would do so, provided that they were granted extra resources for knowledge-sharing activities. Further, the

---

[3] In this article, 'we' is used when referring to collaborative research activities involving the two researchers and the 17 teachers in Team 1. My research colleague was Astrid G. Eikseth.

teachers suggested that project activities should be discussed at their weekly teacher forum and that a leader should be appointed to take responsibility for continuation of the development work. The teachers' suggestions expressed a genuine desire to formalize the knowledge-sharing activities and make them a permanent part of the school's structure. During the period of the development work, a combination of project grants and school grants had enabled the school's administration able to give the teachers extra weekly time resources in order to participate in the development work.

In our R&D project, the point of departure was to establish a common platform and an inter-subjective understanding of what was functioning well and what could be developed in the teachers' practices. For the researchers, it was important to spend time to anchor the project in the teachers' practice from day one, and to ground the research questions in the teachers' wish for practice development. The work started with a dialogue during which we formulated questions and future plans on the basis of present practice. Active teacher and student participation were guiding principles in the project, and therefore action research combined with action learning was a useful approach. In action research, a spiral model of planning, implementation, gathering of data, reflections, and evaluations, and new planning was used (Carr & Kemmis, 1986; Coghlan & Brannick, 2005).

In action learning, ownership, structured reflections, and active participation are critical factors, and both willingness to volunteer and engagement are essential for successful work (Argyris, 2003; Revans, 1982; Tiller, 2006). Accordingly, from the outset, we emphasized that this was the teachers' project and that we were there to guide and support them. Moreover, we would not necessarily give answers, but would be willing to provide input if and when the situation called for it. According to the teachers, the researchers' appointed times for implementations, observations, meeting places, and feedback were significant elements in the progress of their action learning. Opportunities for knowledge sharing among the teachers included meetings on cooperative planning and reflections, held between all 17 colleagues in Team 1, and during observations of colleagues teaching the same classes and subsequent reflection meetings. The researcher(s)[4]

[4] In addition to working collectively with all teachers in Team 1, the reseachers also worked separately with individual teachers and with small groups of teachers. Thus, whereas

took part in all activities. In addition to full-day knowledge-sharing seminars held for members of all three teacher teams at the end of each half year, which were also attended by the leadership[5], the teachers participated in full-day planning meetings and training seminars with invited lecturers.

Before we left the school in the spring of 2008, the teachers and the researchers cooperated to develop simplified strategies for the continued development work. However, some unanswered questions remained regarding the further implementation of the project: Did the teachers continue the project? Did they integrate the new assessment methods in their daily work, or did they return to their earlier practices? How was their development work supported by the new principal? Had the school developed into a learning organization as a consequence of establishing structured systems for knowledge-sharing activities within and between the teacher teams?

The methodological approach of the project drew on a single case study (Creswell, 1998; Denzin & Lincoln, 2000; Stake, 2000). In the empirical study we used multiple sources of information to explore the development work and the process of collective learning. The data were collected during two years of fieldwork, mainly from teacher Team 1, where development of formative assessment methods and learning goals were focused. The data consist of field notes, video- and audio-taped recordings of the following: observations made in classrooms, knowledge sharing, reflection meetings, team meetings, staff meetings, and individual and group interviews with the teachers at the beginning (2006) and end (2008) of the study, and in a follow-up study two years later (2010). In addition, two succeeding principals were interviewed. The researchers were present and participated in all activities that were video or tape recorded, and also took field notes during those times. The frequency of the researchers' visits to the school varied, but on average we spent four to five weeks with the teachers each half year in the course of the two-year period. All recordings were transcribed and analysed using the constant comparative method (Strauss & Corbin, 1998). In order to distinguish particular characteristics in the coding and categorizing process, data were structured and reduced, and in order to understand how the

---

my colleague worked with teachers of grades 1–2 in the first year of the study and 1–3 in the second year, I worked with teachers of grades 3–4 in the first year, and 4–5 in the second year.

[5] In this article, the term 'leadership' refers to the principal and teachers with administrative functions in the school's leader group. Here too, 'leader' is synonymous with 'principal'.

different parties expressed their agency discursively and to analyse how conflicting interests might influence the teachers' continued development work, critical discourse analysis was applied (Chouliaraki & Fairclough, 1999; Fairclough, 1995).

## *Action research – roles, relations, and knowledge- creation processes*

Action research blurs the boundaries between teachers and researchers, 'knowers' and 'doers', and experts and learners. The research role of an action researcher holds multiple and sometimes conflicting functions, as such researchers can function as participant and observer, collaborator and leader, and learner and coach in the same study. At the outset of our project we worked on developing mutual understanding of aims and roles, and on establishing trustful relations. Willingness on the part of teachers to open up to outside researchers the classroom over a long period of time requires trust and confidence (Hargreaves, 2002). In this regard, Punch (1994) provides three useful guidelines for field researchers: (1) the researcher needs social acceptance in order to gain access to and participate in the working community, (2) full identification prevents necessary distance and perspective, and (3) the researcher should bear in mind that they are a guest in the domain of the practitioners, and when their fieldwork ends, their guest role ends too.

In our research project, the knowledge-creation process started with a reflexive learning approach by mirroring the participants' development work. Møller (1996) distinguishes between three levels of reflexivity. The first level is integrated in action, and can only be understood as part of such action. The second level arises when an actor suddenly sees things in a new way, often provoked by a problem. The third level is systematic and continuous meta-reflection, which demands more thorough consideration. In order to contribute to self-development and to ensure that the rate of knowledge creation in action learning exceeds the rate of day-to-day problem solving, it is significant to reflect and dwell upon experience. In our project the teachers reflected collectively on their experiences, and the researchers contributed as 'critical friends' (Carr & Kemmis, 1986). Rewinding audio tape or video recordings of practical situations proved to be a useful tool in reflection meetings. The researcher initiated the processes of knowledge sharing and thereafter the participants collectively reflected on whether the development work was going in the right direction. Reflexive and reflective activity, critical questions, disagreements, and challenges all contributed to the learning process. Disagreement was not considered negative, but rather as possibly generating further developments and new understanding. Valid knowledge is questionable, adjustable, and arises from a contextual reality (Strand, 2001). In our action research, knowledge was created in collective processes of interpretations and negotiations. In these processes, systematic self-reflexivity and self-reflection paved the way for collective learning. Action learning is a successive process where each step rests upon foregoing discussions, decisions, and conclusions. When the process ended, the participants were able to look back on a mutual learning and development process. Process-oriented learning, like action learning, deals with personal development in a social context (Fullan, 2001). This kind of learning takes time, and in order to achieve successful action learning it is imperative to create a context in which participants cooperate and trust each other.

The research role in action research also involves guidance, and this demands sensitivity, involvement, empathy, and closeness to the participants. Furthermore, it demands an understanding of situations, interactions, and relations, and confirmation that ethical dimensions in a research partnership will be preserved. Two separate research fields have contributed to a more severe focus on ethical issues in field research, namely action research and feminist studies (Punch, 1994). The growth in action research has been a major contributor to the building of ethical principles within field research. Within this tradition, research subjects are regarded as active participants in collaborative and deliberative research processes (Carr & Kemmis, 1986; Coghlan & Brannick, 2005). The code of ethics is based on democratic values, equality, and openness. Relations within projects are based on mutual trust and responsibility, and on agreement that private spaces should be respected. Since action research aims at empowering the participants, the demand for honesty is an underlying ethos. The complementary roles in action research imply recognition of participants' resources and differences, and mutual respect is necessary in order to maintain the balance between participants. However, the principle of equality is probably the most important ethic.

The research tradition that has grown out of the women's liberation movement has contributed to more widespread emphasis on dimensions such as identification, trust, empathy, and equal relations, and to an agreement that all kinds of exploitation in research should be abolished. The women's liberation movement has been especially preoccupied with imbalance in power relations in terms of gender, social background, social status, and ethnicity. Hence, solidarity with research subjects has been an important ethos for feminist researchers, and the way that research informants are perceived has shifted from them being viewed as passive objects, to being regarded as equal and active subjects. Subject-object relations, where research participants are devalued to objects produce suppressive positions. In such relations there is little room for dialogical and pedagogical encounters, self–development, and personal growth (Arnesen, 2004; 2012). In feminist research, personal involvement and the establishment of relationships based on mutual trust are significant aims (Arnesen, 1995; Harding, 1986; Smith, 1987; 1990). In our project, the practitioners and the researchers had equal status, and above all, as researchers we wanted to be self-reflexive, listening, and constructive co-workers in the visited research field (Steen-Olsen, 2010).

## *Organizational learning – structural and individual factors*

Nonaka and Takeuchi (1995) offer a useful conceptual framework for approaching organizational learning. By drawing on Polanyi's (1967) distinctions between implicit and explicit knowledge, they have developed a spiral model of knowledge creation. Whereas implicit knowledge is personal and context-specific, explicit knowledge is formal and transmittable. Through processes of sharing, interaction, observation, collective reflection, and reconfiguration, knowledge may be converted from implicit to explicit knowledge through the modes of socialization, externalization, combination, and internalization. In this study, the last three modes are relevant. The mode of externalization means to be able to express implicit personal knowledge, whereas the mode of combination denotes reconfiguration of existing individual knowledge into shared knowledge at organizational level. The mode of internalization refers to making new knowledge personal and applicable. With this in mind, teachers' insights into one another's tacit and implicit knowledge may contribute to their professional development and collective learning.

In organizational learning, structural and individual factors are influential. In the case of structural factors, resources such as time and economy, and also arrangements for regular learning activities are significant (Argyris & Schön, 1978; Fullan & Hargreaves, 1991). Further, in order to establish a learning organization, structural factors such as preparation and arrangements for cooperative learning and knowledge sharing are needed. Moreover, in order to succeed at an organizational level, scheduled time and space for learning activities should be incorporated in schools' administrative plans (Senge, 2007). A school's learning culture is closely tied to its organizational plans for internal learning, and before changes towards a learning organization can be seen, knowledge has to be elevated to an organizational level (cf. the mode of combination). According to Senge (1990), typical traits of a learning organization are mutual obligations between the individuals and the organization, and that new learning is translated into observed behaviour (cf. the mode of internalization). When learning and development, both individual and collective, are integrated in a continuous process in teachers' daily practices, their school is turned into a learning organization. Basic hallmarks of a learning organization are openness, trust, and supportive relations between colleagues. Reciprocal commitment in a community of colleagues makes collective learning more rewarding than learning alone. Collaboration between teachers and management is a decisive factor in this process (Senge, 2007).

In the case of individual factors, ownership, relevance, and professional autonomy are significant (Argyris & Schön, 1978; von Krogh et al., 2000). The core of successful organizational change is individuals' experiences of meaningful change. Even the most convincing school development project may create problems if it reduces the teachers' opportunities to act autonomously (Hargreaves, 2002; Steen-Olsen, 2011). The teaching profession has a long-established tradition of working alone, and teaching has been associated with a high degree of autonomy and independence. In the past, the socialization of teachers has supported the image of an individual professional (Lortie, 1975; Thomson & Halloway, 1997). Also, recent research indicates that teachers' learning is directed more by individual learning than by collective learning (Flores, 2001). Educational research has documented that teachers' tradition of working alone can create conservatism and resistance to collective learning, and that collective learning and lack of real opportunities for choice can be experienced as devaluation of teachers' professional autonomy (Fullan & Hargreaves, 1991; Sachs, 2001). Further, classroom research may be experienced as a threat against the professional self-value of teachers (Hargreaves, 2002). Consequently, the supportive role of school leaders is significant in encouraging and enhancing teachers' professional development. One of the most decisive factors for teachers' professional development is how they are valued by their leaders (Elmore, 2000; Lillejord, 2003; Møller, 1996; Postholm, 2011).

## *Agency, power relations, and discursive practice*

Within critical discourse analysis the central methodological aim is to map connections between text and context, and language and social practice (Chouliaraki & Fairclough, 1999; Fairclough, 1995). Another central point is to recognize power relations taking place in different positions. On the subject of describing power relations, Chouliaraki and Fairclough (1999, p. 24) argue that power in the sense of domination figures at the level of particular practices and relational positions, '*such that some are able to incorporate the agency of others into their own actions and thus reduce the autonomous agency capacity of the latter*'. Discourses are a form of social practice empowered to reproduce and change knowledge, identities, and social relations, including power relations. Within critical discourse analysis, discourses are regarded as a dialectical form of social practice, in which they produce social practice and in turn are reproduced by social practice. Discursive practice is a function of invisible rules of power distribution, controlling what are to be considered 'correct' meanings, values, and policies. When a given discursive practice creates hegemony, other discursive practices might be suppressed or excluded. Such power is productive because it reproduces social practice. In daily life, practices can become so fixed or taken for granted that they no longer are disputed. However, when a social practice becomes fixed, it becomes non-discursive and reproductive, and thus difficult to change.

Critical discourse analysis is used as a theoretical framework, and as a method for identifying power relations in data analysis, and also to provide examples of discursive practices in the establishment of learning organizations.

Analyses of educational discourses can be made by looking at their strength to reproduce power relations and hegemonies within and between groups (Fairclough, 1995). A central point is to recognize changes in power relations and positions of dominance. In the data analysis related to our project, I looked for discursive practices and power relations related to different interests. The methodical and analytical framework used to identify traits and patterns in the data was the study of texts, discursive practices related to group interests, and social practices. As part of the analytical work, discursive practices, as well as the function that these practices have in promoting the interests of individuals and groups were studied. In addition, texts were analysed in the context of the fieldwork. First, I analysed statements in written interview texts. Thereafter, I looked for conflicting interests related to positions and discursive practices, and finally I looked for conflicts related to discursive order and hegemonies expressed by the parties involved. The process of analysis was supported by the video and audio recordings and the field notes. Throughout the data analysis, I looked for discursive and social practices related to group interests and power relations.

In the start-up phase of the project, we noticed that regardless of the teachers' awareness of malfunctioning practices, they did not have time to stop and reflect in order to change them. Instead, they seemed constantly to be trapped in time intensification and in shortness of time. Giddens (1984) refers to how social structures can maintain social practice, even when the practices do not function well, and that practice can be altered through discursive and reflexive actions. Unreflected routines may act as barriers to change, and the taken-for-granted character of daily routines may serve to inhibit change. Instead of looking at the possibility to act in new ways, it may be easier to continue with old habits and routines. Social practice is a function of rules and resources constructed in the meeting between individual and structural properties. Structuring rules and resources contribute to the production of practice contextually, and in turn to reproduce contextual conditions. This is what constitutes the duality of structures. Strategic action is to make use of available rules and resources in order to overcome structural hindrances. Agency, or autonomous action, presupposes strategic action, and agency and strategic action can be means to establish autonomous professional practice. What Giddens aims to show us, is that the properties of given structures do not necessarily restrict agents' alternatives. By acting strategically, an agent can act in new and surprising ways, and thus avoid being a victim of an established system. Giddens' contribution is valuable in order to understand the ruling principles of agency and social practice, but he elaborates little on the distribution of power.

## *Teachers' development of practice – a struggle to be valued*

The focus of this article is an exploration of the teachers' learning experience two years after a development work was completed. In this section, I consider the following questions: Did the teachers continue the development work, or did they return to their earlier routines? Did they have the opportunity to share their knowledge across the teacher teams at the school, and thus to contribute to a learning organization? Did they experience support and recognition of their work from the leadership?

During the development work the teachers applied collective learning activities in collaborative planning and colleague observations, and sharing of knowledge and experience in reflection meetings. Prior to any planned observations, the teachers sent a planning document to their colleagues who would be observing and a copy to the researcher. In the planning document, which contained descriptions of the subject, activities, and aims of the lesson to be observed, they added topics for requested feedback from their observers. This type of collective learning, whereby teachers gained insight into each other's practice, proved successful. The teachers highly valued their colleagues' comments on their practice, and through questions forwarded to them, they were able to reflect on their practice in new ways. One of the teachers said: '*The reflections I shared with my colleagues and the researcher afterwards were very useful because they enabled me to discover things I had not seen before. In fact, they made me see my practice in a new way.*' In this case, the teacher's implicit knowledge had been challenged and externalized. Through systematic observations and reflections the teachers were able to externalize, combine, and internalize knowledge, and they expressed that this was insightful an way of reflecting added to their knowledge development (cf. Nonaka & Takeuchi, 1995); one of the teachers expressed: '*By observing my colleagues' teaching methods, I became more aware of my own*' (cf. Møller, 1996).

Knowledge-sharing seminars across the teacher teams opened up the means for making implicit knowledge explicit. However, due to a slight gap in relations between teachers of lower and higher grades, it was difficult to achieve collaborative learning across the teacher teams. For some teachers, comprehensive cooperation across the teams was not desirable, and consequently knowledge sharing at combination mode level was not as successful as hoped. Teachers of higher grades felt that themes related to lower grades were less relevant to their teaching and that discussing such themes was not the best use of their time. A teacher in teacher Team 3 expressed: '*Probably there is no culture for knowledge sharing across all teacher teams at the school*' (Wiken, 2010, p. 47).

During the first year of the project we often heard that teachers found their days so hectic that they had no time to reflect. Furthermore, team time had to be used for planning purposes, not for reflection purposes (Steen-Olsen & Eikseth, 2010). Close to the end of the development work in the spring of 2008, we noted that the teachers had started to change their work attitudes by reinterpreting demands from management in order to adapt their workload to the time available. By using less time for planning and more time for reflection, the teachers created space for rethinking their work situation and thereby changed their practice from being non-discursive to becoming discursive (Chouliaraki & Fairclough, 1999). Prior to when the teachers developed their ability to reflect and analyse their practice and working conditions, their actions had been driven more by routines than by possibilities to change those routines and to exert influence on the school system. Having developed their ability to reflect on actions, they used agency to create new structures for their work situation. In the conceptual view of 'the dualities of structures' (Giddens, 1984), the teachers created their own rules of actions, which in turn created a basis for discursive practices. By the spring of 2008, the majority of the teachers felt enthusiasm and a sense of ownership of the development work, and almost all of them wanted to continue. This finding is in line with the results of the evaluation made by the new principal in late autumn 2007. Two years later, the number had declined significantly. To understand this change, I had to search for explanations also outside the teacher team.

The new principal's evaluation in the autumn of 2007 expressed a positive attitude towards our project. In an interview with her in the spring of 2008, she stated that her impression was that '*Nine out of ten teachers are very positive, and they say that they have learned a lot.*' However, from her perspective there were some challenges related to the project. First, there was a need to steer and control what was going on in the school. As a new principal, it was imperative for her to point out a new direction for the school's visions in a personal way, and to focus on new projects. In the interview, she underlined, '*When I came to the school I did feel some expectations that I should front a new vision or a new direction.*' Second, after the economic contributions from our project had come to an end, there were fewer grants for development work at the school. This restricted the management's opportunity for giving the teachers extra resources in the form of time and money. Also, the new principal believed that the development work was more self-sustaining than it actually was: '*The project is so well integrated in the teachers' practices that it may survive also without the researchers.*'

In the group interviews held with the teachers in the follow-up study in 2010, we were informed that management decisions did not coincide with the teachers' professional plans, and that the teachers' requests for scheduled time and space for collective learning had been ignored. One of the teachers said: '*I am a member of the leader group now and have applied for scheduled time for project activities on several occasions, but I am not able to make myself heard because such time is not prioritized by the management.*' Also during the interviews, the teachers said that their plan to extend portfolio assessment methods to the other teacher teams at the school had not been fulfilled. During the project period, the teachers had developed plans for grades 1 to 5, and had intended to continue to make plans for higher grades.[6] However, one of the teachers stated: '*The fact is that portfolio assessment has been downgraded at our school.*' Not only had formative assessment methods been a focus area in the teachers' development work for two years, but also the school's leadership had decided that this would be a target area even before we started the development project. Furthermore, formative assessment methods had become the target area for the entire school as from 2010, as a new national campaign (2010–2014)[7] demanded that all Norwegian schools developed learning goals and criteria for goal attainment. This was exactly what we had been doing in our project.

[6] Many of the teachers varied their teaching activities between grades 1 to 10, and in this way they were familiar with teachers' work for other grades.

[7] The Norwegian Directorate for Education and Training: Assessment for Learning (2010–2014).

When conducting the follow-up study in the spring of 2010, during a coffee break we accidentally became observers of a staff meeting where all staff members were assembled. On the agenda was a discussion of the new national assessment directives, and in this regard we noted the formation of a school slogan: the school administration had projected '*This is how we do it in our school*' onto a big screen on one of the walls. This was followed by a lecture by an administrative representative of the leader group. Clearly, the school's leadership was struggling to find a way to meet the new national assessment directives, but without recognizing that a competent group of teachers within the school already knew much about the directives. The knowledge the aforementioned teachers had developed during two years of intensive collaborative work was neither recognized nor acknowledged as a valuable resource at the school.

There might have a number of reasons for the neglect of the teachers' experience of the national assessment directives. One of them might have concerned the school's internal micro-politics and the hierarchical structures among the teachers. Power relations connected to the teachers' instruction level seemed to have created unwritten rules regarding the right to decide the knowledge discourse (Chouliaraki & Fairclough, 1999). Time allocation has long been a central element in the structuring of teachers' work, and time resources mirror status and power relations within school systems, and hence teachers' disposal of time might have micro-political importance (Steen-Olsen & Eikseth, 2010). In schools in general, it has been noted that teachers of lower grades spend practically their entire day working closely with pupils, whereas teachers of higher grades are more independent in their use of time (Hargreaves, 1994). This situation is confirmed by our findings.

Another possible reason for the neglect of the teachers' experience could have been that teaching lower grades is not associated with formal assessment – as pupils in Norway are not graded until they reach a level equivalent to lower secondary school (grades 8–10) – and that the management did not consider assessment skills as a topic that teachers of lower grades knew much about. Although Norwegian schools administer national tests also at lower levels, the greatest pressure in terms of assessment takes place in lower secondary schools. This might have obscured the teachers' assessment knowledge as a valuable resource in the school community. The knowledge discourse at the school was that topics presented by teachers of lower grades were not interesting for teachers of higher grades, and that sharing across all teacher teams was not considered a valuable use of time.

In addition to finding hierarchical structures and contradictions between lower and higher instruction levels at the school, a somewhat more surprising finding in the follow-up study was that there also were contradictions within the teacher teams, indicating conflicting strategies. During the development work, one of the teachers' strategies had been to define their tasks in new ways. Another strategy had been to voice their need for extra resources in order to continue the development work. In the follow-up study in 2010, we noted that a teacher who had continued the development work on her own, and who had managed to integrate the development work into her daily practice – without extra resources – had not received any support from her fellow colleagues. The teacher had been very enthusiastic and an active driving force in Team 1 throughout the project period, but after the end of the project there was evidently pressure exerted by colleagues within the teacher team not to carry out 'extra' work unless they were granted extra resources – a strategy that was in line with their request to the new principal in the autumn of 2007. The above-mentioned teacher's personal strategy seemed to be perceived as a threat against the other teachers' strategy to secure resources.

## *Discussion and conclusion*

Hallmarks of a school as learning organization are sustainable systems of knowledge sharing, a collaborative school culture, and acknowledgement of all knowledge resources in a school (Senge, 1990). Despite the teachers lobbying in the autumn of 2007 for the establishment of permanent systems for knowledge sharing, no such system was enabled after the study project ended in the spring of 2008. The sharing of knowledge across the teacher teams had been an imperative aim of the project, but due to hierarchies among the teams, the mode of combination did not turn out to be successful. Two colleagues, who were working on a cooperating subproject at the same school, commented:

> Evidently, knowledge-sharing activities at the individual and team level at the school allowed for creation moments to occur. However, knowledge did not always flow easily and straightforwardly during activities that were

> meant to enhance knowledge creation across all teaching teams (Rismark & Sølvberg, 2011, p. 157).

At the organization level, structural factors that restricted the teachers' knowledge sharing were hierarchical structures, power relations among colleagues, lack of collaborative sharing systems, and lack of recognition of the teachers' knowledge resources at all instruction levels (Chouliaraki & Fairclough, 1999). At the individual level, I found that only teachers who had demonstrated strong professional autonomy and ownership of the project had continued with the development work. These teachers did not emphasize lack of resources as a major hindrance for doing development work. By contrast, teachers who had been less enthusiastic or active during the project period overemphasized the lack of resources or blamed the leadership for not giving priority to their development work (Giddens, 1984).

In a learning organization, teachers are expected to support each other in collaborative and trustful relations (Argyris & Schön, 1978; Senge, 1990; 2007; von Krogh et al., 2000). However, instead of finding the supportive, collective actions and united commitment of a learning organization, I found division among teachers when some among them struggled individually to establish a learning organization. Despite their battle to be acknowledged as competent teachers, holding knowledge relevant for the entire school, their knowledge resources were not recognized. Paradoxically, their knowledge was overlooked at a time when their expertise was needed in the school. Formative assessment with focus on learning goals, which had been the topic of our subproject, subsequently became the government's new priority programme and the target area for the entire school's development work, but without recognizing the knowledge of teacher Team 1.

The most central factors for knowledge creation on the route to becoming a learning organization can be summarized as follows:

1. *Structural and leadership factors essential to establish a learning organization*

   Organizational systems for reflection and knowledge sharing, efforts to elevate knowledge creation to an organizational level, acknowledgement of competences and knowledge resources in an organization

2. *Individual factors essential for teachers to continue development work*
Agency, strategies to overcome structural obstacles, enthusiasm, initiative and ownership during development work, professional autonomy, and supportive collaborative work.

All of the teachers, regardless of their degree of participation or enthusiasm for the project, agreed that the supportive attitude of the first principal, which had been a significant success factor during the first year of the project, was not followed up the second year. After a positive attitude towards the R&D project in the first autumn of her office, the new principal later had more focus on projects that she had initiated, and more focus on steering and control. In addition, she had believed that the R&D project was more self-sustaining than it actually was.

In retrospect, I am left with the impression that individual teachers had expanded their knowledge, and the knowledge that the most enthusiastic among them had continued the development work on their own. Their request for permanent systems for knowledge sharing reflected awareness of the value of making implicit knowledge explicit (Nonaka & Takeuchi, 1995). With regard to the structural level, the school's effort to develop into a learning organization was less successful. However, process-oriented organizational learning such as discussed above takes time, and the school had made a start towards becoming a learning organization.

Collective learning deals with more than learning; it deals with how knowledge is dispersed and used in a social community. Senge's (1990) fifth discipline, the integrative discipline (cf. the mode of combination) deals with how learning organizations create knowledge. By operating at the system level, such organizations are able to combine knowledge, and by lifting collective learning to a higher level of capacity they are able to enhance new insights. Further, such organizations develop learning communities that bind the members of the organizations together. When there are collaborative exchanges of ideas in which differing perspectives are aired and shared, exchanges of insight gained at individual and group levels may be fully realized at organizational level. In conclusion, school leaders who value and appreciate organizational learning, and who arrange for such learning to take place on an individual basis as well as on a collective basis, contribute significantly to schools as learning organizations. Development-oriented leaders who are able to forward teachers' knowledge and competence in such a way that all colleagues in a responsible way contribute productively to the learning community pave the way to organizational collective learning.

## *References*

Argyris, C. (2003). *Actionable knowledge.* In T. Tsoukas & C. Knudsen (Eds.), The Oxford handbook of organization theory. Oxford: Oxford University Press.

Argyris, C. & Schön, D. (1978). *Organizational learning: A theory of action perspective. Reading,* MA: Addison-Wesley.

Arnesen, A.-L. (1995). *Gender an equality as quality in school and teacher education: Final report from the 3-year Nordic projects on Gender and Equal Opportunities in Teacher Education. Aprostrof Special Edition A/95.* Oslo: Nordisk Ministerråd/Høgskolen i Oslo.

Arnesen, A.-L. (2004). *Det pedagogiske nærvær: Inkludering i møte med elevmangfold [The pedagogic encounter: Inclusion and student diversity].* Oslo: Abstrakt Forlag.

Arnesen, A.-L. (2012). Kjærlighet til menneskene – interesse og engasjement [Love to the people – interest and engagement]. In A.-L. Arnesen (Ed.), *Inkludering: Perspektiver i barnehagefaglige praksiser [Inclusion: Perspectives in preschool practices]* (pp. 254–271). Oslo: Universitetsforlaget.

Carr, W. & Kemmis, S. (1986). *Becoming critical: Education, knowledge and action research.* London: Falmer Press.

Chouliaraki, L. & Fairclough, N. (1999). *Discourse in late modernity: Rethinking critical discourse analysis.* Edinburgh: Edinburgh University Press.

Coghlan, D. & Brannick, T. (2005). *Doing action research in your own organization* (2nd ed.). London: Sage.

Creswell, J. W. (1998). *Qualitative inquiry and research design.* Thousand Oaks, CA: Sage.

Denzin, N. K. & Lincoln, Y. S. (2000). The discipline and practice of qualitative research. In N. K. Denzin & Y. S. Lincoln (Eds.), *Handbook of qualitative* research (pp. 1–28). London: Sage.

Elmore, R. F. (2000). Building a new structure for school leadership. *American Educator*, 23(4), 1–9.

Fairclough, N. (1995). *Critical discourse analysis*. London: Longman.

Flores, M. (2001). Person and context in becoming a new teacher. *Journal of Education for Teaching,* 27(2), 135–148.

Fullan, M. (2001). *The new meaning of educational change* (3rd ed.). New York and London: Teachers College Press.

Fullan, M. G. & Hargreaves, A. (1991). *What's worth fighting for? Working together for your school.* Andover, MA: Regional Laboratory for Educational Improvement of the Northwest & Island.

Giddens, A. (1984). *The constitution of society: Outline of the theory of structuration.* Cambridge: Polity Press.

Harding, S. (1986). *The science question in feminism.* Milton Keynes: Open University Press.

Hargreaves, A. (1994). *Changing teachers, changing times: Teachers' work and culture in the postmodern age.* London: Cassell.

Hargreaves, A. (2002). Teaching and betrayal. Teachers and Teaching: *Theory and Practice*, 8(3–4), 393–407.

Lillejord, S. (2003). *Ledelse i en lærende skole [Management in a learning school].* Oslo: Universitetsforlaget.

Lortie, D. C. (1975). *Schoolteacher: A sociological study*. Chicago: University of Chicago Press.

Møller, J. (1996). *Lære å/og lede: dilemmaer i skolehverdagen [To learn and to lead: Dilemmas in everyday life in schools].* Oslo: Cappelen Akademisk Forlag.

Nonaka, I., & Takeuchi, H. (1995). *The knowledge-creating company: How Japanese companies create the dynamics of innovation.* London: Oxford University Press.

Polanyi, M. (1967). *The tacit dimension*. Garden City, NY: Anchor Books.

Postholm, M. B. (2011). A completed research and development work project in school: The teachers' learning and possibilities, premises and challenges for further development. *Teaching and Teacher Education*, 27(3), 560–568.

Punch, M. (1994). Politics and ethics in qualitative research. In: N. K. Denzin & Y. S. Lincoln (Eds.), *Handbook of qualitative research* (pp. 83–97). Thousand Oaks, CA: Sage.

Revans, R. W. (1982). *The origins and growth of action learning.* Bromley: Chartwell-Bratt.

Rismark, M. & Sølvberg, A. (2011). Knowledge sharing in schools: A key to developing professional learning communities. *World Journal of Education,* 1(2), 150–160.

Sachs, J. (2001). Teacher professional identity: Competing discourses, competing outcomes. *Journal of Educational Policy,* 16(2), 149–161.

Senge, P. (1990). *The fifth discipline field book: Strategies and tools for building a learning organization.* New York: Doubleday.

Senge, P. M. (2007). *Schools that learn: A fifth discipline field book for educators, parents, and everyone who cares about education.* London: Nicholas Brealey.

Smith, D.E. (1987). *The everyday world as problematic: A feminist sociology.* Milton Keynes: Open University Press.

Smith, D. E. (1990). *The conceptual practices of power.* Boston: Northeastern University Press.

Stake, T. (2000). The case study method in social inquiry. In R. Gomm, M. Hammersley, & P. Foster (eds.), *Case study method* (pp. 19–26). London: Sage.

Steen-Olsen, T. (2010). Refleksiv forskningsetikk – den kritiske ettertanken [Reflexive research ethics – the critical reflection]. In T. Lund, M. B. Postholm, & G. Skeie (red.). *Forskeren i møte med praksis: Refleksivitet, etikk og kunnskapsutvikling [Researchers' encounters in the field of practice: Reflexivity, ethics and knowledge production]* (pp. 97–113). Trondheim: Tapir Akademisk Forlag.

Steen-Olsen, T. (2011). Refleksivt blikk på forsknings- og utviklingsarbeid [A reflexive perspective on research and development]. In T. L. Hoel, T. M. Guldal, C. F. Dons, S. Sagberg, T. Solhaug, & K. Wæge (red.), *FoU i Praksis [R&D in practice]* (pp. 429–439). Trondheim: Tapir Akademisk Forlag.

Steen-Olsen, T. & Eikseth, A. G. (2010). The power of time: Teachers' working day, negotiating autonomy and control. *European Educational Research Journal,* 9(2), 284–295.

Steen-Olsen, T. & Postholm, M. B. (2009). (red.) *Å utvikle en lærende skole: Aksjonsforskning og aksjonslæring i praksis [Developing a learning school:*

*Action research and action learning in practice]*. Kristiansand: Høyskoleforlaget.

Strand, T. (2001). Hva er pedagogikk? Pedagogikkens kunnskapstradisjoner og kulturer versus pedagogikkens faglige identitet [What is pedagogy? Pedagogic knowledge traditions and cultures versus pedagogic subject identity]. In T. Kvernbekk (red.). *Pedagogikk og lærerprofesjonalitet [Pedagogy and teachers' professionalism]* (pp. 164–190). Oslo: Gyldendal Norsk Forlag.

Strauss, A. & Corbin, J. (1998). *Basics of qualitative research: Techniques and procedures for developing grounded theory.* Thousand Oaks, CA: Sage.

Thomson, J. M. & Halloway, D. G. (1997). Staff development procedures and a culture of collaboration in primary school. *Teacher Development,* 1(2), 309–326.

Tiller, T. (2006). *Aksjonslæring – forskende partnerskap i skolen: Motoren i det nye læringsløftet (2. utgave) [Action learning – research partnership in schools: The engine in the new Knowledge Promotion curriculum (2nd ed.)].* Kristiansand: Høyskoleforlaget.

von Krogh, G., Ichijo, K., & Nonaka, I. (Eds.) (2000). *Enabling knowledge creation: How to unlock the mystery of tacit knowledge and release the power of innovation.* Oxford: Oxford University Press.

Wiken, J. S. (2010). *Lærere og skoler i utvikling [Teachers' and schools' development].* Master's thesis. Trondheim: NTNU.

AUTHOR: Tove Steen-Olsen is Associate Professor (dr.polit.) of Educational Science at Sør-Trøndelag University College in Trondheim, Norway, where she has been leading R&D for six years. During that time, she has collaborated with Anne-Lise Arnesen, who was a part-time professor at the same institution in the period of 2006-2009. Steen-Olsen has been a member of the Nordic research network NordCrit since 2008, and has collaborated with Anne-Lise Arnesen also through this network. Steen-Olsen has led and contributed to several interdisciplinary research projects in the fields of educational research, organization development, and workplace learning.

Correspondence: tove.steen-olsen@hist.no.

# *Developing competences for diversity*

JULIE ALLAN
University of Stirling, Scotland

ABSTRACT: *This paper reports on a Council of Europe Project, Policies and Practices for Socio-cultural Diversity, undertaken between 2006 and 2009 and led by Anne-Lise Arnesen. The project had three phases and involved a survey of teacher education policies and practices in relation to socio-cultural diversity across Europe, a conceptual analysis and the development of a framework of teacher competences for socio-cultural diversity. The paper charts the process of developing the framework and reports on the engagement with the key stakeholders – policymakers, teachers and students. The features of the competence framework, informed by Levinas and emphasising the teacher's responsibility to the Other, is discussed.*

## *Introduction*

The Council of Europe *White Paper on Intercultural Dialogue: Living Together as Equals in Dignity* (Council of Europe, 2008a), whilst underlining the common responsibility among us all for fostering intercultural dialogue, identifies educators at all levels as playing an "essential role" (p. 32). The role places obligations on teachers to promote tolerance and understanding among diverse populations and to challenge negative attitudes. Yet, as the social capital theorist Robert Putnam (2007) has argued, diversity produces fear and leads people to disconnect from one another. He contends that diversity is a threat to democracy, citing evidence that in areas of high levels of ethnic diversity, people desist from associating with others and "hunker down—that is, to pull in like a turtle" (2007, p. 149). For beginning teachers, diversity produces significant fear and they see themselves as needing to acquire highly specific and narrow skills in order to address the perceived deficits among their pupils and manage diversity in their classrooms (Allan, 2008; Gallagher, 2010; Rizvi, 2009). Many of the textbooks available to beginning teachers reinforce such notions of pupil deficits and expectations about the skills required to respond (Brantlinger, 2006; Sleeter, 1987). The realities presented in these texts bear little resemblance to the children whom the student teachers encounter and the certainty that they command makes them irresponsible (Allan & Slee, 2008; Brantlinger, 2006). The segmented way of presenting particular 'conditions' within the texts and the absence of any regard for the intersections of disability with class, race, gender, sexuality or any other aspect of diversity inevitably limits student teachers' understanding and sense of capability (Connor, 2006; Lewis & Armstrong, 2011) and as Arnesen and Lundahl (2006) point, even the tradition of comprehensive education, especially strong in the Scandinavian countries, produces problems through its associations with "uniformity and cultural homogeneity" (p. 293) and through practices which are in "confrontation" (p. 293) with minority ethnic groups. Furthermore, Arnesen et al (2007) note a strong rhetoric of equality and inclusiveness in Nordic educational policies that is accompanied by a vagueness about difference and in a comparative study of Norway and Finland found that teachers struggled when challenged to think about difference. A narrow view of teaching as involving the management of diversity is unlikely to enable teachers to foster intercultural dialogue and could lead to discrimination and exclusion (Oliver, 1996).

The White Paper's authors, acknowledging the impossibility of prescribing dialogue across cultures and ethnicities in law, offer the White Paper as an "open invitation" (Council of Europe, 2008a, p. 5). This chapter reports on a project undertaken within the Council of Europe, *Policies and Practices for Socio-cultural Diversity*, that has responded to this invitation, although perhaps not as anticipated. It charts the progress of the project and its culmination in the development of a framework of competences for diversity that was influenced by ideas from Levinas' ethics (1969; 1999). It reports on the engagement with the key stakeholders—policymakers, teachers and students—throughout the project and on how their interests were both recognised and responded to. The framework of competences for teachers that was developed within the Council of Europe project, with its emphasis on values and teacher capacities to respond to diversity, was a response to this invitation that in Levinisian terms was both ethical, through its concern with the teacher in relationship to their students, and responsible, through its efforts to intensify and strengthen that relationship.

## *The council of Europe project: dialogue with (a) difference*

The Policies and Practices for Socio-cultural Diversity project commenced in 2006 and was co-coordinated by the Council of Europe's Head of the Division of Citizenship, Human Rights and Diversity and Secretary to the Steering Committee for Education, within the Directorate of Education and Languages, Villano Qriazi, and chaired by Anne-Lise Arnesen. The project team included Julie Allan (Scotland), Elizabeth Furch (Austria), Siyka Chavdarova (Bulgaria), Karmen Trasberg (Estonia) Pavlina Hadjitheodoulou Loizidou (Cyprus) Angelos Vallianatos (Greece) and Bernard Dumont (France) participated. Eva Simonsen (Norway) was special adviser to the project and Cesar Birzea (Romania) was involved in the initial phases of the project. The project was undertaken in three phases and began with a survey of teacher education programmes within Europe, examining how well diversity was covered. Phase 2 developed an analysis of concepts, principles and challenges for teacher education for diversity and the project concluded, in Phase 3, with the establishment of a framework of competences for diversity. The framework was taken to a series of national consultation tables, held in Austria, Bulgaria, Cyprus and Estonia and involving member state officials, government officers, teacher educators, managers, researchers, principals, teachers and students. Following discussion in each of these consultation tables, the framework of competences was revised.

The survey, carried out in Phase 1, found that in many parts of Europe initial teacher education did not adequately prepare beginning teachers to cope with the diversity that they met in their classrooms (Council of Europe, 2008b). In analysing the concepts, principles and challenges for teacher education, the project participants identified a number of problems which made the development of effective teacher education for diversity a complex task (Council of Europe, 2008b). One key issue was the increasing complexity and diversity of European societies and the limited, partial and outdated understandings of these societies, the needs and issues of particular groups within them, and the appropriate educational responses (OECD, 2005; Rizvi, 2009). A second issue concerned structural causes of inequalities and exclusion, including inadequate educational policies and legal frameworks. These are important in underlining responsibilities and obligations towards building diverse democratic societies but may themselves produce inequalities and exclusion or place constraints on the development of diversity within countries. If these structural barriers are not addressed by member states, too much of a burden is placed upon teacher education to support beginning teachers in responding effectively to diversity. The capacity of teacher education institutions to develop teacher competences was identified as a problem: The survey of teacher education institutions found that the experience and expertise of the teacher educators themselves was limited and there was a lack of relevant institutional policies.

Whilst these issues clearly made the task of improving teacher education in relation to diversity a significant challenge, the project team viewed it as one which could be taken up. There was an expectation, from within the Council of Europe, that the response to the challenge would take the form of the establishment of teacher competences for diversity, which could "serve as a common denominator" (Council of Europe, 2009, p. 12). The project team viewed competences, and governments' and organizations' attraction to them, as part of a complex "governance turn" (Ball 2009, p. 537; Ozga, 2009), catching teachers and teacher educators in a web of accountability that emphasises proving rather than improving (Ball, 2000). We envisaged scope for reframing and reorienting competences and this was undertaken in relation to ethics and is discussed below.

## Becoming competent, becoming ethical

Before outlining the particluar understanding of competence that was the basis of the Council of Europe project, a brief review of the development of the notion of competence is offered.

The origins of the term competence can be seen in the Greek notion of *arete*, meaning excellence, in the sense of being fitting and thorough, and the Latin term *virtus*, a kind of moral excellence. Competence can be attributed to individuals, social groups or institutions, and the words "competence," "competency" or the plural form "competencies" are often used interchangeably. The term has a large variety of meanings, and it can be captured by the terms "ability," "aptitude," "capability," "effectiveness" and "skill" (Weinert, 2001).

Competence can be attributed to individuals, social groups or institutions possessing or acquiring attributes that enable them to meet demands presented by the external environment (Weinert, 2001). However, the notion of competence and its plural, "competences," have, in recent years, been replaced by the narrower version of "competency," or the plural form "competencies," denoting discrete skills and activities which individuals can perform. Arnesen (2011) notes the emergence of the *competent child,* evolving through a series of technologies (Popkewitz, 2004) and which serve to order, classify and make distinctions between children and to specify the appropriate pedagogical response (Arnesen and Lundahl, 2010).

Competence surfaced as a concept within teacher education in the early 1990s and has become firmly embedded within standards frameworks for the accreditation of teachers across Europe. However, the standards have been recognised as being problematic. Roy (2003) argues that they envelop the student teacher within rigid stratifications, which deny complex thinking and firmly entrench their novice and incompetent identities. They have been viewed as invalid indicators of good teaching (Smyth & Shacklock, 1998; Mahoney & Hextall, 2000) and as part of the "struggle over the teacher's soul" (Ball, 2003, p. 217). When the standards have been applied to diversity, the effects have been sinister, pushing the new teacher towards the management of, rather than engagement with, difference. Teachers merely have to perform the diversity-related standards, without necessarily committing to the values associated with them. And since there has been little attempt to specify what effective engagement with diversity might look like, it is inevitable that scrutiny of these particular standards will be *light touch* compared with the attention given to those associated with the more visible aspects of teaching such as classroom management. Such a framing of competences is irresponsible because it makes few demands on beginning teachers to engage with the diversity in his or her classroom other than by problematising it and seeking to limit its impact. This problematising of diversity creates, as Critchley (1999) suggests, a forgetfulness of the Other and produces inequality and injustice.

The White Paper takes up competences as a necessity for promoting intercultural dialogue but suggests that these competences "are not automatically acquired: they need to be learned, practised and maintained throughout life" (Council of Europe, 2008a, p. 29). The paper identifies three key competence areas: democratic citizenship, language and history. These are detailed as important areas of experience both in and out of school, but what is not made clear is the nature of teachers' competence in order to facilitate these. However the warning against using history teaching as "an instrument of ideological manipulation, of propaganda or … for the promotion of intolerant and ultra-nationalistic, xenophobic, racist or anti-Semitic ideas" (p. 30) gives some indication of what teachers are expected *not* to do.

In considering the competences required by teachers for diverse democratic societies within the project, we posed the questions, What do we want our teachers to understand? To be? To do? Our understanding of teacher competence for diverse democratic societies is that these cannot reasonably be viewed as consisting of fixed amounts of knowledge, skills or behaviours to be acquired by teachers, but must be responsive to the changing nature of the society in which the teacher works and subject to the teacher's continuous reflection and adaptation.

The notion of competence developed within the project can be interpreted, following Levinas (1969; 1999), as a relationship of responsibility, directed at all students within the classroom and as a readiness to meet diversity in any shape or form. Such an approach has its basis in a Levinasian ethics and constitutes a reorientation to human subjectivity. It stems from a disappointment at the failure to be responsible for the Other, and at the forgetfulness of that Other, especially that Other who is different in some way, and aspires to "be able to face and face down the iniquities of the present" (Critchley 2007, p. 88). An ethics has as its core an absolute responsibility to the Other and the relationship is experienced, because of an inadequacy in the face of the Other, as asymmetrical (rather than as one of equals, which the White Paper advocates) and as not benign, but as a responsibility that "persecutes me with its sheer weight" (Critchley 2007, p. 59). This produces an absolute imperative towards the Other which is a "gratuitous and non-transferable responsibility, as if they were chosen and unique—and in which the other were absolutely other, i.e … still incomparable and thus unique" (Levinas 1999, p. 170). The responsibility, according to Levinas, is inescapable:

> to be a "self" is to be responsible before having done anything…I am not merely the origin of myself, but I am disturbed by the Other. Not judged by the Other, but condemmed without being able to speak, persecuted (Levinas, 1996, p. 94).

The responsibility to the Other is both "indeclinable" (Levinas, 1998, p. 134), so we cannot say "no" to it, and infinite:

> The idea of the infinite consists precisely and paradoxically in thinking more than what is thought while nevertheless conserving it in its excessive relation to thought. The idea of the infinite consists in grasping the ungraspable while nevertheless guaranteeing its status as ungraspable (Levinas, 1969, p. 19).

The responsibility that one has to the Other operates at three levels: responding *to* the Other; responding *for oneself* to the Other and responding *for the Other*, by substituting oneself for the other person in his or her responsibilities (Hutchens, 2004). And whilst these are heavy responsibilities, as Butler (2004) reminds us, being disturbed by the obligation of the Other is a vital part of what it is to be human: "Let's face it. We're undone by each other. And if not, we're missing something" (p. 43). Biesta's (2008) notion of "pedagogy with empty hands" (p. 198) is an extremely useful way of thinking about education from an ethical point of view. It requires teachers to approach students within their classroom without ready solutions or "tricks of the trade" (p. 208), derived from textbooks, research or elsewhere, and to ask "what do you think of it?" (p. 208). This notion of constant readiness is something of a departure from the idea of a teacher whose lessons, activities and outcomes are planned ahead and whose actions in class can be predicted. It does, however, appear more likely to enable teachers to respond to diversity in whatever shape or form it surfaces.

The approach to competence within this project differs significantly from other frameworks of teacher competence, such as that offered by Westera (2001) which focuses on operational aspects and include knowledge, skills, attitudes, metacognition, or by Shulman (1986) who distinguishes three types of knowledge as being at the heart of teacher competence, namely content knowledge, pedagogy content knowledge and curriculum knowledge. These frameworks indicate what is to be acquired by teachers in order to become competent. The framework developed here, in contrast, emphasises values of openness and readiness both to children and their diversity.

The representation of the competent teacher as in a relationship of responsibility to students and with an attitute of readiness to diversity met with a positive response from the participants in the consultation tables, especially the teachers, teacher educators and students, and indeed one teacher from Estonia offered an image of the teacher as gardener. This kind of teacher, she explained, had to be always ready and adaptive to the different demands of the various species in her classroom. She had to be prepared to provide different amounts of water, nourishment and protection to each individual and to recognise that they would flourish in different ways. Above all, the teacher had to love each one of her charges. The image of the teacher as gardener resonated well with the development of competences which were ethical and which principally concerned the relationship between the teacher and his or her learners.

The framework, in its final form, contains three clusters of competences. In the centre, and central, is *Communication and Relationships*. The competences within the clusters which flanked *Communication and Relationships*, *Knowledge and Understanding* and *Management and Teaching*, would, we argued, be of a second order to, and developed from the acquisition of competences in, *Communication and Relationships.* Fundamentally, we argued, these competences were not finite skills that could be demonstrated, but required continuous development and review. Table 1 outlines the framework of teacher competences for diversity.

The framework was published in the third of the project's reports (Council of Europe, 2010a) and is now in the public domain. It was launched at a conference in Norway in October 2009, organised by Council of Europe in co-operation with the Ministry of Education of Norway, Oslo University College and the Wergeland Centre. The conference brought together senior officials from member states governments with responsibilities for teacher education, teacher educationists, researchers and representatives from international Non-Governmental Organisations. The aim of the conference was to give participants the opportunity to enlarge their vision of key issues concerning diversity and inclusion in the field of teacher education and to identify new perspectives for work at European level. The conference focused on the work and outcomes of the Council of Europe project and concentrated on the conditions of implementation and adaptation to national contexts of the framework of teacher competences for engaging with diversity, developed within the project.

| Knowledge and understanding | Communication and Relationships | Management and teaching |
|---|---|---|
| **Competence 1**<br>Knowledge and understanding of the political, legal and structural context of socio-cultural diversity | **Competence 7**<br>Initiating and sustaining positive communication with pupils, parents and colleagues from different socio-cultural backgrounds | **Competence 13**<br>Addressing socio-cutural diversity in curriculum and institutional development |
| **Competence 2**<br>Knowledge about international frameworks and understanding of the key principles that relate to socio-cultural diversity education | **Competence 8**<br>Recognising and responding to the communicative and cultural aspects of languages used in school | **Competence 14**<br>Establishing a participatory, inclusive and safe learning environment |
| **Competence 3**<br>Knowledge about different dimensions of diversity eg ethnicity, gender, special needs and understanding their implications in school settings | **Competence 9**<br>Creating open-mindedness and respect in the school community | **Competence 15**<br>Selecting and modifying teaching methods for the learning needs of pupils |
| **Competence 4**<br>Knowledge of the range of teaching approaches, methods and materials for responding to diversity | **Competence 10**<br>Motivating and stimulating all pupils to learn individually and in co-operation with others | **Competence 16**<br>Critically evaluating diversity within teaching materials, eg textbooks, videos, media |
| **Competence 5**<br>Skills of inquiry into different socio-cultural issues | **Competence 11**<br>Involving all parents in school activities and collective decision-making | **Competence 17**<br>Using a variety of approaches to culturally sensitive teaching and assessment |
| **Competence 6**<br>Reflection on one's own identity and engagement with diversity | **Competence 12**<br>Dealing with conflicts and violence to prevent marginalization and school failure | **Competence 18**<br>Systematic reflection on and evaluation of own practice and its impact on students |

Table 1: Framework of teacher competences for diversity

Anne-Lise Arnesen set the tone of the conference with her keynote address, The complex of sociocultural diversity – challenges for teacher education (Arnesen, 2009). Here, she outlined the dimensions of sociocultural diversity and the significance of the challenge for teacher education. She criticised the reduced focus on equality and social justice within educational policy and the simplistic and unreflective use of the concept of diversity. In spite of this, Arnesen underlined the potential of education as one of the major institutions for enhancing progress and preventing unemployment and social exclusion; as contexts for children and young people to learn to live together across differences; and of huge significance for those living difficult lives. Arnesen argued for philosophical engagement with the nature of difference and for a high level of reflexivity and outlined a number of challenges for teacher education. Above all, she argued for recognition of reality as plural, complex and dynamic, with teachers as part of that plurality, complexity and dynamic. It was necessary to start the process of teacher education by building understanding among teacher students about themselves, their circumstances and their position in a world of diversity. Teacher education thus needed to shift the focus from the differences of individuals to the factors which maintain differentiation and discrimination in social life. It was also necessary to emphasise the promotion of inclusive environments for all children and young people, recognising that some are particularly vulnerable and at risk of marginalisation or exclusion and calling for an engaged pluralism (Greene, 1993). The greatest challenge, according to Arnesen, was to develop in teacher students a sensitivity towards the tensions between diversity and unity and here Arnesen was implicitly articulating what Derrida (1992a) refers to as an aporia, a double-contradictory imperative.

Pavlina Hadjitheodoulou-Loizidou (2009), one of the project team members, provided a comprehensive overview of the project, its findings and the implications for future policy and practice and highlighted how much of the existing knowledge and assumptions about sociocultural diversity had been unravelled in the course of the project. She indicated the project team's view that there was much satisfaction to be taken from this, given the inadequacy of current policy and practice and the knowledge and assumptions which guide it. Fazal Rizvi (2009), an invited speaker from the US, outlined the ways in which diversity was changing in transnational contexts and illustrated this from his own experience. In spite of these changes, he suggested, teachers were still working with notions of immigration from the 50's and 60's and therefore had outdated understandings of diversity. He invited conference participants to imagine a scenario in which diversity was the norm rather than the exception and posed questions for reflection during the conference. These concerned how to develop sensitivity to diversity and understand specifics rather than textbook versions of it; how to avoid assuming categories – how to listen; and how to get teachers to understand that talk of diversity is socially constructed and can have both positive and negative consequences.

After being introduced to the framework of competences, conference participants were asked to address three specific questions during workshop discussions:

- How will the framework for engaging with diversity, as proposed by the project group of the Council of Europe, work for you?
- Could you identify the main areas where reform or changes are necessary?
- What are your main priorities for further work in relation to the practical implementation of such a framework?

The working groups were structured in relation to the three clusters of competences in the framework and each were chaired by members of the project team and featured case studies, presented by experts and illustrating particular competences. On the final day of the conference, a panel discussion took place with distinguished experts offering their specific 'agenda for change'. The presentations and discussions were provocative and raised fundamental issues for the participants. These concerned:

## *The role of the teacher*

The socio-cultural development of the teacher's role was a key concern, as was the question of whether the teacher was a teacher of a subject, a language/culture teacher or something more. Some participants reflected on whether the expectations associated with socio-cultural competence were too great for teachers and there was discussion in several groups about where responsibilities for promoting a socio-cultural democratic society lie – with society itself or with the school, the community, individuals or the media.

### *Diversity*

Participants reflected extensively on the nature of diversity. Theyresponded positively to the invitation by Fazal Rizvi to consider diversity to be the rule rather than the exception. There was recognition that diversity could be frightening to teachers and therefore a problem, but that it could also be a stimulus for thinking about the teaching of all children and thus an opportunity, especially for student teachers. There was discussion of how diversity is recognised and named and of the misrecognition and non-recognition of diversity. The cultural specificity of language and the potential for misinterpretation was also acknowledged and questions were raised about national policy frameworks and their sensitivity to diversity. Some concern was expressed that we might 'tire diversity out' by talking about it too much.

### *Teacher education*

Considerable concern was expressed about teacher educators and their understanding and experience of diversity. Concerns were also expressed about where diversity sits within teacher education and within universities, which are organised in relation to various disciplines (eg psychology/sociology/pedagogy). The deep conservativism within universities was identified as a potential problem and questions were raised about the teacher education curriculum and whether it can accommodate the competences framework.

### *The competences framework*

There was considerable enthusiasm for the competences framework, although some participants raised questions about the actual competences and whether they were too individualistic, while others suggested they were not individualistic enough. There was also a suggestion that psychological aspects were missing from the competences. Participants raised questions about the relationship between the competences, teacher education and society and about whether all national contexts would be able to incorporate the competences.

## *Putting the competences framework into practice*

Participants envisaged the framework working, not in a revolutionary way, but through a gradual process of change. It was viewed as a tool to inform, not direct, practice and as providing more of a cultural than a social frame. It offered a vision, based on an ethical view of society, to see the complexity of diversity in teacher education. There were suggestions that the framework might work more effectively with some of the competences grouped differently (within the clusters), but a recognition that these adaptations could be made to suit particular contexts. There was agreement that the successful implementation of the framework was dependent on exposure to new learning by student teachers especially of language and even with 'unlearning' – with the suggestion that it may be necessary to implore student teachers to 'forget your knowledge'.

Participants identified a number of areas for reform in order to ensure teachers were adequately prepared for responding to diversity and promoting inclusion.

- The *involvement of the policymakers* – the decision makers – in dialogue, debate and action is crucial. There was recognition of the need to educate the policymakers about the significance of diversity and inclusion and to support their understanding of the complex challenges associated with preparing teachers to respond adequately.
- *Schools* need to be supported and encouraged to become engaged in implementing the competences framework. It was acknowledged that schools could be potentially receptive or hostile to competences. It was also recognised that the greater autonomy being extended to schools in many contexts may lead to greater exclusion rather than inclusion and could make the implementation of the competences framework difficult. This needs to be addressed.
- The importance of *working with families*, improving and expanding communication (in and beyond school), was underlined. At the same time, it was acknowledged that home-school relations were complex and potentially negative in some contexts. This called for great sensitivity, understanding and care.

- The need for *student mobility*, to facilitate exposure to diversity, especially minority languages, was stressed.
- *Taking diversity into the academic arena,* and developing dialogue about diversity and inclusion within universities and encouraging reform was considered to be of the utmost importance.
- There was a call for *research* to map patterns of diversity, document practice and build knowledge about diversity.
- *Extending intercultural dialogue across Europe* was also considered to be crucial.

Participants outlined what they considered to be the main priorities for action for the implementation of the competences framework and for enhancing the capacity of teacher education to support student teachers in responding effectively to diversity:

1. Obtaining concrete examples of sensitivity to diversity
2. Recognising both knowledge (about diversity) and sensitivity (to it)
3. Considering (but not targeting) specific groups, eg children with special needs, Roma children
4. Engaging colleagues in own countries in dialogue about the importance of implementing competences
5. Establishing a critical mass of people in own member states who can understand and communicate competences
6. Presenting issues relating to diversity and inclusion in the universities
7. Co-ordinating disciplinary knowledges within universities (including pedagogy)
8. Selection/attraction of teachers with an openness to diversity
9. Providing student teachers with intercultural experiences
10. Evaluation of teacher education programmes.

The discussions among the participants focused frequently on the fundamental nature of education and what it means to be human. Alongside the more pragmatic areas for reform and priorities, outlined above, participants emphasised the need for substantial shifts in how diversity and inclusion is conceptualised and enacted. The required shifts are:

- From nice words to action
- From diversity as the exception to diversity as the norm
- From target groups to design for all
- From needs to rights (human rights, children's rights)
- From children as becoming to children as being
- (But) from student teachers as being to student teachers as becoming.

These shifts, while fundamental, did not appear to the participants to be unattainable and the ending of the conference was characterised by strong resolve on the part of the participants to take responsibility for embedding the competences framework in their own member states and to promote dialogue and debate about the issues concerning diversity and inclusion. Villano Qiriazi announced the Council of Europe's intentions to extend the programme of work on *Policies and practices for teaching socio-cultural diversity* and this news ensured that the conference ended on an extremely positive - and committed - note.

The essence of the ethical approach informed some of the advice in support of the 23rd Council of Europe Ministerial Conference, Teacher Education for a Sustainable Democratic Society, which took place in June 2010 in Ljubljana, Slovenia. Ministers were invited to consider teacher competences alongside the status and conditions of teachers and partnership working. Acting in the role of Expert Adviser to the Council of Europe and taking responsibility for teacher competences, I conveyed the ethical approach to competences to the Ministers, but did not name it as such. The inappropriateness of a developing a fixed notion of skill for the purpose of managing difference was justified as unsustainable and the Ministers were instead treated to the Estonian teacher's image of the teacher as gardener. The choice of language was important and was influenced by Solis and Connor's (2006) warning that much of the conversation within academic studies is inaccessible outside of academe.

Although many of the Central and Eastern European Ministers had a background in education, it was important not to assume this and it was a significant challenge to find words that provided solidity and reassurance within a familiar discourse of competences but which also conveyed a sense of openness and responsiveness to difference. Derrida's (1992a) notion of an aporia - a double contradictory imperative, implicitly invoked by Arnesen in relation to the tension between diversity and unity - was deployed as a strategy whereby Ministers were encouraged to understand that decisions were not necessarily resolvable or reducible to one single choice and indeed that it was the very process of keeping two apparently oppositional questions open that was at the heart of justice. Derrida (1992b) argues that it is the point at which decisions are made, when only one option is selected, that closure is created and injustice is produced:

> When the path is clear and given, when a certain knowledge opens up the way in advance, the decision is already made, it might as well be said that there is none to make; irresponsibly, and in good conscience, one simply applies or implements a program . . . It makes of action the applied consequence, the simple application of a knowledge or know how. It makes of ethics and politics a technology. No longer of the order of practical reason or decision, it begins to be irresponsible (pp41-45, original emphasis).

Questions were thus framed and presented to the Ministers as aporias, for example asking them to consider how, on the one hand, student teachers might learn to develop as autonomous professionals, and on the other hand learn to depend on others for support and collaboration; or how new teachers might work to maximise the achievement of students, with an eye on performance profiles and at the same time ensure that all students improve and that no student is excluded.

Ministers were advised that although the challenge of developing competences for diverse democratic societies was both enormous and complex, there was clearly much that member states could do which was not dependent on vast amounts of resources, specialised technical knowledge or personnel, but which involved finding ways of simultaneously creating opportunities and removing barriers to dialogue and participation. Their response was one of recognition and desire and although such formal events can be more memorable for their ministerial platitudes than for their evidence of transformatory thought, the subsequent declaration which the Ministers' signed up to expressed a significant commitment to, and responsibility for, the Other and an intent to remove barriers to intercultural dialogue:

> RECOGNISING that, in times of global economic crisis, European societies are facing many challenges such as increasing inequality and social exclusion, which threaten the fundamental principles of socially sustainable societies including equal opportunities and social justice .... CONSIDERING that all teachers and other education professionals are one of the essential pillars of the process of building sustainable democratic societies and need to develop the necessary transversal competences; these

> are interrelated knowledge, skills and attitudes enabling teachers to model democratic and participatory processes based on respect for human rights, diversity and human dignity (Council of Europe, 2010b, pp. 2–3).

Beyond the formal language of the declaration, the Ministers can be seen highlighting the centrality of teachers as agents of intercultural dialogue and signaling the importance of teacher education in equipping teachers effectively and appropriately - enabling them to *be* democratic citizens in order to cultivate these values and attributes among their students. Ethics, even if they were just implied, had been invited along to the ministerial dialogue and appeared to have been a welcome guest.

## *Conclusion: infinitely competent?*

> [Ethics] being utopian does not prevent it from investing our everyday actions of generosity or goodwill towards the other: even the smallest and most commonplace gestures, such as saying "after you" as we sit at the dinner table or walk through a door, bear witness to the ethical (Levinas, 1986, p. 32).

The Council of Europe, in its White Paper on Intercultural Dialogue, has issued a challenge to address the inequalities produced by an education system that insists that "everyone do better than everyone else" (McDermott, 1993, p. 274). The pathologising and naming of individual deficits within that system represents what Thomas (2008) calls a "closure on learning" (p. 7), which produces and reinforces disabled, ethnic, class and gendered identities as failures and, as Gillborn and Youdell (2000) have documented, there is a channeling (and rationing) of educational support away from these individuals and towards those most likely to benefit. Teachers, through no fault of their own, lose sight of the Other or, worse still, become afraid of the diversity that the Other brings and beginning teachers are encouraged to think of diversity as a problem to be *managed* within the classroom.

Levinas' ethics offers the possibility of rethinking the relationship between teachers and students *as a dialogue* and diversity, within such a dialogue, becomes a central and inevitable element. It was possible to introduce a framework of competences that was characterized by a relationship with, and responsibility to, students and a readiness for diversity through a series of contingent elements.

First, there was the Council of Europe and its commitment to dialogue beyond a rhetorical level. The Council of Europe's relative lack of power compared with the European Union is its strength, as it leaves it free to guide in a more ethical and responsible way. Villano Qriazi, as the Council of Europe's manager of the project, allowed it to proceed, under the Chairmanship of Anne-Lise Arnesen, as an intercultural dialogue and to develop along these ethical lines. At the same time, however, he had the utmost regard for the expectations of the Council of Europe and a detailed knowledge of how best to communicate complex ideas to policymakers and politicians. Anne-Lise Arnesen took up the responsibility for chairing a project and co-ordinating a disparate and spirited group of academic colleagues. In this position of responsibility she fostered dialogue among the project group and with stakeholders and resisted the kind of closure that must have, at times, been tempting. Anne-Lise's willingness to engage with uncertainty combined with a strong conviction about the importance of doing justice in and through our work challenged and stretched all of us and while we all, including Anne-Lise, experienced considerable frustration at having to abandon some of our false starts, we were all committed to an outcome that properly did justice. The researchers who participated in the project, whilst not all familiar with Levinas' ethics, brought a commitment to helping teachers towards greater recognition of, and confidence with, diversity. As we engaged together with this uncertainty, there was a growing awareness of our shared understanding and commitment and our collective responsibility for representing the competences in a way that allowed for teacher-student relationships as openings. Thus, an ethical approach was possible, within the structure and ethos of the Council of Europe and through a dialogue that was itself intercultural and, above all, responsible.

Three particular challenges were posed by working with a framework of competences that were concerned with an openness and a readiness to students and to diversity. The first challenge was methodological and related to the dialogical working methods we adopted in developing the framework. We did not set out systematically to 'test' the framework but to 'try it out' with key stakeholders. As we proceeded through the dialogues, the framework was further developed and refined rather than tested. Whilst this may not have enabled us to 'prove' the framework's validity we emerged confident that it was allowed to develop in ways that made it meaningful to those who might put it to use.

A second significant challenge emerged in relation to the way in which the framework sought to trouble the 'stuck places in our thinking about difference' (Ferri, 2006, p. 304). In so doing, it may have disappointed those looking for greater clarity and certainty in supporting students in the management of difference. We remained firm in our resolve throughout the project that such clarity and certainty merely creates closure around diversity and Anne-Lise Arnesen provided exemplary and unapologetic leadership in this regard.

A final challenge concerns the invitation that the competences framework poses to member states to put it to work in their specific contexts. This potentially makes the framework appear incomplete but this is, we believe, a necessary state of affairs in order that the framework may be adapted and developed appropriately throughout Europe.

The ethical framework of competences were presented as far from being a solution to the *problem* of diversity; rather, diversity itself, and teachers' relationship with it and with the Other, was its own solution, gently steering away from assumed knowledges about both students with diverse backgrounds and what their teachers need to manage them. Diversity was repositioned as interesting and as something for teachers – and indeed governments – to be curious about. This reorientation to difference as positive was experienced, not as disruptive, but as inviting and the notion of decisions being multiple and, in Derrida's sense, aporetic, came as something as a relief to the administrators and Ministers. Furthermore Levinas' ethics allowed for a rethinking of the relationship between teachers and students *as a dialogue. The stakeholders remained unaware of how the pushing of their thinking had been informed by Levinas and there was never any mention of ethics. Nevertheless, respondents became taken with the idea of teaching as a dialogue and with how* diversity, within such a dialogue, becomes a central and inevitable element and something that the teacher must be ready - and eager - to respond to. Teacher education, in preparing the beginning teacher's readiness, inevitably also has to take the form of a dialogue within which they can articulate anxieties and questions, rather than rehearse the dogma of tolerance. Re-presenting competences as ethical, using the recognisable language and structures of the competences themselves, appears to have engaged, then redirected that engagement, in more responsible ways. It remains to be seen whether this particular competences framework will be *used* in the way we have intended, and as Levinas has suggested, to develop a teaching relationship in which the teacher, as well as the student, is taught. One might hope that it can at least provoke, among teachers and teacher educators, a dialogue that has at its heart responsibility.

## References

Allan, J. (2008). *Rethinking inclusive education: The philosophers of difference in practice*. Dordrecht: Kluwer.

Allan, J., & Slee, R. (2008). *Doing inclusive education research*. Rotterdam: Sense.

Arnesen, A.L. (2009). The complex of sociocultural diversity – challenges for teacher education. Keynote address to *Diversity and Inclusion: Challenges for Teacher Education: Final conference of the Council of Europe Project, Policies and Practices for Socio-cultural Diversity,* Oslo, Norway.

Arnesen, A.L. (2011). International politics and national reforms: The dynamics between 'competence' and the 'inclusive school' in Norwegian education policies. *Education Inquiry*, 2(2), 193-206.

Arnesen, A.L., Lahlema, E., & Mietola, R. (2007). Language of inclusion and diversity: Policy discourses and social practices in Finnish and Norwegian schools. *International Journal of Inclusive Education*, 11(1), 97-110.

Arnesen, A.L. & Lundahl, L. (2006). Still social and democratic? Inclusive education policies in the Nordic welfare states. *The Scandinavian Journal of Educational Research,* 50(3), 285-300.

Arnesen, A.L. & Lundahl, L. (2010). Standardized individualisation: Text-mediated Relations of Governance in Two Nordic Welfare Institutions. In S. Kvam, K.P. Knutsen & P. Langemeyer (Eds.) *Textsorten und kulturelle Kompetenz: Interdisziplinäre Beiträge zur Textwissen- schaft.* Münster & New York: Waxmann, 147-171.

Ball, S. (2000). Performativities and fabrication in the education economy: Towards the performative society? *Australian Educational Researcher, 27*(2), 1–23.

Ball, S. (2003). The teacher's soul and the terror of performativity. *Journal of Education Policy, 18*(2), 215–228.

Ball, S. (2009). Editorial: The governance turn! *Journal of Education Policy, 24*(5), 537–538.

Biesta, G. (2008). Pedagogy with empty hands: Levinas, education and the question of being human. In D. Egéa-Kuehne (Ed.), *Levinas and education: At the intersection of faith and reason*. New York: Routledge.

Brantlinger, E. (2006). The big glossies: How textbooks structure (special) education. In E. Brantlinger (Ed.), *Who benefits from special education? Remediating (fixing) other people's children*. Mahwah, NJ: Lawrence Erlbaum.

Butler, J. (2004). *Precarious life*. London: Verso.

Connor, D. (2006). Not so strange bedfelows: The promise of disability studies and critical race theory. In S. Gabel & S. Danforth (Eds.), *Disability & the politics of education: An international reader*. New York: Peter Lang.

Council of Europe (2008a). *White Paper on intercultural dialogue: "Living together as equals in dignity"*. Strasbourg: Council of Europe.

Council of Europe (2008b). *Policies and practices for teaching sociocultural diversity: A survey report*. Strasbourg: Council of Europe.

Council of Europe (2009). *Policies and practices for teaching sociocultural diversity: Concepts, principles and challenges in teacher education*. Strasbourg: Council of Europe.

Council of Europe (2010a) *Policies and practices for teaching sociocultural diversity: A framework of teacher competences for engaging with diversity*. Strasbourg: Council of Europe.

Council of Europe (2010b). *Declaration on the conference theme: "Education for sustainable democratic societies; The role of teachers"*. 23rd Session of the Standing Conference of Ministers of Education. Retrieved from http://www.coe.int/t/DG4/EDUCATION/STANDINGCONF/MED-23-14%20E%20Declaration.pdf

Critchley, J. (1999). *The ethics of deconstruction*. Edinburgh: Edinburgh University Press.

Critchley, J. (2007). *Infinitely demanding: Ethics of commitment, politics of resistance*. London: Verso.

Derrida, J. (1992a). Force of law: The mystical foundation of authority. (trans M Quaintance). In D. Cornell, M. Rosenfield & D. Carlson (Eds.), *Deconstruction and the possibility of justice*. New York/London: Routledge.

Derrida, J. (1992b). *The other heading: Reflections on today's Europe*. (trans. P. Brault & M. Naas). Bloomington/Indianapolis: Indiana University Press.

Ferri, B. (2006). Teaching to trouble. In S. Danforth & S. Gabel (Eds.). *Vital questions facing disability studies in education*. New York: Peter Lang.

Gallagher, D. (2010). Hiding in plain sight: The nature and role of theory in learning disability labelling. *Disability Studies Quarterly, 30*(2). Retrieved from http://www.dsq-sds.org/article/view/1231/1278

Gillborn, D. & Youdell, D. (2000). *Rationing education: Policy, practice, reform and equity*. Buckingham, England: Open University Press.

Greene, M. (1993). *Diversity and inclusion: Towards a curriculum for human beings*. Teachers College Record, 95(2), 211-221.

Hadjitheodoulou-Loizidou, P. (2009). Looking back, stepping forward - Presentation and evaluation of the project. Main results and lessons learnt. Keynote address to *Diversity and Inclusion: Challenges for Teacher Education: Final conference of the Council of Europe Project, Policies and Practices for Socio-cultural Diversity*, Oslo, Norway.

Hutchens, B. (2004). *Levinas: A guide for the perplexed*. London: Continuum.

Levinas, E. (1969). *Totality and infinity*. Pittsburgh, PA: Duquesne University Press.

Levinas, E. (1986). Dialogue with Emmanuel Levinas [Interview by Richard Kearney]. In R. A. Cohen (Ed.), *Face to face with Levinas* (pp. 13–33). Albany: State University of New York Press.

Levinas, I. (1996). *Basic philosophical writings* (Eds. A. Perperzak, S. Critchley, & R. Bernasconi). Bloomington: Indiana University Press.

Levinas, E. (1998). *Collected philsophical papers* (trans. A. Lingis). Pittsburgh, PA: Duquesne University Press.

Levinas, E. (1999). *Alterity and transcendence*. Columbia University Press: New York.

Lewis, A. & Armstrong, A. (2011). Editorial: The intersection of gender and disability: An international perspective. *Review of Disability Studies,* 7(1), 3-5.

Mahony, P. & Hextall, I. (2000). *Reconstructing teaching: Standards, performance and accountability*. London: RoutledgeFalmer.

McDermott, R. P. (1993). The acquisition of a child by a learning disability. In C. Chaiklin & J. Lave (Eds.), *Understanding practice: Perspectives on activity and context* (pp. 269–305). New York: Cambridge University Press.

OECD (2005). *The definition and selection of key competencies*. Retrieved from www.oecd.org/dataoecd/47/61/35070367.pdf

Oliver, M. (1996). *Understanding disability: From theory to practice*. Basingstoke, England: Macmillan.

Ozga, J. (2009). Governing education through data in England: From regulation to self-evaluation. *Journal of Education Policy, 24*(2), 149–162.

Popkewitz, T. S. (2004). The alchemy of the mathematics curriculum: inscriptions and the fabrica- tion of the child, *American Educational Research Journal* 41(1), 3–34.

Putnam, R. (2007). *E pluribus unum:* Diversity and community in the twenty-first century; The 2006 Johan Skytte Prize lecture. *Scandinavian Political Studies, 30,* 137–174.

Rizvi, F. (2009). *Working with diversity in transnational contexts*. Keynote address to Diversity and Inclusion: Challenges for Teacher Education: Final conference of the Council of Europe Project, Policies and Practices for Socio-cultural Diversity, Oslo, Norway.

Roy, K. (2003). *Teachers in nomadic spaces: Deleuze and curriculum*. New York: Peter Lang.

Shulman, L.S. (1986). Those who understand: Knowledge growth in teaching. *Educational Researcher,* 15(2), 4-14.

Sleeter, C. (1987). Why is there learning disabilities? A critical analysis of the birth of the field in its social context. In T. Popkewitz (Ed.). *The formation of school subjects: The struggle for creating an American institution*. London: Falmer Press.

Solis, S. & Connor, D. (2006). Theory meets practice: Disability studies and personal narratives in school. In S. Danforth & S. Gabel (Eds.), *Vital questions facing disability studies in education*. New York: Peter Lang.

Smyth, J. & Shacklock, G. (1998). *Remaking teaching: Ideology, policy and practice*. London: Routledge.

Thomas, G. (2008). *Theory and the construction of pathology*. Paper presented at the American Educational Research Association Annual Meeting, New York.

Weinert, F. E. (2001). Concept of competence: A conceptual clarification. In D. S. Rychen & L. H. Salganik (Eds.), *Defining and selecting key competencies*. Seattle: Hogrefe & Huber.

Westera, W. (2001). Competences in education: A confusion of tongues. *Journal of Curriculum Studies,* 33(1), 75-88.

AUTHOR: Professor Julie Allan is Depute Head of Department in the School of Education, University of Stirling, Scotland, UK and Visiting Professor at the University of Borås, Sweden. Her research and teaching interests encompass inclusive education, diversity, disability and children's rights and her books include *Rethinking inclusion: The philosophers of difference in practice* (2008, published by Springer) and *Doing inclusive education research* (2008, with Roger Slee and published by Sense) Julie participated in a Council of Europe Project, led by Anne-Lise Arnesen, *Policies and practices for socio-cultural diversity.*
Correspondence: j.e.allan@stir.ac.uk

APPENDIX I

# *Professor Anne-Lise Arnesen's research projects*

1979 – 1981: *Differensiering og tilpasset opplæring* [Differentiation and adapted learning]. Project leader in co-operation with Unn Sollie, funded by the Department of Education and Research.

1985 – 1987: *Equal opportunities and teacher education in Europe: A curriculum framework.* ATEE, Equal Opportunities Unit of the Commission of the European Communities, with co-director Dearbhal NíCharthaigh.

1990 – 1991: *Kjønns- og likestillingsperspektiv i utdanningsforskningen* – en Kunnskapsoversikt [Gender- and equality perspectives in educational research – an overview of knowledge]. Project leader, funded by the Department of Education and Research.

1990 – 1994: *Project: Publication series on equal opportunities in teacher education.* 4 volumes published by Pavic Press, Sheffield Hallam University. Project Leader, funded by the EU Commission.

1992 – 1998 *NORD-LILIA – Nordisk utviklingsprosjekt* [Nordic Development Project, which included 62 research and development projects. Nordic project leader, funded by the Nordic Council of Ministers.

1994—1995 *Vurderingsgrunnlag for sammensatte mål i videregående opplæring: kjønn og likestilling i videregående opplæring [Evaluative criteria for complex goals in secondary learning: gender and equality in secondary learning]*. Project leader, funded by the Department of Education and Research.

1995 – 2001 Member of the board of the Association for Teacher Education in Europe (ATEE). Coordinator for 22 research networks in the association.

1996 – 2001 *Ulikhet og marginalisering i skolen – med referanse til kjønn og sosial bakgrunn* [Difference and marginalization in school – with respect to gender and social background]. Project leader, funded by the University of Oslo and Oslo University College.

2000 Coordinator for EERA's network 'Social Justice and Intercultural Education'.

2002 – 2004 *Gender, Complexity and Diversity in Pedagogical Institutions for Children Aged 0 – 10.* Collaborative project with Professor Jeanette Rhedding-Jones at Oslo University College, funded by the Norwegian Research Council.

2002 – 2006 *Inkludering og ekskludering i lys av profesjonsutøvelse i sosiokulturelt perspektiv: Institusjonelle relasjoner og dilemmaer i skolen* [Inclusion and exclusion in light of professional practice in a sociocultural perspective: Institutional relations and dilemmas in School]. Funded by the Norwegian Research Council.

2006 – 2007 *Multiplicity, Diversity and Inclusive Education*, in cooperation with Professor Joron Pihl, Oslo University College, funded by Oslo University College.

2006 – *Ungas makt och välfärd. Livet i skolan och efter skolan i kritiskt klass-, köns och Mångfaldsperspektiv* [The power and social wellbeing of youth. Life in school and after school from the critical perspective of class, gender and diversity]. Collaborative research network with Lisbeth Lundahl, Elisabet Õhrn and Anne-Lise Arnesen, funded by Umeå University.

2006 – 2009 *Policies and Practices for Teaching Sociocultural Diversity.* Chair of the International Expert Group, funded by the European Council.

2007 – *Nordic Research Network: Young People, Welfare and Education.* University of Umeå, University of Helsinki, University of Gothenburg, Borås University College & Østfold University College.

2007 – Expert on the EU's and Europa Commission's Joint Programme on Fostering the Culture of Human Rights in South Caukasus and the Ukraine.

2008 – 2010 *Barnehagens arbeid for inkludering av barn med nedsatt funksjons-evne i et profesjonsperspektiv* [The kindergarten's efforts to include children with reduced functional abilities, from a professional perspective]. Project leader, funded by Norwegian Research Council.

APPENDIX II

# *Professor Anne-Lise Arnesen's bibliography*


Arnesen, Anne-Lise & Skare, Lars Olav. (1976). *Integrering av funksjonshemmede: En teoretisk tilnærming og en kasuistisk studie av tiltak i grunnskolen [Integration of the physically disabled: A theoretical approach and a casuistic study of initiatives in compulsory schools]* (Hovedoppgave, Universitetet i Oslo). Oslo: A.L. Arnesen.

Arnesen, Anne-Lise. (1983). Handlingsplanen for likestilling - utdanning og yrkesvalg [Action plan for equality – education and career choice]. *Forsøksnytt [Research News],* 14(5/6), 176-177.

Arnesen, Anne-Lise. (1984). Likestillingsarbeidet i skolen må styrkes [Efforts towards equality in the school must be strengthened]. *Skoleforum [School Forum],* 83(2), 30-31.

Arnesen, Anne-Lise. (1986). Likestilling mellom kjønnene: Handlingsplanen for 1986-1990 [Equality between the sexes: Action plan for 1986-1990]. *Skolens årbok [The School's Year Book],* 1986, 9153-9166.

Arnesen, Anne-Lise. (1986). Språk, kjønn og makt [Language, gender and power]. *Rådgivernytt [Advisor News]*, (3), 10-13.

Arnesen, Anne-Lise. (1986). Tiltak og virkemidler i likestillingspolitikken [Initiatives and means in the politics of equality]. *Rådgivernytt [Advisor News],* (4), 6-12.

Arnesen, Anne-Lise & Ni Charthaigh, Dearbhal (ed.). (1987). *Equal opportunities for girls and boys in education: A curriculum framework for teacher education with guidelines for action.* Brussels: The Association for Teacher Education in Europe.

Arnesen, Anne-Lise. (1987). Handlingsplan for likestilling [Action plan for equality]. *Videregående opplæring [Secondary School Learning]*, (4), 34-35.

Arnesen, Anne-Lise. (1988). Bevisstgjøring må til: Om departementets handlingsprogram for likestilling [Awareness is needed: About the Ministry's action plan for equality]. *Videregående opplæring [Secondary School Learning]*, (3), 10-11.

Arnesen, Anne-Lise. (1988). Likestilling i lærerutdanningen: Et europeisk prosjekt [Equality in teacher training: A European project]. *Videregående opplæring [Secondary School Learning]*, (3), 34-35.

Arnesen, Anne-Lise & Markussen, Eifred. (1988). Liv laga: Om likestillingssekretariatets arbeid: Anne-Lise Arnesen intervjuet [It works: About the work of the equality secretariat: Anne-Lise Arnesen interview]. *Videregående opplæring [Secondary School Learning]*, (3), 22-24.

Arnesen, Anne-Lise & Pettersen, Kjellaug. (1990). *Framtidsdrømmen og virkeligheten: Jenter og gutter velger utdanning og yrke [Future dreams and reality: Girls and boys choosing educations and careers]*. Oslo: Friundervisningens forl.

Arnesen, Anne-Lise. (1990). *Kjønns- og likestillingsperspektiv i utdanningsforskningen [Perspectives on gender and equality in education research]*. Oslo: Likestillingssekretariatet, Utdannings- og forskningsdepartementet.

Arnesen, Anne-Lise. (1991). 1.-3. klasseprosjektet som likestillingsstrategi og etterutdanningsmodell [The 1st to 3rd grade class project as a strategy for equality and a model for continuing education]. *Nytt om kvinneforskning [News about Women's Research]*, 15(2), 44-49.

Arnesen, Anne-Lise. (1991). Internasjonalisering og likestilling [Internationalization and equality]. *Videregående opplæring [Secondary School Learning]*, (1), 8-11, 42.

Arnesen, Anne-Lise, Feldberg, Karen Brit & Li, Grethe. (1992). *Internasjonalt samarbeid: Med særlig relevans for lærerutdanning [International cooperation: Particularly as regards teacher education]*. Oslo: Bislet høgskolesenter, Lærerutdanning.

Arnesen, Anne-Lise & Ni Chárthaigh, Dearbhal. (1992). *Pathways to change: Gender and curriculum development in teacher education.* Sheffield: Pavic Publications.

Arnesen, Anne-Lise (ed.). (1994). *Likestilling i lærerutdanningens innhold og arbeidsmetoder [Equality in the contents and work methods for teacher education]*. Oslo: Bislet høgskolesenter.

Arnesen, Anne-Lise (ed.). (1995). *Gender and equality as quality in school and teacher education: The final report from the 3-year Nordic project on gender and equal opportunities in teacher education.* Oslo: Oslo College, School of Education.

Arnesen, Anne-Lise. (1995). *Kjønn og likeverd i videregående opplæring: Et vurderingsgrunnlag og en sammenfatning av forskning om kjønn og likestilling med relevans for videregående opplæring [Gender and equality in secondary school learning: A basis for evaluation and a summary of research on gender and equality in the context of secondary education].* Oslo: Høgskolen i Oslo.

Arnesen, Anne-Lise (ed.). (1998). *Likt og ulikt: Kjønnsdimensjonen i pedagogisk tenkning og praksis [Alike and unlike: The dimension of gender in pedagogical thinking and practice].* Oslo: Høgskolen i Oslo.

Arnesen, Anne-Lise. (2000). Marginalisering i skolen: En tekst- og diskursanalytisk studie av beretningen om en lærer-elevkonflikt [Marginalization in the school: A text- and discourse-analytical study of an account of a teacher-pupil conflict]. *Nordisk pedagogic [Norwegian Pedagogics],* 20(4), 206-218.

Arnesen, Anne-Lise. (2000). Masculinities and ethnicities at play: A discourse analysis of conflict in a Norwegian classroom. Pedagogy, *Culture and Society,* 8(2), 157-172.

Arnesen, Anne-Lise. (2000). To stemmer - to versjoner: Kollisjon mellom elevers og læreres virkelighetskonstruksjon i skolen [Two voices – two versions: Collision between pupils' and teachers' constructions of reality in the school]. *Bedre skole [Better Schools],* (2), 4-13.

Arnesen, Anne-Lise. (2001). *Aktør- og strukturperspektiver anvendt på forståelse av marginalisering i skolen: Vitenskapsteoretisk essay om forklaringsmåter innen metodologisk individualisme og sosial strukturteori [Actor- and structure perspectives applied to the understanding of marginalization in the school: A scientific-theoretical essay about explanatory models in methodological individualism and social structure theory].* Oslo: Høgskolen i Oslo.

Arnesen, Anne-Lise. (2001). Den vet best hvor skoen trykker som har den på?: Refleksjoner om kunnskap, sannhet og forskningsperspektiver i studier av skolen [The person wearing the shoe knows best how it feels?: Reflections on knowledge, truth and research perspectives in studies on schools]. *Norsk pedagogisk tidsskrift [Norwegian Pedagogical Journal]*, 85(5), 383-398.

Arnesen, Anne-Lise. (2002). Forskerblikk på blikket i klasserommet [A study of the gaze in the classroom]. *Norsk pedagogisk tidsskrift [Norwegian Pedagogical Journal]*, 86(6), 460-472.

Arnesen, Anne-Lise. (2002). *Ulikhet og marginalisering: Med referanse til kjønn og sosial bakgrunn: En etnografisk studie av sosial og diskursiv praksis i skolen [Unequality and marginalization: With reference to gender and social background: An ethnographic study of social and discursive practices in the school]*. (Doctoral thesis, Universitetet i Oslo). Oslo: Unipub forl.

Arnesen, Anne-Lise. (2003). Construction of an "outsider": Contradictions and ambiguities in institutional practices. In D. Beach, T. Gordon, & E. Lahelma (eds.), *Democratic education: Ethnographic challenges* (s. 52-65). London: Tufnell Press.

Arnesen, Anne-Lise. (2003). De "sårbare" barna og de "farlige" kategoriene i skolen [The "vulnerable" children and the "dangerous" categories in the school]. In E. Befring (ed.), *Sosiale og emosjonelle vansker hos barn: Problemer, utfordringer og muligheter [The social and emotional difficulties of children: Problems, challenges and possibilities]* (s. 51-59). Oslo: Organisasjonen Voksne for barn.

Arnesen, Anne-Lise & Sollie, Unn. (2003). *Differensiering og tilpasset opplæring: Om forutsetninger og hindringer for å realisere Mønsterplanens intensjoner om å ta hensyn til elevforskjeller i skolens undervisning [Differentiation and adapted learning: About preconditions and hindrances to realizing the master-plan's intention to pay heed to the differences between pupils in the school's teaching]*. Oslo: Høgskolen i Oslo.

Arnesen, Anne-Lise. (2004). *Det pedagogiske nærvær: Inkludering i møte med elevmangfold [The pedagogical presence: Inclusion encounters pupil diversity]*. Oslo: Abstrakt forl.

Arnesen, Anne-Lise. (2004). Kommunikasjon - mer enn ord [Communication – more than words]. In P. Arneberg, J. H. Kjærre, & B. Overland (eds.), *Samtalen i skolen [The conversation in the school]*, (s. 95-114). Oslo: Damm.

Arnesen, Anne-Lise, Dingstad, Pål E., Rhedding-Jones, Jeanette & Rossholt, Nina. (2004). Strengthening partnerships locally and internationally:

Experiences and reflections from a Norwegian research project. *New Zealand Research in Early Childhood Education Journal,* 7, 149-162.

Arnesen, Anne-Lise & Lundahl, Lisbeth. (2006). Still social and democratic?: Inclusive education policies in the Nordic welfare states. *Scandinavian Journal of Educational Research*, 50(3), 285-300.

Arnesen, Anne-Lise, Mietola, Reetta & Lahelma, Elina. (2007). Language of inclusion and diversity: policy discourses and social practices in Finnish and Norwegian schools. *International Journal of Inclusive Education,* 11(1), 97-110.

Arnesen, Anne-Lise (ed.). (2007). *Pre-service teacher education on socio-cultural diversity: Report on the first phase of the project: Policies and practices for teaching socio-cultural diversity: Volume 1.* Strasbourg: Council of Europe, Division of the European Dimension of Education.

Arnesen, Anne-Lise, Birzéa, Cézar, Dumont, Bernard, Essomba, Miquel Angel, Furch, Elisabeth, Vallianatos, Angelos & Ferrer, Ferran. (2008). *Policies and practices for teaching sociocultural diversity: A survey report*. Strasbourg: Council of Europe Publ.

Arnesen, Anne-Lise, Lahelma, Elina & Öhrn, Elisabet. (2008). Travelling discourses on gender and education: The case of boys' underachievement. *Nordisk pedagogic [Norwegian Pedagogics],* 28(1), 1-14.

Arnesen, Anne-Lise, Hadzhitheodoulou-Loizidou, Pavlina, Birzéa, Cézar, Essomba, Miquel Angel & Allan, Julie. (2009). *Policies and practices for teaching sociocultural diversity: Concepts, principles and challenges in teacher education.* Strasbourg: Council of Europe Publ.

Arnesen, Anne-Lise & Solli, Kjell-Arne. (2009). Spesialpedagogiske tiltak i barnehagen skjer ofte ureflektert [Special educational measures in kindergartens are often not reflected over]. *Første steg [First step],* (3), 36-38.

Arnesen, Anne-Lise, Lahelma, Elina, Lundahl, Lisbeth & Öhrn, Elisabet. (2010). Introduction: Agency in a changing educational context: Negotiations, collective actions and resistance. *European Educational Research Journal,* 9(2), 159-163.

Arnesen, Anne-Lise & Lundahl, Lisbeth (eds.). (2010). *Metoder i forsknings- og utviklingsarbeid i utdanning og lærerutdanning: Rapport fra en konferanse mellom Høgskolen i Østfold og Universitetet i Umeå [Methods in research- and development work in education and teacher education: Report from a conference for Østfold University College and the University of Umeå].* Halden: Høgskolen i Østfold.

Arnesen, Anne-Lise, Hadjitheodoulou-Loizidou, Pavlina, Allan, Julie, Trasberg, Karmen, Chavdarova-Kostova, Siyka, Furch, Elisabeth, & Qiriazi, Villano. (2010). *Policies and practices for teaching sociocultural diversity: A framework of teacher competences for engaging with diversity*. Strasbourg: Council of Europe.

Arnesen, Anne-Lise & Lundahl, Lisbeth. (2010). Standardized individualisation: Text-mediated relations of governance in two Nordic welfare institutions. I S. Kvam, K. P. Knutsen, & P. Langemeyer (eds.), *Textsorten und kulturelle Kompetenz: Interdisziplinäre Beiträge zur Textwissenschaft [Text type and cultural competence: Interdisciplinary contributions to text studies]* (s. 147-171). Münster: Waxmann.

Arnesen, Anne-Lise. (2010). The complexity of diversity: Challenges for teacher education. In C. O. Europe (ed.), *Policies and practices for teaching sociocultural diversity: Diversity and inclusion: Challenges for teacher education* (s. 21-34). Strasbourg: Council of Europe.

Arnesen, Anne-Lise. (2011). Barnehage og skole: Arena for inkludering og marginalisering [Kindergarten and school: Arena for inclusion and marginalization]. In H. Larsen, & S. Seim (eds.), *Barnefattigdom i et rikt land: Kunnskapsoppsummering om fattigdom og eksklusjon blant barn i Norge [Child poverty in a rich country: Knowledge review on poverty and exclusion amongst children in Norway]* (s. 119-138). Oslo: Høgskolen i Oslo, Sosialforsk, Avdeling for samfunnsfag.

Arnesen, Anne-Lise. (2011). International politics and national reforms: The dynamics between "competence" and the "inclusive school" in Norwegian education policies. *Education Inquiry*, 2(2), 193-206.

Arnesen, Anne-Lise & Simonsen, Eva. (2011). Spesialpedagogikk - merkevare i epistemisk drift?: Refleksjoner i et barnehageperspektiv [Special education – brand-name product epistemically adrift?: Reflections from the perspective of kindergartens]. *Norsk pedagogisk tidsskrift [Norwegian Pedagogical Journal],* 95(2), 115-128.

Arnesen, Anne-Lise, Kolle, Tonje & Solli, Kjell-Arne. (2012). De problematiske kategoriene i institusjonelle sammenhenger [The problematic categories in institutional contexts]. In A.-L. Arnesen (ed.), *Inkludering: Perspektiver i barnehagefaglige praksiser [Inclusion: Perspectives on practices in the kindergarten profession]* (s. 79-100). Oslo: Universitetsforl.

Arnesen, Anne-Lise. (2012). Den komplekse inkluderingen og pedagogisk nærvær [The complexity of inclusion and pedagogical presence]. In A.-L. Arnesen (ed.), *Inkludering: Perspektiver i barnehagefaglige praksiser [Inclusion: Perspectives on practices in the kindergarten profession]* (s. 247-271). Oslo: Universitetsforl.

Arnesen, Anne-Lise. (2012). Inkludering i det utdanningspolitiske barnehagelandskapet [Inclusion in the landscape of kindergarten education policy]. In A.-L. Arnesen (ed.), *Inkludering: Perspektiver i barnehagefaglige praksiser [Inclusion: Perspectives on practices in the kindergarten profession]* (s. 56-78). Oslo: Universitetsforl.

Arnesen, Anne-Lise. (2012). Inkludering: Perspektiver i barnehagefaglige praksiser: En innledning [Inclusion: Perspectives on practices in the kindergarten profession: An introduction]. In A.-L. Arnesen (ed.), *Inkludering: Perspektiver i barnehagefaglige praksiser [Inclusion: Perspectives on practices in the kindergarten profession]* (s. 13-33). Oslo: Universitetsforl.

Arnesen, Anne-Lise (ed.). (2012). *Inkludering: Perspektiver i barnehagefaglige praksiser [Inclusion: Perspectives on practices in the kindergarten profession].* Oslo: Universitetsforl.